D1602933

THE PUBLIC VOICE IN A
DEMOCRACY AT RISK

THE PUBLIC VOICE IN A DEMOCRACY AT RISK

Edited by Michael Salvador
and Patricia M. Sias

Under the auspices of the Eisenhower Leadership Program

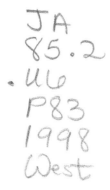

PRAEGER

Westport, Connecticut
London

Library of Congress Cataloging-in-Publication Data

The public voice in a democracy at risk / edited by Michael Salvador
   and Patricia M. Sias ; under the auspices of the Eisenhower
   Leadership Program.
      p.   cm.
   Includes bibliographical references and index.
   ISBN 0–275–96013–7 (alk. paper)
     1. Communication in politics—United States. 2. Communication—
Political aspects—United States. 3. Democracy—United States.
I. Salvador, Michael, 1957– . II. Sias, Patricia M., 1959– .
III. Eisenhower Leadership Group.
JA85.2.U6P83   1998
324.6'3'0973—dc21   97–22809

British Library Cataloguing in Publication Data is available.

Library of Congress Catalog Card Number: 97–22809
ISBN: 0–275–96013–7

First published in 1998

Praeger Publishers, 88 Post Road West, Westport, CT 06881
An imprint of Greenwood Publishing Group, Inc.

Printed in the United States of America

The paper used in this book complies with the
Permanent Paper Standard issued by the National
Information Standards Organization (Z39.48–1984).

10 9 8 7 6 5 4 3 2 1

Copyright Acknowledgments

The editors and publisher gratefully acknowledge permission for use of the
following material:

"Opryland Recruiting Expands to Ireland," by Heather Newman. *The Tennessean*,
November 21, 1995, A-1. Copyrighted by *The Tennessean*, 1995.

"Secretary Accuses Lawmaker of Harassment," by Kriste Goad. *Nashville Banner*,
June 20, 1995, A-1, A-2.

After the News Column and *Special-to-the-Banner* material: "When to use Anonymous
Sources a Judgment Call," by Richard A. Pride. *Nashville Banner*, August 8, 1995, A-5;
"Opryland Employment Story Misses Deeper Issue," by Richard A. Pride. *Nashville
Banner*, November 28, 1995, A-9; and "TV News Often Sheer Melodrama," by
Richard A. Pride. *Nashville Banner*, June 19, 1995, A-11.

Contents

PART III: *Collaborations*

PART IV: *Reflections*

PART I

DEMOCRACY AND COMMUNICATION

own functioning community weekend helps them feel good about what they are accomplishing together. Collaboration skills need to be taught early and continuously in the schools. Collaboration must be modeled in the way that the schools are administered as well.

Experience

Citizenship skills cannot be learned in the abstract. Sound leadership and followership theories must be taught, but lessons in theory must be reinforced with practice. Students from kindergarten through graduate school must be challenged with real opportunities to test the theories they learn against the real problems they face in their communities. The "real world" provides a tremendous civics laboratory where students can apply their citizenship skills through every other academic discipline. Teachers, administrators, and students must be supported by each other and their community as the desired experiences of their developing leadership [...]

Reflection

Students must be given the opportunity for guided reflection about the things they experience and learn. Reflection is the means by which students cognitively internalize their affective learning experiences. Reflection itself brings meaning to a learning experience which in turn needs to be improved reflection. It is sound to teaching students who will become citizens how to deal with the challenges of citizenship that face [...] communities. Citizens must think for themselves [...] tible to simple, appealing solutions offered by those who only want to hold office or obtain power.

RECOMMENDATIONS

The five principles discussed are the foundation for the five recommendations that the [...] has forwarded. Following is a listing of those recommendations and annotations about each one. Drawing from the group's report, and from a former member of the [...] the author has provided his own interpretations of the intent of each recommendation.

Recommendation One: Promote the New Model

The basic paradigm of leadership that needs to be taught in our schools and colleges has to be one that will be workable in the twenty-first century. The one that may have been workable in the twentieth [...]

Chapter 1

Practicing Democracy

Michael Salvador

In March 1996, the Eisenhower Leadership Group (ELG), in partnership with the U.S. Department of Education's Leadership Development Program, presented its findings on the status of citizenship and leadership in the United States at a national press conference in Washington, D.C. After interviewing authorities from across the nation—from professors at Harvard University to the Mayor of Missoula, Montana—the study group declared that ours is a democracy at risk:

American democracy is at risk. Too many of us—either from complacency or despair, inertia or ignorance—are leaving the work of civic engagement to others. Too many of us are expecting someone else to carry all the water. The upshot? A democracy in which too few people do the public business, leaving many disengaged and disenchanted. (ELG, 1996, p. 1)

The report echoes complaints voiced in numerous recent books. Some note the increasing discontent and cynicism of Americans, as in *The System* (Johnson and Broder, 1996), *Democracy's Discontent* (Sandel, 1996), or *Demanding Democracy* (Schmuhl, 1994). Others decry the mediated dramaturgy that passes for democratic discussion, as in *Dirty Politics* (Jameson, 1992), *The Electronic Republic* (Grossman, 1995), or *The Power of the Press* (Schudson, 1995). Still others call for a more informed and critically prepared citizenry, as in *Coming to Public Judgment* (Yankelovich, 1991), *Politics for the People* (Mathews, 1994), or *Breaking the News* (Fallows, 1996).

A common theme in all these critiques of American democracy centers on the ways citizens participate in and deliberate issues of public concern. Most agree in principle that a healthy democracy is a *participatory* democracy: one in which voters are more than pliable spectators of political marketing and passive consumers driven by narrow self-interest; one in which informed citizens with at least some concern for the public good take an active role in articulating the important issues of the day and formulating potential solutions to common problems. Most of these writers also recognize that simply *more* participation is not necessarily *better* participation. For example, while Mathews (1994) calls for greater citizen participation in policy making (he calls it "putting the public back in politics"), he notes that "the public in this case refers to a deliberative body of citizens, not a mass of individuals" (p. 5).

The difference between mass opinion and effective public participation in democratic decision making centers on the ability of citizens to deliberate in a thoughtful and democratic manner. The ELG addressed one aspect of developing such a deliberative body of citizens in its call for increasing public school education about democracy, citizenship, and leadership. This book focuses on another, and we think central, element in fostering a citizenry equipped for participatory democracy, for the process of public deliberation is first and foremost a process of *communication*. Effective deliberation in a participatory democracy demands that citizens are able to have a voice in the discussion, that they are able to consider the voices of others, and that they can recognize the many subtle forces that impact how those voices are communicated in our mediated and technological world.

The processes and products of communicating about matters of common interest, of deliberating about public issues, make up what we call the *public voice*. Actually, the public voice is made up of many competing voices: a never-ending, turbulent, competitive, euphonious cacophony of debating perspectives contributing to some semblance of a marketplace of ideas. To talk about the public voice and how to strengthen the public voice is to address the awareness, values, knowledge, and skills that citizens must have to constructively contribute to the process and outcome of civic deliberation. Since most of the information we are exposed to and use in our public deliberation is filtered through the media, this book addresses how media practices impact the public voice. Since much of our public deliberation revolves around political campaigns of one form or another, this book also explores the role of campaign communication in the public voice. And since public deliberation necessarily involves conflicting positions and the diversity of perspectives that exist in the United States, this book also notes cultural, social, political, and economic factors that impact the public voice.

All the contributors to this book are nationally recognized authorities on public communication and the processes of democratic deliberation. They have published numerous articles and books on subjects ranging from American political culture to the practices of journalism, from presidential politics to the history of women's struggles for access to public influence. But beyond their academic expertise, these authors have been deeply involved in frontline efforts to improve America's public voice. They have conducted workshops, written columns, facilitated public forums, taught school children and their teachers, developed curricula, and advised media outlets on how to foster better public discussion of important issues and better democratic deliberation of public policy.

And more than rehashing complaints about the faults of our public voice, these authors draw upon their expertise and real-world experiences to offer specific solutions to the problems they address. While it is easy to note problems, too few commentaries on American democracy provide tangible suggestions for improvement. This book does not call for a return to some mythological golden age when a utopian democratic dialogue ruled the public voice, for such an age never existed in America. Nor does it assume that change will be easy or complete or that such a utopia is possible, even if we follow the advice offered. Its hope is that the analysis and suggestions advanced will provide guidelines for citizens to practice democracy: practice in the sense of striving to improve and practice in the sense of actually operationalizing the principles of democratic decision making. Paraphrasing Jameson, such practicing of democracy might not change the outcome of any specific election. "But it could better project the who, what, and how of governance. In the process, it would invite citizens to commit themselves to policies that will effect their lives. And, as my grandmother was fond of saying, what's the harm in that?" (1992, p. 238).

OUTLINE OF BOOK

This book is divided into four parts. Part I introduces the major issues and obstacles challenging our abilities to effectively deliberate matters of public concern. The next three parts each focus on a specific area which impacts the public voice and identify measures that may enhance effective citizenship communication. Part II focuses on *education*, with each chapter illuminating ways that we can better prepare citizens to deal with the information age and the complexities of our media-saturated society. The chapters in Part III concentrate on the practices of the mass media, and identify potential *collaborations* between media organizations, political institutions, and citizens that enhance civic dialogue and public deliberation. Finally, Part IV focuses on the kinds of critical *reflections* all of us, if we are to be truly informed and involved citizens, must consider about our own role in practicing democracy.

In Chapter 2, "Creating Civic Connections," Robert Schmuhl surveys the general terrain before us, noting many current and persistent obstacles to effective citizen participation in civic debate. He argues, "Although a citizen today can follow political and governmental affairs more closely than ever before, hearing America's public voice is difficult because a cacophony of babel surrounds it." That "cacophony of babel" emanates from individuals who are overwhelmed with the speed and volume of information availability, from voters who lack a basic understanding of how government and media institutions operate, and from the apathy and indifference fostered by such ignorance. Schmuhl sounds the three themes addressed in this book as he highlights the need for increased voter knowledge (education), media responsibility (i.e., collaboration), and citizen awareness (critical reflection). "Once a person leaves school," Schmuhl notes, "the media collectively assume the potential of becoming a, if not *the*, significant link to civic life. The person, however, needs to bring to the media's messages an informed understanding of what the words and images mean as well as how they contribute to a citizen's knowledge of government and politics."

In Chapter 3, "Two Questions for Populists," Charles Arthur Willard articulates another fundamental issue demanding consideration when suggesting ways to enhance civic dialogue and democratic participation. It stems from the debate—dating to the founding of the United States and earlier—about whether average citizens are fully able to assume the responsibilities of democratic governance, or if that governance is best left to elites with the necessary expertise and experience to make informed and reasoned judgments. Given the technical and complex nature of many if not most contemporary public issues, Willard questions whether we can expect general citizens to sufficiently understand, and nonspecialized media to adequately explain, all problems of public policy. Using the examples of the capital gains tax-cut debate and the creationism versus evolution controversy, Willard lays out a continuum of public communication ranging from general messages which appeal to the broadest possible audience to the most technical and complex messages understood only by the most specialized of audiences. He argues that most matters of public policy fall somewhere along the middle of the continuum, and he suggests that it is improbable that a generalized mass-public voice can adequately deliberate all matters of public concern.

Schmuhl and Willard advance important challenges for the remaining chapters. How can we better prepare citizens to face the realities of contemporary politics and mass-mediated society? How can the media better explain complex issues without oversimplifying and obscuring important facts and disputes? What types of self-awareness must citizens develop to function in a democratic fashion? The last three parts of this book face these challenges head on, and offer both an assessment of where we are and a vision of potential improvements.

Part II focuses on education, and opens with Chapter 4, "The Significance of Critical Communication Skills in a Democracy," by Jodi R. Cohen. This chapter explains the essential need for critical viewing skills among the citizenry. Starting from the model of classical rhetoric, she articulates a framework for interpreting contemporary media messages that recognizes the role communication plays in sustaining the political and economic relations of contemporary society. "Socio-cultural groups become dominant when powerful agents of socialization, such as the media, government, and education, assume their view of the world and hail all others according to that view," Cohen notes. "Being an active participant among communication power struggles is absolutely necessary to a participatory democracy." Chapter 4 outlines the types of skills students need to acquire to assume the responsibilities and opportunities of citizenship in our media-dominated society.

Chapter 5, "Building Citizenship Skills through Media Literacy Education," by Renee Hobbs, explains the agenda of most media literacy projects, noting that while our dependence on the mass media has grown, our general understanding of the workings and impacts of the media has remained impoverished. "As a result of modern communication technology, we have become so enmeshed in a sign system that the very system itself has become invisible to us," she writes. "As media literacy techniques help refresh our vision, we are invited to 're-vision' ourselves, our families, our neighbors, our communities and all our social institutions in ways that reflect the spirit of democratic problem solving through mutual respect, rational discourse and critical inquiry." Hobbs details a curriculum of media literacy education that includes the following four phases: (1) building awareness of personal choice in media exposure; (2) developing critical viewing skills; (3) analyzing the political, economic, and cultural contexts of media practices; and (4) exploring media advocacy, media action, and social change.

In Chapter 6, "Citizenship: The Forgotten Trust That Puts Democracy at Risk," John S. Burns details the progressive decay of citizen-education in the United States. "While we may still believe that somehow our children are being educated to become productive, active and involved citizens," Burns admonishes, "the empirical evidence proves this is one of the greatest (and perhaps one of the most dangerous) of our society's myths." Burns advances "applied civics"—an interdisciplinary curriculum designed to develop leadership and citizenship knowledge, skills, and conviction among students in America—as a partial corrective to our lethargic citizen-education efforts. He identifies the following five guiding principals: (1) democratizing schools and classrooms, (2) emphasizing critical thinking, (3) focusing on collaborative leadership, (4) utilizing experiential learning, and (5) fostering thoughtful self-reflection.

The chapters in Part III turn their attention to how the mass media can better facilitate public understanding and deliberation of public issues. These chapters illustrate specific types of collaboration among media outlets, public and private organizations, and citizens which foster greater attention to and understanding of the genuinely important issues of the day. In "Collaborating to Hear Public Voices," Karlyn Kohrs Campbell uses the Clarence Thomas and Anita Hill Senate hearings to illustrate how citizens voicing their discontent can combine with thorough media coverage to produce a vigorous and constructive dialogue about important public concerns. Campbell notes that politicians and reporters often fail to communicate the complexities of public issues, opting instead for simplified, confrontational narratives which make for more exciting, if not informative, news stories. "Deliberation on issues in all their complexity is perceived by news people as boring," she writes, "and nuanced positions on these issues are condemned as wishy-washy." Both the press and political candidates seldom see any advantage in participating in events designed to emphasize the extended and complex discussion of issues. Campbell describes the types of collaboration among citizens, politicians, and the news media needed to foster a more effective public voice.

In Chapter 8, "Does Civic Journalism Have a Future?," Edmund B. Lambeth concentrates on civic journalism, a growing national movement to institutionalize collaboration between the press and the public. Drawing upon examples from Spokane, Washington, to Madison, Wisconsin, Lambeth illustrates emerging and "still experimental" efforts at civic journalism, including the use of polling to determine community priorities for news coverage, joining print and electronic newsrooms into a collective effort, or entering into partnerships with public and private organizations to foster community interaction. While still controversial, Lambeth argues that civic journalism offers useful opportunities to enhance the coverage and discussion of people's deepest concerns. "Civic journalism makes a greater effort than traditional journalism to identify these concerns, report them with fidelity and link them to questions of public policy," he writes. "Its search is for ways to help stimulate public deliberation and help maximize the likelihood that citizens will generate the will to inform themselves and act in their own and in the public interest."

Richard A. Pride discusses a third type of media collaboration in Chapter 9, "Media Critics and Newsgroup-Embedded Newspapers:

Making Attentive Citizens Attentive." Pride echoes Cohen, Hobbs, and Burns in calling for educational curricula designed to develop students' awareness and critical thinking abilities concerning the mass media and contemporary political processes. He writes, "Potential citizens need two things if they are to grow into full citizenship: (1) knowledge of the way government and media interact and (2) a place where they can encounter the views of other citizens." Pride calls for a collaboration among public educators, serving as media critics, and media outlets using interactive technologies. Pride envisions the use of electronic newspapers with embedded news groups (interactive forums where individuals participate in ongoing discussions) to create a new kind of town square where civic debate can flourish. Drawing upon his own experiences as an educator and media critic, Pride illustrates how such collaborations may simultaneously educate the public and provide a viable arena for healthy, democratic debate.

The chapters in Part IV focus on basic understandings of communication, human action, cultural identity, and social and political conflict. They discuss the kinds of issues which must be addressed if our educational agendas and media collaborations are to advance a democratic public voice rather than simply reproducing obdurate and sterile patterns of social interaction. In Chapter 10, "On Discursive Amnesia: Reinventing the Possibilities for Democracy through Discursive Amnesty," Wen Shu Lee and Philip C. Wander focus on one of the most critical struggles that hinder a truly democratic public voice. They focus not only on the media but on the communication practices we employ in our everyday lives. Lee and Wander demonstrate how dominant patterns of discourse marginalize less powerful groups in our society by discounting alternative perspectives of our history and social reality. Resonating Cohen's concern that powerful institutions, such as the media, government, and education reinforce a narrow range of communicative possibilities, Lee and Wander see a current public voice robbed of its potential vibrancy and democratic diversity. They advance their notion of "discursive amnesty" as a way to open up our civic deliberations to new possibilities and perspectives and to reinvigorate our public interaction. As Lee and Wander write, "What we have before us is not Democracy, but the possibility and the glory of acting democratically— of actually deliberating and acting as a people to solve problems and doing so in ways that respect inalienable rights, which are more consistent than those our founding fathers accorded to Mankind in one section and reserved for land owning, white, males in another."

Roderick P. Hart draws attention to another struggle facing our efforts to enhance civic deliberation in Chapter 11, "The Search for Intimacy in American Politics." Hart explores the changing character of presidential politics, illustrating a turn to what he calls the "language of intimacy." Faced by a turbulent world that demands flexibility, and by complex policy issues that are difficult to explain in quick sound bites, politicians increasingly rely on communicating feelings rather than ideas or positions. "The world politicians inhabit—the real world that is—provides few things they can manage with confidence. A president therefore is constantly overpedaling to keep from back-pedaling. The language of intimacy gives him an edge. With it, a president can show he knows what he feels even if he does not know what to do," Hart writes. The result of this reliance on the language of intimacy is that it turns citizens into spectators of an emotional drama rather than involved, democratic workers in public decision making. Hart argues for increased critical reflection about what it is we reward politicians for giving us.

   Chapter 12, "Continuing the Conversation in a Democracy Always at Risk," discusses many of the recurring issues and persistent problems addressed in the previous chapters. While noting the promise of the solutions offered, the concluding chapter by Patricia M. Sias also notes some of the challenges to be faced and some of the philosophical tensions between the various points of view offered throughout the collection. It concludes not with a final pronouncement but with an invitation to continue the ongoing dialogue about America's public voice: to consider, debate, modify, or implement whatever suggestions you can in order to develop more capable citizens and a more democratic public voice for the twenty-first century.

REFERENCES

Eisenhower Leadership Group (ELG). (1996). Democracy at risk: How schools can lead. Unpublished report to the U.S. Secretary of Education. College Park, University of Maryland. March.

Fallows, J. (1996). *Breaking the news: How the media undermine American democracy*. New York: Pantheon.

Grossman, L. K. (1995). *The electronic republic*. New York: Viking.

Jameson, K. H. (1992). *Dirty politics*. New York: Oxford University Press.

Johnson, H., and D. Broder. (1996). *The system*. Boston: Little, Brown.

Mathews, D. (1994). *Politics for the people*. Urbana: University of Illinois Press.

Neuman, W. R., M. R. Just, and A. N. Crigler. (1992). *Common knowledge*. Chicago: University of Chicago Press.

Postman, N. (1995). *The end of education*. New York: Knopf.

Sandel, M. J. (1996). *Democracy's discontent: America in search of a public philosophy*. Cambridge: Harvard University Press.

Schmuhl, R. (1994). *Demanding democracy*. Notre Dame: Notre Dame University Press.

Schudson, M. (1995). *The power of the press*. Cambridge: Harvard University Press.

Yankelovich, D. (1991). *Coming to public judgment*. Syracuse: Syracuse University Press.

Chapter 2

Creating Civic Connections

Robert Schmuhl

As incongruous and even paradoxical as it might sound, the closer American democracy draws to the nation's citizenry, the further many citizens withdraw from civic enlightenment and engagement. Despite more participatory electoral procedures, more open government practices, and more availability of information about public life, citizens in alarming numbers find the activities of democracy cause for—to use words from just the first letter of the alphabet—alienation, anger, anxiety, or apathy. Books that recently appeared discuss "democracy's discontent" and "the breaking point" of the American political system (Sandel, 1996; Johnson and Broder, 1996). Although troubling today, this democratic distemper is potentially more ominous if it foreshadows greater decline in citizenship for the future.

A consequence of our current condition is a quandary with a prime question: How can individuals and institutions create stronger, more vital connections to the workings of democracy in all of their robust, at times rowdy, variety? Interestingly, the possibilities for designing an appropriate, hope-fulfilling response have never been more promising. Thanks to the expanding availability of information technologies and what they offer, professionals in education and the media—as well as citizens at large—can probe virtually any subject with a political or government dimension. Cognizance of an issue has the potential to become the foundation for purposeful action of one kind or another.

Conceptually, the briefly sketched process could, without undue effort, link people to the democracy, fostering knowledge and participation. Practically, however, several forces and phenomena intersect to make an effective and enduring civic connection more difficult to achieve. Education, the media, and public life in general are currently in states of turbulent change as a result of what has been occurring among people and throughout technology in recent years.

Since the 1960s, many educators have attempted to right previous wrongs by focusing on the experiences of particular groups—notably, women, African-Americans, Native Americans, Hispanics, and Asian-Americans—rather than the "all American" approach of the past that emphasized the less-inclusive Western heritage of this nation's life and thought. Necessary though they might be, efforts to place in perspective what has happened to and with specific groups come at a cost. In studying history and government (to pick the most relevant fields), there is not only more concern with identifying or analyzing acts of commission and omission that draw into question fundamental democratic principles. There is also the risk that overly particular attention to different groups might stand in the way of developing nuanced understanding of common characteristics and qualities Americans share.

Simultaneously with the new emphases in education and their broader consequences throughout society, the media environment changes so quickly and with such regularity that trying to keep up with the messengers and their messages requires the endurance of a long-distance runner who never stops. From a relatively small number of print and broadcast sources as recently as two decades ago, people now face a dizzying choice of information and entertainment outlets. Fallout from this technological explosion includes not only splintering from fragmentation but the endless jousting of competition. Although a citizen today can follow political and government affairs more closely than ever before, hearing America's public voice is often difficult because a cacophony of babel surrounds it.

Even with easy access to civic information, there is a question to what extent the people want to know about public life. A recent study by *The Washington Post*, Harvard University, and the Kaiser Family Foundation revealed that only 25 percent of people surveyed trusted "the government in Washington to do the right thing" on a consistent basis (Morin and Balz, 1996, p. A1). Back in 1964, 76 percent trusted Washington, but that, of course, was before the Vietnam War, Watergate, Iran-contra, and the absorption in political scandal involving private lives as well as public business. If an overwhelming majority of the citizenry lacks trust in the national government, will they be disposed to spending time studying issues related to civic affairs?

Taken together, what has been occurring in education, communications, and public life forces reconsideration of traditional approaches to citizenship. At a time of abundant change, where do the people turn for the leadership and guidance necessary in creating a civic connection that recognizes these new realities and their consequences? More pointedly is the question, Is the America of today so different from yesterday that tomorrow our most basic principles and practices of self-governance will be considered anachronistic?

Curiously enough, because of their diversity, our educational system and the media offer the most promising opportunities for developing and sustaining the appropriate civic connection in the future. In the same public opinion study already cited, respondents revealed startling ignorance of elementary information about government and political life in general. Some findings are as follows: 67 percent did not know who represented them in the House of Representatives; 54 percent were unable to name their state's two senators; and 58 percent thought more public money was spent on foreign aid than on Medicare (Morin, 1996).[1] Such percentages are particularly troubling when viewed in context over time and in relation to the availability of factual information from such a wide variety of sources. As Morin notes in his analysis of the data, "Overall, surveys indicate that Americans know about as much about politics and government today as they did during the 1940s. But these results hide a more distressing trend: In the past 50 years, the average number of years an American spends in school has increased from less than nine to more than 12, yet political knowledge has not grown" (1996, p. A6).

Clearly, educators responsible for teaching about politics and government need to devote more attention to explaining fundamental concerns related to representative government and to the role individual citizens can and should play in the American system. Without such knowledge and its significance, the danger exists that people will never understand or appreciate what is possible for them to do, both theoretically and practically. Even with the growing emphasis on the importance of particular groups and the influence of multicultural approaches, teaching civics should not be dismissed or denigrated as an old-fashioned exercise whose time passed with the "anything goes 1960s" and their aftermath. Elementary as it might sound, it is important to know how government works, where public money is being spent, who is running in election campaigns, and what specific links exist between citizens and public life.

Education has the responsibility to begin a process of civic awareness that the media in subsequent years will sustain. Introducing the results of the recent survey, Morin perceptively observes that

Knowing basic facts about politics does matter. The survey suggests that information is one of democracy's golden keys: Without basic facts about the players and the rules of the game Americans tune out politics and turn off to voting.

In addition to not voting, the survey found that these less informed Americans are far more likely to believe their country is in decline. They consistently say that the country's biggest problems have worsened in recent decades, including air and water quality that actually have improved. And they are less likely to know that the annual budget deficit and the number of federal workers have gone down—not up—in recent years.

As a consequence, less knowledgeable Americans are much more likely to believe that actions by the federal government invariably make every problem worse, a rigid cynicism that the survey found transcends party identification or political ideology. (1996, p. A1)

Besides recognizing the connection between the individual citizen and the community, citizenship means making the effort to keep informed and to act with the community interest in mind. Without basic facts and a framework for seeing how they relate to each other, people in a civic sense feel isolated, and they are more inclined to nurse personal grievances and prejudices, factually founded or not. The need for civics education that initiates long-term commitment is particularly acute for younger people today. According to the most recent survey of the Higher Education Research Institute at the University of California at Los Angeles, only 28.5 percent of this year's college freshmen think it is "important to keep up with politics"—half the number of thirty years ago—and 34 percent believe one person can do little to change society—a ten-year high (Riechmann, 1996, p. A5).

Whether disinterested, uninterested, or prematurely cynical, the young have their reasons for their attitudes and opinions. Until they realize the value to themselves and to others of maintaining a continuing connection to civic life, we can probably expect to see the disengagement and disaffection that currently exist. However, substantive and compelling educational programs in elementary grades and high school could help create an appropriate foundation and springboard for the future. Work, of course, is already being done in this area, but statistical trends suggest that a focused effort would meet an urgent need.

Properly designed, teaching about citizenship and civic life need not be a recitation of rules about the legislative process and the mysteries of the electoral college. Of greater potential benefit would be an approach that stressed an individual citizen's stake—philosophically and practically—in the nation. Going hand in hand with this approach would be an emphasis on the role media play in communicating information about public affairs. Once a person leaves school, the media collectively assume the potential of becoming a significant link to civic life. The person, however, needs to bring to the media's messages an informed understanding of what the words and images mean as well as how they contribute to a citizen's knowledge of government and politics.

Just as there needs to be attention given to the basic facts of our self-governing democracy, a program in citizenship and civic life should answer such questions as these: How does a news story come into being? What process is involved in selecting something deemed newsworthy? Who chooses what we read, see, and hear? Why do certain stories merit coverage while others fail to appear? How do media differ in transmitting information, and what do those differences mean to citizen understanding?[2]

Media literacy has a central place in a civics curriculum. For instance, in *The Electronic Republic*, Lawrence K. Grossman observes, "Journalism's biases lie mostly in five areas: in favor of what is new, what is bad, what is dramatic, what is most readily available, and what can be readily understood" (1995, p. 89). These biases, a teacher might inform students, elevate change, controversy, and simplicity in a journalist's mind, subordinating such characteristics as compromise and complexity. The same teacher could ask, Is it any wonder why we tend to be exposed to so much partisan or personal conflict in the coverage of politics and government rather than efforts at harmony or consensus? Does the perception of a polarized political life help contribute to the mounting sense of mistrust that government is incapable of performing in the public interest?

Especially in a presidential election year, it would be instructive to examine the candidate nominating procedure and how that process is presented to us through different forms of media. Theodore H. White notes, "There was a terminal madness to the primaries of 1980—the madness of a good idea run wild" (1982, p. 284). After explaining that the post-1960s system is "a classic example of the triumph of goodwill over common sense" (p. 285), the noted chronicler of presidential campaigns writes this:

There was no longer any way of making a simple generalization about how Americans chose their candidates for the presidency. What was worse, no school, no textbook, no course of instruction, could tell young Americans, who would soon be voting, how their system worked. And if we of the political press had to cram such rules into our heads as we moved from state to state, each with two parties, and each state differing—how could ordinary voters understand what professional observers had such difficulty grasping? (p. 289)

White's book appeared in 1982. The system has become even more maddeningly complicated since then, with states continuing to jockey for more advantageous positions for varying reasons. Though originally intended to foster democratic openness and citizen participation, the current design defies simple explanation by the media or anyone else, and voter turnout is generally quite low. Residents of the states later in the process feel as though they have little or no voice in a process that rewards the people who were able to participate earlier. Greater awareness of the myriad weaknesses of the ever-changing procedure could ultimately yield concern throughout the citizenry that election to our national offices (president and vice president) demands a methodically designed and implemented nationwide nominating system (Schmuhl, 1990, pp. 7–13). Until this happens, however, the media—complete with their characteristics and biases—will continue to be responsible for *nationalizing* the contests that take place in the individual states, idiosyncratic as they tend to be.

It could be argued that heavy coverage of a chaotic process contributes to the chaos, making matters and how they are perceived even worse. Journalists, though, could frequently point out the undemocratic lunacy of change, contingency, and personality orientation the current procedure tends to promote for the nation as a whole. In *Breaking the News*, James Fallows writes the following:

The ultimate reason people buy the *New York Times* rather than *People*, or watch World News Tonight rather than Entertainment Tonight, is a belief that it is worth paying attention to public affairs. If people thought there was no point even in hearing about public affairs—because the politicians were all crooks, because the outcome was always rigged, because ordinary people stood no chance, because everyone in power was looking out for himself—then newspapers and broadcast news operations might as well close up shop too, because there would be no market for what they were selling. If people have no interest in politics or public life, they have no reason to follow the news. It doesn't concern them. (1996, pp. 243–244)

Although somewhat limiting in defining news, particularly in a multisource environment, Fallows's statement suggests that information with a political or public dimension should mean something in the lives of the people. Simultaneously, as consumers of media messages and citizens, people need to see the relevancy of the news for themselves, such as the case in nominating presidential candidates. Otherwise there is the danger that people will assume the role of spectators and (in times of scandal) voyeurs, watching the passing scene without recognizing any personal or civic connection to it.

Breaking the News is a catalog of complaint and criticism, explaining—in the words of the book's subtitle—"How the Media Undermine American Democracy." Fallows is unsparing in charging journalists with an overemphasis on the sensational, superficial, and strategic instead of the substantive and salient.

His final chapter, "News and Democracy," offers the possible hope that interest in what is called *public journalism* will help news consumers and citizens understand their own stake in politics and public life. Whether public journalism will exorcize the "mood of fatalistic disengagement" Fallows describes is debatable (1996, p. 243). The rationale animating the movement is laudable; however, some of the practices—like having news institutions perceived to be forcing candidates to respond to concerns presented by the media—are questionable. Yet having journalists aware that serious problems exist in the coverage of politics and public life is the first step in rethinking what might be appropriate ways for the media to serve as effective intermediaries between the people and the broader civic community.

Even if the news media dramatically change their approach to presenting information about public affairs, education will still play a critical role in preparing Americans for the duties and obligations of citizenship. Fallows and other commentators note that the speed with which news now circulates makes thoughtful deliberation of subjects more difficult than previous times. This situation affects how public figures respond to what might be occurring, but there is also another consequence of this unending rush of words and images. A citizen's attention span is often relatively brief these days because the media's attention span is often relatively brief.

Designed methodically, a civics curriculum (especially for high school and college students) could provide a counterbalancing force to the media's overwhelming urgency. Classrooms provide the perfect setting to examine ideas and issues with care over time. Teachers and students can keep an eye on the media, but they also have the opportunity to take the longer view. Ideally, discussion of individual concerns and how they are portrayed in news coverage would lead to larger and lasting conclusions that create models for use away from school in later years. A discriminating, questioning consumer of news will most probably be a concerned and active citizen. Making that connection meaningful should be a priority of education on the same plane as the traditional goals of literacy, compositional aptitude, and numerical proficiency.

In preparing for the future, it is important to realize that the changing communications environment will place new and different demands on the citizenry. The proliferation of media outlets means constant competition for a person's attention and the finite amount of available time one can spend with the media's messages. With so much information and entertainment from which to choose, people will have to be more active in seeking out news about politics and public affairs. Unless they already understand the significance of their involvement in civic life, they might be inclined to seek any of the multitude of diversions the same media offer in abundance.

Interestingly, with CNN, C-SPAN, web sites on the Internet, and many other sources, the average citizen has a virtually unlimited opportunity for access to data about every aspect of American democracy.

Worries about coping with the information overload notwithstanding, the most compelling concern centers on the following question: Will individuals—except for the self-interested engaged in politics and government—take the initiative to study issues and ideas relevant to democratic deliberation? In recent years, as the number of television channels has grown and the use of the remote control operator has become more popular, the phenomenon of "zapping" messages without immediate appeal has increased. Somehow or other, the slow-moving and complicated processes of public life will have to be perceived as worthy of continuing consideration, or the public knowledge central to purposeful action will suffer even greater decline (Schmuhl, 1994, pp. 108–128).

The proliferation of sophisticated communications technologies has also led in recent years to a chorus of calls proposing that the people use interactive capabilities of these technologies to participate in decision making about government issues. During his 1992 presidential campaign and more recently, Ross Perot has talked—to the enthusiastic approval of listeners—about the value of electronic town hall meetings with people providing feedback on public issues and questions. In his book *Arrogant Capital*, Kevin Phillips praises the new methods of political action made possible by modern communications. Phillips writes the following:

Futurists Alvin Toffler and John Naisbitt emphasize two reasons for rightly calling our system of representative government outdated: First, what used to be true representative government is being swallowed up by the Washington presence of more interest groups than the world has ever before seen in one place. Representative government has become interest-group government. Second, new electronic technology now gives governments an unprecedented wherewithal to empower the ordinary voter directly. We should use it. (1995, pp. 189–190)

If we are to believe such thinking, electronic plebiscites loom over the horizon, providing a continuous flow of opinions or judgments to elected and appointed government officials.

In theory, the idea of direct democracy in some form appeals to a primordial characteristic of American citizenship. Getting together in town meetings to discuss and resolve problems goes back to the early years of the nation. Also, there is the romance that anyone, with or without experience, can recognize what is in the best interests of the people and act accordingly. An innocent, well-meaning amateur—like Jefferson Smith in Frank Capra's film *Mr. Smith Goes to Washington*— quickly learns how to confront antidemocratic activity and work on behalf of the citizenry. An attitude of "anybody can do it" is common among Americans. Especially at a time of widespread public mistrust, the sense of control that comes from a greater say in political life is alluring.

However, the theory and romance of direct democracy quickly collide with the realities of the public ignorance and relatively low rates of voting in existing electoral procedures already discussed. At jeopardy in any plan to conduct regular referenda with the people deciding is the basic character of our representative system. It is hopelessly idealistic (and misguided) to imagine that the average citizen, as a matter of daily routine, will study complex legislation and initiatives to prepare to vote on an ongoing basis. As David Mathews explains in *Politics for the People*, "Almost half of the bills that come before the U.S. Congress include highly technical and specialized scientific data" (1994, p. 73).

Cheerleading from the likes of Ross Perot, Kevin Phillips, Alvin Toffler, or John Naisbitt notwithstanding, that technology makes direct democracy possible does not mean we should create such a process. The dawning of a new century provokes an abundance of futuristic speculation; however, sober-minded remembering of the nation's first two centuries reveals the enduring value that comes from a system stressing balanced and deliberative governance. While the modern media work with wondrous speed, people in political life need to guard against making decisions when public opinion is highly volatile and still shifting with the transmission of new information. To be sure, only a contemporary Luddite would reject out-of-hand any use of the new information technologies in our politics and government. Throughout *The Electronic Republic*, Grossman argues that we need to reinvigorate our commitment to citizenship at the same time we consider what role these technologies might play. He concludes his book with the following reasoned statement:

As we go about the complicated task of reshaping representative government and redistributing political power in the electronic republic, we must retain the delicate constitutional balance between local and national, between private interests and the public good, and between minority freedom and majority rule. Those will not be easy tasks. But we cannot afford to miss the opportunity to use these new means of communication for the public benefit. We must harness the inter-active telecommunications system to help make modern deliberative democracy satisfy the needs of far more citizens than it does today. (1995, p. 254)

American political life and the world of popular communications have been intertwined since the days of pamphleteering and the Partisan Press. The two realms influence and have impact on each other with the public placed in a role akin to "observer-participants" or "consumer-citizens." In *The Road Ahead*, computer guru and entrepreneur Bill Gates makes the following remarks:

Each media advance has had a substantial effect on how people and governments interact. The printing press and, later, mass-circulation newspapers
changed the nature of political debate. Radio and then television allowed
government leaders to talk directly and intimately with the populace. Similarly, the information highway will have its own influence on politics. For the
first time politicians will be able to see immediate representative surveys of
public opinions. Voters will be able to cast their ballots from home or their
wallet PCs with less risk of miscounts or fraud. The implications for government may be as great as they are for industry. (1995, p. 271)

But how far should we go? Can democratic action be carried to an
extreme that ultimately becomes self-defeating or dangerous? After
discussing how "the highway will bestow power on groups of citizens
who want to organize to promote causes or candidates," Gates consid-
ers the possibility of carrying that power to its furthest point, what he
calls "total 'direct democracy'":

Personally, I don't think direct voting would be a good way to run a government.
There is a place in governance for representatives—middlemen—to add value.
They are the ones whose job it is to take the time to understand all the nuances of
complicated issues. Politics involves compromise, which is nearly impossible
without a relatively small number of representatives making decisions on
behalf of the people who elected them. The art of management—whether of a
society or a company—revolves around making informed choices about the
allocation of resources. It's the job of a full-time policy-maker to develop expertise. This enables the best of them to come up with and embrace nonobvious
solutions direct democracy might not allow, because voters might not understand the tradeoffs necessary for long-term success. (p. 272)

Astutely and appropriately, Gates draws the line at using the bur-
geoning technologies in ways that fundamentally and irrevocably alter the traditional relationship between the citizen and government.
No one disputes the value of using whatever the communications media
offer as a way to be better informed and more participatory. Such work
is, indeed, commendable and should be strengthened through programs
on all levels of education and by efforts supported within the communications industry. If the media can help cultivate a more knowledgeable, engaged electorate over time, democracy itself would be a
beneficiary. Possibly there would be less public discontent and more
reason to maintain an active as well as vital civic connection.

Near the end of his life, James Madison wrote in a letter to a friend,
"A people who mean to be their own governors must arm themselves
with the power which knowledge gives" (Grossman, 1995, p. 228).
Modern media make the potential for that kind of power more accessible than Madison, or Thomas Jefferson, or any of the founders ever
imagined. People in education and communications share the duty of

transmitting political information that leads to knowledge. For the vitality of American democracy now and in the future, citizens must actively assume the responsibilities such knowledge and power make obligatory for effective, purposeful self-governance. To do otherwise would not only endanger our political system but place at risk our distinct—and distinctive—civilization.

NOTES

1. The people polled thought foreign aid accounted for 26 percent of the federal budget, when in actuality it amounts to less than 2 percent, while Medicare accounts for about 13 percent (Morin, 1996).

2. In the mid-1970s, with support from the Ford Foundation, Indiana University's Poynter Center began the Citizen and the News project to help academics in the humanities and social sciences integrate the study of news in college-level courses (Schmuhl, 1979).

REFERENCES

Fallows, J. (1996). *Breaking the news: How the media undermine American democracy.* New York: Pantheon.

Gates, B. (1995). *The road ahead.* New York: Penguin.

Grossman, L. K. (1995). *The electronic republic.* New York: Viking.

Johnson, H., and D. S. Broder. (1996). *The system: The American way of politics at the breaking point.* Boston: Little, Brown.

Mathews, D. (1994). *Politics for the people.* Urbana: University of Illinois Press.

Morin, R. (1996). Who's in control? Many don't know or care. *The Washington Post,* January 29, p. A6.

Morin, R., and H. Balz. (1996). Americans losing trust in each other and institutions. *The Washington Post,* January 28, p. A1.

Phillips, K. P. (1995). *Arrogant capital.* Boston: Back Bay Books.

Riechmann, D. (1996). College freshmen found apathetic. *South Bend Tribune,* January 8, p. A5.

Sandel, M. J. (1996). *Democracy's discontent: America in search of a public philosophy.* Cambridge: Harvard University Press.

Schmuhl, R. (1979). *The classroom and the newsroom.* Bloomington: Poynter Center, Indiana University.

Schmuhl, R. (1990). *Statecraft and stagecraft.* Notre Dame: University of Notre Dame Press.

Schmuhl, R. (1994). *Demanding democracy.* Notre Dame: University of Notre Dame Press.

White, T. H. (1982). *America in search of itself: The making of the president 1956–1980.* New York: Harper & Row.

sound bites or rallies or the slick "interchanges" that characterize "Crossfire," something they have rarely been willing to deal with opportunity. Sound bite campaigning at best stifles, does not prepare candidates to deliberate about issues, which is one reason they avoid the involvement that issues require. The 1992 presidential debate in Richmond was a creditable effort to refocus the concerns of ordinary voters. It should be repeated, but the format of other debates could be changed to facilitate more extended policy statements and challenges. Also, confronting candidates with their own advertisements, as was done in the South Carolina Republican primary debate, is an effective way to compel candidates to take responsibility for the charges and claims made in them.

Finally, the public also has responsibilities. As Americans, we tend to believe that in former times there must have been an ideal public sphere through which the public participated more fully in politics. In *The Power of News*, Schudson (1995) addresses the question of whether

there was an time when such a public sphere existed in the United States. He also concludes that the news media are ill-equipped to facilitate its creation because their commercial character largely . . . the mass audiences they seek to deliver to advertisers, is the antithesis of . . . citizenship. . . .

If Schudson and Lippmann are right, the links connecting together content and the citizenry are those entities known as intermediary associations. In the past, these consisted primarily of political parties, labor unions, churches, and civic associations. At present, political parties and labor unions as well as many civic associations are in decline, and they are not performing this function well. According to . . . many Americans, the primary or only link to government is . . . Congress and its representatives. Yet, if citizens wish to have their voices heard . . . The voices of citizens who are not associated with groups . . . will find it more difficult . . . voluntary associations diminishes the ability of publics to have their views heard . . . here the public has full responsibility.

. . . that the public acknowledges . . . responsibility for news content is evident in recent studies investigating what viewers are or wish to

Chapter 3

Two Questions for Populists

Charles Arthur Willard

Whether enhanced public participation is seen as an end in itself, as a check against elite oligarchy, or as a counterforce to technocracy, one indispensable assumption is that public issues are to some extent accessible; that without special training, some greater portion of the lay public can participate beneficially in political life. But to what extent can the knowledge needed to run a complex civilization be democratized? To what extent can expert knowledge be translated into a common parlance and judged by nonexperts? These questions are most remarkable for the confidence with which many people answer them.

Noam Chomsky says, for instance, "Compared to intellectually complex tasks [public knowledge] is pretty slight. It's not like the sciences where there are so many things you have to study. . . . By and large, what happens in political life is relatively accessible. It doesn't take special training or unusual intelligence" (1989, p. 54). One conspicuous intellectual tradition would reply to Chomsky's claim by huffing in the opposite direction. Richard Hofstadter would call it demagoguery. Walter Lippmann and Joseph Schumpeter would call it preposterous. And even Thomas Jefferson (1813) would call it dubious: "There is a natural aristocracy among men [of virtue and talent, not wealth]. . . . May we not even say that that form of government is best that provides the most effectually for a pure selection of these natural aristoi into the offices of government?" To this end, Jefferson proposed an educational system that would teach "the three Rs" to everyone but select only the best and brightest for higher education. He championed the public as one check in a system of checks and balances, but Jefferson was not, in any modern sense of the expression, a "Jeffersonian democrat." He envisioned what can only be called government-by-Harvard men, and were he among us today, he would belong to the school of thought political scientists call pluralism. Most pluralists today would snort derisively at Chomsky's claim. They would say that done properly, which is to say done by experts and by splendidly trained public actors, policy disputes are technical affairs that demand special training and unusual intelligence.

This schism between America's republican and egalitarian instincts is democracy's oldest dispute. It engaged the Federalists, enraged the Jacksonians, and since the progressive era, as I have argued in a recent book, it has presented every symptom of a debate gone bad.[1] Bristling with class antagonisms, marked more by rancor than evidence, the debate about the public has sparked a spiral of escalating hyperbole. Fixed on one another's most outrageous claims, each side has drawn away from the other. Opponents who once might have profited from one another's criticism have turned inward, talking only to fellow travelers. As their reading habits became increasingly incestuous, the two camps have become hermetically sealed discourses, self-referential and self-confirming. This ideological self-assurance has resulted in an "is not–is too" squabble, a clash of dueling pronouncements that allows even very dubious claims to pass as obvious.

Claims such as Chomsky's (1989), for instance, at least are possibilities populists should consider. Pluralism may be a Potimkin village, as I argue, and perhaps there are no reasons to trust the rule of experts or the unembarrassed power elite espoused by the Federalists. But when human discourse aspires to be something nobler than a contact sport, the weaknesses of one's opponents do not necessarily vindicate one's own case. If Chomsky's claim is an equal and opposite caricature, as I suspect even some populists would say it is, then it is important to consider the extent to which public issues are technical, or have technical dimensions, and the degree to which technical appearances are deliberately obscurant or unavoidably arcane. In this spirit, I ask even the most committed populists to put aside their pique with the pluralists. However rankling that Brahman self-assurance may be, populists still need to know whether Chomsky's claim is defensible. And no one, neither pluralist nor populist, knows the degree to which knowledge can be democratized, or the degree to which technical knowledge can be translated into a general parlance.

To prove these claims, I will consider two rather different examples, namely, the capital gains tax and the creation science debate that played itself out in *McLean v. Arkansas*. I do not have the faintest idea whether they are typical public issues. They both affect the general public directly and are controversial, but it is hard to say whether they are typically complex. The former is technical, certainly. The latter does not seem to be exceptionally so. But in choosing these examples I hope to avoid the kind of loaded dice by which pluralists most annoy populists—arguing, for instance, that the debate about the supercollider is a typical public issue, and then conjuring the spectacle of "Bubba" and "Joe Sixpack" pondering the mysteries and deciding the future of particle physics. But neither should our examples be too easy. Flag burning, welfare Cadillacs, and Pat Buchanan's fortress America may be as accessible, as Chomsky says, but they are not, I should think, examples populists will like. They are demagogue fodder; their essence *is* their simplicity. Typical or not, I will begin an example that at least has the grace of drabness.

• • •

What would a senator or citizen need to know to assess a proposal to reduce the capital gains tax? A rational decision, Robert Solow (1990) says, would rest on an estimate of the pattern of losses and gains to the U.S. Treasury, a demographic understanding of how the effects of the tax change would be distributed across the population, and a sense of the tax's effectiveness in stimulating capital investment and research and development—"exactly the stuff of academic research papers and Ph.D. theses," media riddled with technical jargon, arcane assumptions, and mathematical procedures. One would think "that a body of interpretive economic journalism would fill the gap and mediate between policy-oriented research and policy-interested citizens. There is indeed some [but] there is not nearly enough serious economic journalism and the average quality is pretty poor" (p. 9).

One might infer that the problem lies partly with economists, who are more recondite than they need to be, and with journalists, who are less expert than they should be. Both might do better at translating the enigmas of the dismal science into a general parlance. But the drift of Solow's argument is that only economists have the epistemic wherewithal to do the translation. For what must be translated is not a body of self-evident facts but a series of deep disputes. Economists disagree, to put it mildly, about macroeconomic models and simulations, about how to read the historical record, and about how to determine the degree to which future investment will replicate the past. There are disagreements about how to calculate the effects of cutting capital gains taxes on gross domestic product, unemployment rates, household income, and stock prices. There are deep—and deeply political—differences about whether (and about the degree to which) the benefits of cuts would flow mostly to the wealthy or to middle-income taxpayers or even to lower-income taxpayers. The competing advocates often have impeccable economic credentials, and judged by squint-of-eye, a more or less equal distribution of tainted appointments (if I may so characterize positions in conservative or liberal think-tanks). To reliably represent such disputes, we might infer from Solow's (1990) argument that one would need dissertation-level expertise in economics, which suggests that the onus for improving economic journalism lies not with journalists but with economics itself.

Still at the tip of the iceberg, however, is the problem that some aspects of economic policy lie outside the economist's expertise. Consumer confidence, for instance, is a necessary condition for spending, investment, and upswings in the business cycle, but for economists it is a mysterious contingency not unlike the weather that calls for the expertise of several social sciences. The performance of agencies—calculating, for instance, the bureaucratic drag that inhibits the achievement of goals—calls for another sort of expertise. The performance of capital venture firms and of the diffusion of innovation call for still others. Overarching all these considerations is the unfathomable tar pit economists call "political interference." Regarding economic policy, Chomsky (1989) has it backwards: It is harder to juggle the disparate and sometimes incommensurable claims of different expert fields than it is to work within any single specialty. Economic policy is a more difficult, less accessible subject matter than economics and arguably requires public actors of extraordinary ability. The economic journalist would need to be an economist with peripheral vision, one with a technically capable grasp of a number of expert fields and of the policy process itself. Unicorns of this sort do exist. At *Newsweek*, Robert Solow and Robert Samuelson, and before them Paul Samuelson, have produced columns that, for thirty years or so, have arguably been exemplars of economic journalism. Though their columns have varied from week to week in complexity of subject matter and in the number of technical concepts used without explanation, one would scarcely call them, on the whole, broadly accessible.

One would not call them populist, either. They are paradigm cases of authority-dependence. They argue chiefly at a conclusory level— one side says this, another side says that, here is the correct view— without fully surveying the empirical evidence or technical problems of interpreting that evidence. Whether this is a flaw or an inevitable feature of the discourse depends largely on how much the readership can be expected to know. Economic journalism may not need a reader who is fully conversant with Keynesian investment theory and elasticities of price and demand. But the *Newsweek* essays have sometimes presumed that readers understand the Phillips Curve, monetary and fiscal policy, multiplier effects, money market equilibrium, and—at least once—stochastic shock.

When one cannot evaluate the soundness of the reasons standing behind claims, one is reliant on the author's authority. This is often for the best. No one can fully understand every idea in the world. There are too many knowledge claims and too many that cannot be understood without considerable expertise. So where medieval logicians held that it was fallacious to accept an idea not on its substantive merits but on the authority of its advocate, in our own time, acquiescing to authority is more often than not the rational thing to do. But this is, withal, a mixed blessing because it demands a trust in credentials and the institutions that bestow them. This trust is sometimes strained when professions seem like predatory turf tenders and professors seem like true believers. But even with impeccable behavior (the *Newsweek* columns have been unfailingly civil) and ideal credentials (Solow and Paul Samuelson bear the imprimatur of Massachusetts Institute of Technology and both are Nobel laureates), the *Newsweek* columnists may or may not be speaking for the rational consensus of their discipline. Since most readers cannot assess the state of consensus in economics, they are left solely with an invitation to trust.

This authority-dependence is the predicament of even splendidly trained intellectuals. Without having inspected the fossil record, one believes in Darwin; without knowing how it works, one believes a statistical procedure; and without any idea of their bases, one believes in the "Big Bang" and in the existence of quarks and leptons. Had we but world enough and time, we might come to understand the rational bases for every belief and the whole of human knowledge. But what is striking is the aplomb with which ordinary mortals claim to do so: "Knowledge of society as a whole involves not merely the acquisition of useful insights from neighboring disciplines but transcending the disciplinary boundaries altogether" (Bellah, 1985, p. 300). Claims of this sort are not treated gently in this book. Transcending the disciplines suggests a reliable understanding of them and something of a reading load. One has presumably kept up with 74,000 science journals, or at least with what *Newsweek* calls "the top 4,500" journals. One has presumably read the 2,000 to 3,000 books published annually in science and technology and the 6,000 to 8,000 books published annually in sociology and economics (R. R. Bowker, 1996). And since this panoptic span of vision is a philosophical undertaking, one is presumably conversant with the 15,000 or so articles in U.S. journals, 12,000 English articles published abroad, and more than 5,000 books published between 1940 and 1976 (R. R. Bowker, 1996). Many people infer from this paper tonnage that most of what is published is mediocre, but these sweeping pronouncements are never buttressed by what would surely be the mother of all spectacles, namely, proof. A proper proof would require an unmanageably expansive corporate enterprise, not to mention the felling of the redwoods to print the result. This suggests, piquantly enough, that what humanists are wont to call "general knowledge" is a blustering not unlike whistling in the dark. The very vocabulary of liberal education may be the acme of all ironies, an illusion of intellectual mastery, and a false consciousness masquerading as reflective thinking. That possibility, at least, suggests the wisdom of a public works project. Given the magnitude of what has been written, and the vastness of what is going on behind our backs, the following should be chiseled in Latin above the entrance to every humanities building: "Omniscience Underdetermined by Data."

One gathers from Chomsky (1989) that "public knowledge" is like academe's general knowledge, only easier. I submit that public knowledge is like its academic cousin, only more so. Specialists need to worry only about how the rest of the world impinges on their specialties, but senators and citizens move from topic to topic to topic. Like Gypsies, they are always on someone else's turf. Given the constraints of time and daily agendas, and given the opportunity costs of background research, they are more or less inevitably and more or less comprehensively dependent on experts and specialists. This is why, I imagine, political interference comes so easily. When the evidence and experts are more or less unintelligible, then inside the Beltway, at least, most anything seems possible.

Outside that peculiar and inbred world there is a sticky republican feel to the rule of experts and trickle-down epistemology. However quixotic it may seem to expect the public to do what intellectuals cannot do, one can sympathize, certainly, with populists who notice how out-of-the-loop most citizens are. Chomsky traces this disempowerment back to the Federalists' distrust of the people, the goal being to reduce the masses to "apathy and obedience, allowing them to participate in the political system, but as consumers, not as true participants. You allow them a method for ratifying decisions that are made by others, but you eliminate the methods by which they might first, inform themselves; second, organize; and third, act in such a way as to really control decision-making" (pp. 40–41).

He certainly has the plot right. The Federalists envisioned the public as a weak check; a small, politically active elite, perhaps the 8 to 10 percent of the populace that actually tracks public issues might choose among options formed by experts (Neuman, 1986, p. 6). This public would be more appreciative than activist. It would be a "coached judge" of a carefully staged competition among elites in the marketplace of ideas. But though Chomsky, in his many writings, has certainly documented instances of the control of information, one does wonder in general whether the truth would set us free or merely bog us down. The National Archives reportedly has 325 million pages of classified documents (*The Washington Post*, 1994, p. A12), a figure that does not include current classified documents kept by various federal agencies and none of the fabled corporate databases often thought to contain the keys to the kingdom. Come the revolution, then, exactly how will all these secrets be brought to public light? It is now technologically feasible to imagine seven or eight cable networks devoted exclusively to publicizing government secrets, a like number devoted to publicizing the contents of corporate databases, and another ten or so networks devoted exclusively to deliberating about the meaning of all that information. The result, I predict, will either be the numbing of the American mind, and utter falsification of the liberal theory of the press, or a dramatic increase in channel surfing whereby MTV will begin to look more and more like the center that will hold.

It may take even heavier lifting to get economic information to the people. Where the depredations of the CIA may be as easily comprehensible as Chomsky says, the case of economic policy is less clear. There is arguably too much rather than too little publicly available information, so much that the opportunity costs of surveying it all may be too high even for economists.[2] And however clear and self-evident it is made to seem in public discourse, economic data rarely if ever have a transparent, self-evident meaning—a proposition you can test for yourself by perusing Internet sites focusing on economics like Renard's WWW database or the estimable FRED maintained by the Federal Reserve Bank of St. Louis.[3]

None of this is to say that economic journalism cannot be improved, or that we have arrived at the ultimate limit to translating economic knowledge into a general discourse. But we have arrived at some limit, temporary or not, that has three quite unpopulist implications. First, Chomsky's claim is mistaken. Economic policy is not a readily accessible subject matter. The second implication is that the onus for improving economic journalism rests with economists. I think, indeed, that the onus for improving public discourse about any number of subjects lies with academic fields. There is ample posturing in academe about empowering the public, yet "popularizing" is generally frowned on. No discipline I know of regards the democratization of its knowledge as an integral feature of its professional practices. The usual view is that popularizing is easier and therefore less estimable than scholarly writing. But if economic policy is in fact harder than economics, then economists—or at least the "Jeffersonian democrats" in their ranks—might want to rethink the conventional wisdom.

The third implication brings us to trickier, or at least unexplored, terrain. No one knows whether the current state of economic journalism is as good as it gets. It is not inconceivable that the prose of economic journalism has found its optimum level, that economists cannot further translate their subject matter into a more broadly accessible language. Popular physics, especially quantum dynamics, has probably reached that point, for there are only so many analogues for publicly describing quantum realities (Willard, 1996). And since economic policy is at minimum a more factious subject matter than quantum physics, populists should consider the possibility that the failures of what Solow calls poor economic journalism stem from attempts to translate technical knowledge into overly sparse codes. And it is with the comparative richness and poverty of vernaculars that the answers to our two questions may begin.

• • •

To know whether technical issues can be made more accessible, we must ask the following two antecedent questions: *to whom* and *into what language*? To see that these are not simple questions, imagine a continuum of what might be called *demographic sweep*. At its left pole are mass communications, messages comprehensible to millions; at its right are the most esoteric, intricate, and recondite messages, comprehensible only to specialists. The suggestion I want to make is that the translation of expert knowledge into a generally accessible parlance has never been, and likely cannot be, from the extreme right to the extreme left poles. In between the poles are any number of gradations, or *latitudes of comprehension*, and to salvage any version of Chomsky's claim, populists must pick their turf by focusing quite concretely on the latitude that contains a code rich enough to make the technical aspects of public knowledge accessible.

Latitude One, *mass communication*, is the sparsest imaginable code because it seeks to be comprehensible to the broadest imaginable audience. It is best suited to light entertainment, for the lower the common denominator, the greater the code's dependence on narrative and pictorial images. And since the mass audience is a demographic potpourri, mass communication prefers a comparatively limited list of topics. It favors goosebump events—war, crime, nationalism, personalities—and comes by its tabloid traits naturally. Given the code, mass politics is and can be little else than the marketing of mass commodities, and mass journalism can be little more than a contradiction in terms. Given the breadth of its demographic sweep, the best the code can do is report elections as horse races, as many critics have pointed out, and reduce opinion and argument to matters of "*x* says *n*; *y* says not *n*; and here is an expert's opinion." With the fog index pegged to the lowest common denominator, broadcast news should have what "Psychic Friends" and "Astrology Now" have showing continually under the picture "for entertainment purposes only."

Even for marketing and advertising purposes, mass communication has limited utility. Americans are remarkably heterogeneous, so most public discourses are demographically segmented by income, race, lifestyle, education, locale, values, religion, beliefs, and interests. Moving rightward on our continuum and narrowing the breadth ,of any particular audience, we find Latitude Two: *big targets*, wherein messages are strategically fitted to the abilities and predispositions of particular publics. Self-help and popular business books differ in message complexity. *Rolling Stone* is written more simply than *High Fidelity*. The "CBS Evening News" is more like "Hard Copy" than "McNeil–Lehrer." In this latitude, variations in message complexity become the rule. For each discourse, *fog indexes* are used to keep content pegged to a common denominator that is determined by measuring the composite cognitive complexity of a cross section of a potential public.

In social scientese, cognitive complexity refers to vocabulary size, the number of contrasts and similarities a person is able to draw, the relationships a person sees among ideas, and the gradations of meaning, the shades of grey, a person is able to call upon. Cognitive complexity is domain specific: One may know much about Italian Renaissance art but nothing at all about auto mechanics. With complexity comes nuances, gradations, and shades of grey. One is more tolerant of ambiguity and of cognitive dissonance. Indeed the hobgoblin of little minds is more powerful in the simplest domains of one's cognitive system. One uses fewer distinctions, and is more prone to lump people, ideas, and events into *all-liked* and *all-disliked* categories. This is why in Latitude One, where mass interest in politics and economics is very low, one finds the language of heroes and villains, slogans and counterslogans, horse races, and scandals. And it explains, from Latitude Two onward toward the right, why publics form around interests and competencies.

Indeed further rightward on our continuum is Latitude Three, which I will call for lack of imagination, *smaller targets*. This latitude is best illustrated by magazines, though magazines span most latitudes on the continuum. Specialism is the driving force of the magazine world, and to appreciate the extent of its heterogeneity, one can profitably stand at some central point in the magazine section of a large general purpose bookstore. It need not be one of those monsters. A mere thousand or so magazines will do. For as one struggles to find *The Public Interest* or *Public Opinion Quarterly*, one's eyes will roam over hundreds of publications, many quite sophisticated. As a rule, the greater the specialization, the more arcane the content. One needs specialized knowledge to read *Chess Life and Review, Flying, Yachting,* or *Antiques*, and professional-caliber expertise to read *Flight International* or any of the thousands of trade magazines one is unlikely to find in a bookstore.

This specialization exonerates television of what some see as its highest crime. The complaint—in essence—is that television is not more like magazines, that it lacks the seriousness and depth of *The New Republic* or *The Commonweal*. By pandering to the lowest common denominator, television sharpens the schism between elites and masses: The former read magazines and are empowered, the latter watch television and are disenfranchised. This scenario seems plausible because one can point to readerships of esoteric magazines who are unquestionably participants in a higher level of discourse characterized by a greater reliance on written material. There is, for instance, a scientifically interested public—its core perhaps embodied by the 700,000 subscriptions to the most arcane popular science magazine, *Scientific American* (Bennett, 1986). But there is less to this criticism than meets the eye. Indeed the critique of television is empty bombast unless the critics can prove—by doing it—that *Scientific American*'s content can be translated into the sparse codes at Latitudes One and Two. It should be said that the case against television is rapidly becoming a straw man. It is directed at NBC not CNBC, at CBS not CNN, and ignores how like magazines television is becoming. C-SPAN, for instance, gives its audience an unprecedented window on Washington, as close to Dewey's public sphere as one can imagine, and cable news networks have expanded the range and depth of available information. Cable is already mimicking the specialization of magazines, and even allowing for considerable hyperbole in the marketing of satellite dishes, the multiplication of new networks will likely continue. Amid this abundance, some specialized and perhaps sophisticated networks will emerge. We already have a network for physicians whose commercials are more or less completely unintelligible to nonphysicians, so it is not inconceivable that CNBC or someone will spawn a macroeconomics channel. If programs such as, "Keynesian Kingdom" (tonight's episode, "Liquidity Preference and the Stock of Money"), fail to attract an audience of commercially viable size, one can well imagine "The Money Channel." Aimed more or less at Solow's current readership, its programming might well take us upward to another discourse level.

At the upper end of the magazine and cable worlds, there is Latitude Four, *elite targets*. The Money Channel may be diluted economics, but its prose will still be at a level of complexity that is in some respects indistinguishable from trade books. Indeed the difference between the most arcane magazines and trade books may be chiefly quantitative: Book-length treatments permit more detail and focus than magazines. Abundant detail and focus should mean greater sophistication, for trade books can target their audiences narrowly and rely on the knowledge and abilities of their readers. As a journalistic realm, this latitude's implied readership is the so-called *educated public*, people who can read, say, *Habits of the Heart*, *The Best and the Brightest*, or *Betrayers of the Truth*. It includes books that find popular audiences for esoteric ideas (*The Cosmic Code*). The Money Channel, I think, will find its home here, as do some of Solow's columns in the higher reaches of the latitude. But where The Money Channel will mind its fog indexes, to remain commercially viable, some of Solow's columns deploy a richer code.

The home of this code, again with no clear demarcation from the previous level, is Latitude Five, the *general discourse of academe*—roughly the level at which academic committees function. It is a general discourse in the sense that any reasonably educated academic can read *The Structure of Scientific Revolutions* or *The Mismeasure of Man*. And some writers (e.g., Jane Goodall, Richard Leakey, and Stephen Jay Gould) follow Darwin's lead and write for a general but high level public. This realm doubtless has many levels differentiated by the degree to which readers can unpack and interpret the reasoning behind conclusions. Nonphilosophers can read Richard Rorty's books, for instance, but are perhaps unable to evaluate the reasons behind his conclusions. Lewis Thomas's *The Lives of a Cell* is lucid for splendidly educated readers. Most translations of esoterica are into this general but high level discourse. Lavoisier popularized the field he invented; Heisenberg translated quantum mechanics for philosophers; and Gamow popularized the Big Bang. These translations are often successful but no one would mistake them for the esoteric knowledge. They are something else: more authority-dependent, metaphorical, and sparse. They are couched in a different language that conceals what may have been lost and added in the translation.

Moving further right on the continuum, there is Latitude Six, the *discourse of professions and disciplines*. This level is not the sole locale of literary density, but it is dense enough to be analogous to a black hole. Ideas rarely escape its gravity and are able to do so only at the price of transformation into language appropriate to Latitudes Four or Five. The media of this latitude might be called *esoteric mass communications* or *relatively mass media*. Relatively mass media are the specialized books and journals. Their audiences are tiny compared to the audiences of magazines and television but enormous compared to interest groups and research programs. These media are characterized by their implicit allusion to more clearly defined bodies of knowledge and their ability to referentially capitalize on commonly known ideas.

And finally, at the far right pole, we arrive at Latitude Seven: the *quantum domain—esoteric cores*. These are discretely defined localities. They are smaller, more focused, and characterized by more frequent face-to-face interaction. Their members are more adept at catching errors in each other's work and more prone to appreciate each other's virtuosity. Their published work is more idiomatic, more elliptical than most professional writings, and more likely to rely on specialized media, namely, newsletters, fax machines, and in the brave new world of the Web, discussion groups and bulletin boards. Their vernacular may need some translation even for fellow professionals.

This sketch is admittedly speculative, and in all likelihood too gross. Finer distinctions may be needed to decide which analogies hold and which explanations are necessary and possible in given latitudes. The intuitive idea is that translation involves transformation; sparser codes lose the detail and precision of esoteric codes; and for some subjects, there in all likelihood comes a point where any further broadening of demographic sweep becomes counterproductive. Just as a jet reaches a point at which any increase in performance entails a fatal loss of stability, every public topic may have its "coffin corner," a point in a code's performance envelope beyond which the topic not only cannot be correctly explained but becomes, in some important way, misleading. After 1909, when *The London Times* announced that relativity had overthrown the certainty of the ages, Albert Einstein spent much of his life protesting that relativity described a reality incomprehensible to ordinary people and that bore no relationship to ordinary life. It is now a platitude in popular physics books—speaking squarely within Latitude Six—that quantum phenomena are so alien from ordinary experience that workable analogies are hard to find. Whether the likes of capital gains, monetary policy, and demand elasticity have similar limits, or whether they can be leaned into codes sparser than Latitudes Five and Six, is an open question and one worthy of some concrete experimentation.

● ● ●

Of course one issue does not a *civitas* make. The capital gains tax, like the North American Free Trade Agreement (NAFTA) or nuclear engineering, may be unusually technical and unusually vulnerable to glibness and demagoguery. One can imagine cases in which Chomsky really ought to be right, issues that at least seem to belong to Latitudes Three or Four. At some such altitudes, I should think, scientists ought to be able to explain the nature of science—not any particular scientific claim, but what science is and is not and the activities that can or cannot be properly called scientific. In this day and age, especially after *McLean v. Arkansas* brought a number of prominent scientists into the public spotlight, one would think that a substantial working majority of the American public would understand why "creation science" is not science (Taylor and Condit, 1988). Yet by all evidence, though the scientists carried the day in court, they lost in the court of public opinion. If polls are to be trusted, a working majority of American voters believe that creationism should be taught in the schools, and some of this, one gathers from a study of *McLean v. Arkansas* by Taylor and Condit (1988), can be blamed on the rhetorical ineptness of the scientists in translating their arguments into a popular idiom. The deeper problem, however, was an accident of Latitude Two ethics. The creationists' plea for fairness squared with the journalists' populist visions, so the distinction between scientists and ministers became invisible. A commitment to objectivity "produced a journalistic leveling which rhetorically transformed competing discourses into equivalent ones" (Taylor and Condit, 1988). The journalist's fairness ethic pitted "Dr. X" against "Dr. Y," and gave equal space and time to each, equating the legitimacy of "mudroad Mullahs" and fully credentialed scientists. "As the story evolved in the mass media, creation science appeared as the equal competing theory to evolution that the creationists claimed it to be" (p. 306).

One would have thought that John T. Scopes and Clarence Darrow put this matter to rest more than seventy years ago. Though the evolutionists lost in court, they were canonized in H. L. Mencken's columns, a Broadway play, and an Oscar-winning movie. But dirt roads pave slowly. Even now, the Tennessee State Legislature is considering a bill that would make it a crime to teach evolution as a fact. Teaching it as a "theory" would be permissible, for in the hermetically sealed discourse of creationism, theory is virtually synonymous with "myth." Darwin's reading of the fossil record would be put on a par with anyone else's opinion; and Mississippi crackpots, as Mencken might say, would be indistinguishable from Berkeley professors.

From cases such as these, pluralists infer one of their most rankling arguments. It is the "irony of democracy," they say, that the *vox populi* may be undemocratic. The political reasoning of the mass is primitive and infantile. The instincts of the least educated are authoritarian, illiberal, and barbarian. Given full voice in a free and open plebescite, the American public would divide along homicidal lines of race, ethnicity, and religion. It would abolish most of the Bill of Rights and trample the most fundamental democratic values. Public apathy is a hidden virtue, for it is the public's taste for tabloid simplicities that has reduced mass discourse to the mean-spirited circus Mencken made a career of denouncing. At the risk of paling by comparison, I will quote the following from my own book:

One can, with grounds, revive Aristotle's pessimism about the "depraved character" of the Athenians. These grounds are often called the *Lazarsfeld tradition* . . . a body of research that improves the odds on Mencken's wager that nobody goes broke betting on the ignorance of the American public. Using research methods likely to understate citizens' flaws (Neuman, 1986), it reports irrationality, frivolousness, primitive passions, infantile reasoning, ignorance, and an attention span that can be likened to Hobbes' view of life: brutish, nasty, and short. (Willard, 1996, p. 342)

This is why politics in America is professional wrestling pursued by other means. Mencken's circus of oompah bands and rottweiler rhetoric is a discourse that has found its level. Advertising and public relations techniques dominate political life because they are rhetorically appropriate to their audiences (Willard, 1996, p. 342).

Without swallowing this portrait whole, one can nonetheless weigh the possibility that American political life has tried to play itself out before the wrong audience and the advocates of increased citizen activism ought to be careful what they wish for. By all evidence there is, along the bayous and back roads of the Bible Belt, a sizable and by no means negligible political movement that has turned its collective attention directly to America's schools. And however overwrought the irony argument may be, the possibility that creationists might affect science education is worth taking seriously. If some of the blame rests with the scientists themselves, who out of hubris or rhetorical naivete failed to clearly explain the nature of science, then even this relatively accessible case is an exception to Chomsky's generalization. For it at least seems for the moment that evolution cannot be correctly translated into Latitude Two prose. The fossil record can perhaps be discussed at Latitudes Five or Six—Stephen Jay Gould's books come to mind. But if studies of scientific illiteracy are to be trusted, the problem is not merely that a working majority of Americans believes that the sun orbits the earth and that the earth is the center of the solar system. The deeper problem is that a horrifying percentage of college graduates cannot answer even elementary questions about science (Trefil and Hazen, 1994). This may mean that Latitude Five is as good as it gets and that any further leaning of the code will make creationism and science seem to be coequal competitors. If we can define precisely the point at which they do seem coequal, and cannot be made otherwise, we will have found the outer limits of Dewey's public sphere.

SUMMARY

Democracy's oldest dispute has been warped by rhetorical excesses, so the last thing in the world I have meant to do in this essay is prompt populists to gesture toward the wisdom of the people or to reply with grandiose empowerment arguments and gestures of defiance to the pluralists. My argument has chiefly been about ignorance: No one entirely knows how democratic democracies can and should be, for both sides have been cavalier about the problem of translating technical knowledge into more accessible parlances. Chomsky is guilty on several counts, but the pluralists, for their part, airily dismiss the possibility that serious issues could be discussed seriously before any but the most select public. I have tried to raise in a concrete way the possibility that two sorts of issues may not be as democratizable as populists might wish, but the chief implications of these examples are twofold. The first, I submit, is that Latitude One journalism was a noble experiment, roughly as effective as prohibition. Some version of Chomsky's claim may be salvageable somewhere along our continuum, but the claim that the capital gains tax, or even the nature of science, can be adequately represented in that code now seems as preposterous as the pluralists say. On the other hand, we have only the vaguest idea of how expansive democracy's vistas might be. The challenge is to find out—a gauntlet, I believe, that is best thrown at the feet of the academic disciplines.

NOTES

1. Much of the material and all of the ideas in this chapter are taken from Willard (1996), and I thank the University of Chicago Press for permission.

2. One can appreciate the reading load by glancing through the 285 pages of Sichel and Sichel (1986).

3. Some suggestive sites for economic data (as of March 13, 1996):

   1. http://renard.com/~johnfox/index.html#Other
   2. http://www.stls.frb.org/fred/dataindx.html
   3. http://www.webcom.com/~yardeni/economic.html

   and for census bureau statistics:

   4. http://www.clark.net/pub/lschank/web/cendoc.html

REFERENCES

Bellah, R. N. (1985). *Habits of the heart.* Berkeley and Los Angeles: University of California Press.

Bennett, W. (1986). The medium is large, but how good is the message? In *Scientists and journalists*, ed. S. M. Friedman. New York: The Free Press.

Chomsky, N. (1989). Interview. In *Bill Moyers: A world of ideas*, ed. Betty S. Flowers. New York: Doubleday.

Jefferson, T. (1813). Letter to John Adams, October 28.

Neuman, W. R. (1986). *The paradox of mass politics.* Cambridge: Harvard University Press.

R. R. Bowker Company. (1996). *Bowker annual library and book trade almanac.* New York: R. R. Bowker.

Sichel, B., and W. Sichel. (1986). *Economics journals and serials: An analytic guide.* Westport, Conn.: Greenwood.

Solow, R. M. (1990). Can economics be made easy? *New York Times Book Review*, March 4.

Taylor, A. T., and C. M. Condit. (1988). Objectivity and elites. *Critical studies in mass communication* 5: 293–312.

Trefil, J., and R. Hazen. (1994). *The sciences: An integrated approach.* New York: Wiley.

The Washington Post. (1994). May 15, p. A12.

Willard, C. A. (1996). *Liberalism and the problem of knowledge: A new rhetoric for modern democracy.* Chicago: University of Chicago Press.

PART II

EDUCATION

Chapter 4

The Significance of Critical
Communication Skills in a Democracy

Jodi R. Cohen

The complaints are well known: The media glorifies violence and over-uses sex; the media gives us empty messages; it entertains instead of informs, and numbs more than sensitizes. Everyone, from national presidential candidates to local parent–teacher associations, is asking the media to become more responsible for the messages it creates. As one who studies communication and educates the students who become "the media," I do not necessarily disagree. However, I believe that responsibility must also be placed on the audiences who make the messages meaningful. Words, images, and sounds do not mean anything in themselves. We ultimately allow a message to have meaning.

In this chapter, I am specifically concerned with how we can educate ourselves to communicate in ways that are conducive to democracy. The classical approach to communication, what the ancient Greeks called "rhetoric," remains relevant to the task, providing some adaptations to the technological and philosophical challenges of contemporary times. I have organized this chapter into three major parts. First, I will review the classical approach to rhetoric and its relevance to informed and active citizenry. I will then discuss limitations of the classical approach imposed by today's communication-saturated world, and with specific attention toward visual media, suggest directions for change. Overall, the study of rhetoric today should emphasize the practice of thinking critically about the communication that shapes our lives.

THE DEMOCRACY–RHETORIC CONNECTION:
THEN AND NOW

The ancient Greeks considered public communication to be vital to active, democratic, public life. In fact, the role of informing and persuading the public in a democracy led to the formal study of communication, or *rhetoric*, in Classical Greece. Twenty-five hundred years ago, the study of rhetoric emphasized the practice of speaking to the public. Since then rhetoric has evolved into a system for studying all communication processes, from formulating ideas to social action.

The nature of communication in society shapes the way we study it and vice versa. The citizens of democratic Athens regularly gathered in the courts and town squares to speak about legal and policy issues (Agard, 1960). Public speaking was the primary means of shaping public opinion and therefore essential to the entire democratic decision-making process. Policy making and legal decisions were believed to involve a special kind of thinking based on public opinion and probability. The most feasible military action or taxation policy cannot be determined with certainty, and we must persuade one another to agree with our opinions. It is through rhetoric, or "persuasive communication," that publics form and effect social action. Writing approximately twenty-four hundred years ago, Isocrates (1956) asserts the significance of public speech to democratic life in particular, and human existence in general:

Because there has been implanted in us the power to persuade each other and to make clear to each other whatever we desire, not only have we escaped the life of wild beasts, but we have come together and founded cities and made laws, and invented arts; and, generally speaking, there is no institution devised by man which the power of speech has not helped us to establish. . . . Through [the power of speech] we educate the ignorant and appraise the wise; for the power to speak well is taken as the surest index of a sound understanding, and discourse which is true and lawful and just is the outward image of a good and faithful soul. (p. 328)

It was in this context that schools of rhetoric developed to educate the democratic citizenry. Over time, the curriculum has changed, sometimes emphasizing speech presentation and other times the substance of speech. The system of rhetoric that has been historically adopted by democratic societies emphasizes the substance or ideas of speech and acknowledges that if not presented in a convincing manner, great ideas may be of little value. Historically, the ideal role of public communication in a democracy is—as Isocrates (1956) viewed it—a mediator of public thought and social action.

For instance, in his *Rhetoric*, Aristotle (1954) asserts rhetoric to be the means through which Greek society will distinguish expedient from harmful political actions, just from unjust proposals, and honorable from dishonorable people. During the Renaissance, Giambattista Vico (1968), a professor of rhetoric and philosophy, argued that all human thinking and knowledge was bound to language. During the period of Enlightenment, philosopher George Campbell claimed rhetoric was a psychological instrument that coordinates the faculties of the mind. In the vocabulary of eighteenth-century faculty psychology, Campbell said rhetoric was necessary to "enlighten the understanding, to please the imagination, to move the passions, or to influence the will" (1963, p. 1).

Much contemporary thought on public communication maintains the emphasis on the substance, ideas, or meanings that are shaped through communication. I. A. Richards (1936) claimed rhetoric to be the study of how language creates misunderstandings among people, and how to overcome them. Richard Weaver (1948) believed all language entails human values and we use it to align our ideals with our practical actions. Kenneth Burke defined rhetoric as a process in which people use language "to form attitudes or induce actions in other human agents" (1969, p. 41). The most recent influence of critical-social theorists, who study how institutions produce meaning (Foucault, 1972; Habermas, 1979), maintains the emphasis on ideas. As long as we have been studying communication, some have held to the belief that our freedom as human beings rests in the substance of our rhetoric.

In spite of the persistence of the classical view of rhetoric, democracies and rhetorics have changed. The next two sections of this chapter address some significant changes in the symmetry between democracy and public communication as we move into the twenty-first century, and some strategies for how we might best adapt to the changes.

CHALLENGES TO THE
DEMOCRACY–RHETORIC CONNECTION

There are many challenges to the possibility of a democracy based in public decision and debate. Today's problem of the "inactive," "silenced," "powerless," "voiceless," or "dead" public is widely accepted in critical-social and critical-communication studies (Dewey, 1954; Habermas, 1975; Lasch, 1984; Meyrowitz, 1985; Sennett, 1976). Here I am concerned with those aspects of the problem that are directly related to public communication and that might be "fixed" by educating citizens in public communication. Specifically, I will illustrate how our lack of a sense of public identity and empowerment are facilitated by technological and philosophical changes in communication. These changes are challenging democracy and the ways we educate ourselves as citizens.

The Technological Changes

Greek democracy was fueled by face-to-face communication among people who were more similar to one another than they were different. Now, given changes in technology, communication is everywhere, unavoidable, and often impersonal, bringing people from all over the world together into what some have called a *global community*. This global community should not be confused with the kind of public identity necessary to democracy.

One significant change in our community today is that it essentially exists within the space and time of communication technology. While we once gathered together into a physical place, such as a courtyard, a schoolhouse, or a church, to define ourselves and the issues of the day, today we are nowhere and everywhere (Meyrowitz, 1985). A series of conversational exchanges between my landlady and me illustrates this paradox. She disapproved of my volunteer work at a soup kitchen just three blocks from where we lived. Her disapproval took the form of snide remarks about the people who ate there. She hollered from her back door whenever I returned home from working at the kitchen. One day as I was climbing the steps to my apartment, she called me into her home to share her grief over an earthquake on another continent. She had seen the pictures and the people on television and was now crying and setting out her canned goods to send to the people there. Clearly, she identified with people living on another continent more than with those living in her neighborhood.

We have, in fact, no sense of place, because communication technology has blurred the private and public realms (Meyrowitz, 1985; Sennett, 1976). We once clearly delineated "backstage" from "on-stage" communication behaviors. Cameras did not capture politicians arguing with their lovers in their own backyards. Similarly, the public has become personal. Political candidates today win more points by exposing their personal feelings and personalities than discussing issues. We learn the lessons of life from how celebrities cope with family and sexual dysfunctions, and we have more active relationships with the doctors on NBC's "ER" or "Friends" than with those people in the house next door (Gumpert and Cathcart, 1986). We listen to our political leaders, up-close and personal, from our living rooms. As with my landlady, we come physically closer to those on television and in magazines than to those who we pass on the street. Quite simply, the private is public and the personal is political, but we can never be quite sure which is which.

Yet another paradox of communication technology, with implications to the disappearing public, is that technology makes us all the same while making us different from one another. The focus on difference reveals itself in talk of "cultural diversity" and "multiculturalism." It is unfortunate that these labels have become thoughtless clichés for real changes in our sense of ourselves and our relationships with others. There is no denying that our political and economic relationships have been globalized, as have our social relationships. Most people in the United States today interact with people from, or in, faraway places. They do so in the actual space of work and school, and in cyberspace. We notice, and perhaps dwell on, the differences between ourselves and others. David Zarefsky, a professor of speech communication, goes so far as to suggest that the emphasis on cultural distinctions "balkanizes our public life" (1995, p. 5).

The contemporary accent on the differences within our country is also being applied to the individual. Patricia Williams (1991), for instance, an African-American woman, lawyer, and professor of legal studies, unpacks her many contradictory, identities in her recent autobiographical work, *The Alchemy of Race and Rights*. We have lost confidence in the idea that psychologically healthy individuals have one unified and consistent identity. Similar to Williams, we all have several, sometimes overlapping and contradictory identities. We participate in many cultures. Cultures—formed when people develop shared codes of meaning over time—are created, reflected, changed, and maintained in communication (Fiske, 1989). Our cultural identities range from the formal and conscious systems of religious beliefs, to the informal and less-conscious myths of a generational culture. Most Americans describe themselves in terms of ethnicity, race, religion, sexual identity, gender, social class, geographical location, and more.

We are further divided into demographic and psychographic identities, literally created in the marketplace of the media. We are "baby boomers" or "generation-Xers." We are double income, no children (DINCs). We are sports enthusiasts, pro-lifers, or working mothers; we are health conscious, premenstrual, or premenopausal. It is billboards, bulletin boards, catalogs, magazines, television, films, and computer networks that define us and differentiate us from one another.

Some researchers suggest we have media identities, created by our membership in *interpretive communities* (Lindlof, 1988). Interpretive communities are groups of people who share particular media or media systems, rules for making meaning, and meanings. Those who regularly use America Online are an interpretive community, as are physicians who read the same periodicals, subscribe to the same electronic services, and keep in contact with other physicians through the American Medical Association. Whether we talk about identities as cultures, demographics, psychographics, or interpretive communities, we are a bundle of complex, overlapping, and often contradictory identities.

Communication technology constantly creates new identities and communities, but it also masks or overshadows the differences with a mass identity. Meyrowitz explains, "A large portion of [media] content is shared by most people in the country" (1985, p. 145). Popularizing ideas is necessary to the economics of media. The producers and advertisers who support, if not create, ideas must package them to be meaningful to as many people as possible. It costs money to print a newspaper, make a film, or even hire a teacher; money that may not be recovered in a television news hour that only rings true for overclass, democratic, Latino men in their sixties.

In this process of popularizing information, ideas are commodities. It makes the most economic sense, where airtime equals dollars, to produce the most information for the most people in the smallest amount of space and time. We do not have the time or the money to explore the details of immigration policies so we are saturated with abstractions of ideas with mass appeal, such as family values, the underclass, and diversity. Multiculturalism is packaged in a Benetton advertisement. Buying a Benetton sweater is an expression of identity and a political act.

One need only look around to see that there are not many differences among us. Unfortunately, our commonalities (and therefore our differences) are often banal. We may wear baggy, hip-hop jeans; ripped, grunge jeans; or bib-overall, farmer jeans. But, we are all simply wearing jeans.

Our public identity may very well be lost in the paradoxes of communication technology. The public has no place to define itself, its issues, and its policies. If it exists at all, it perhaps more appropriately takes the form of wandering publics, always changing place, space, and identity.

Nevertheless, we spend so much of our time as audiences that we cannot separate our ideas and identities from communication itself. The omnipotence of communication, and how it saps us of social power, will be discussed.

The Philosophical Changes

The second challenge to the traditional relationship between communication and democracy, not distinct from the technological changes, is a philosophical one. Traditionally, communication is believed to reflect and influence thought and action. It was believed that the world was endowed with meaning and truths that were mediated through communication. People have a different view of communication today; a view that blurs the difference between language and thought, language and action, language and identity, and language and reality. Postmodern thinking, a philosophical movement or perspective sweeping the arts, social sciences, and humanities, believes communication is to today what religion was to the Middle Ages and what science was to the Modern period. Communication is considered to be the source, if not the essence, of who we are, what we know, and what we do. Because I have discussed how communication constructs our identities, I now focus on the relationship between communication, knowledge, and action, arguing that our difficulty—sometimes inability—to step out of communication allows the symbolic processes to take control of our meanings and actions.

We know about the way it was before we were born through the stories of "old timers," museums, textbooks, films, television, paintings, music, and literature. Quite simply, knowing is shaped through words and other symbols. Even our sense of sight and taste are shaped through communication. Cultures may not even have words for objects and events that are deemed insignificant or go unrecognized. Recent debate over the nature of sexual harassment illustrates the close relationship between what we say and what we see. The term was not used twenty years ago, although certainly events that are today perceived as "sexually harassing" took place. The struggle over the meaning of sexual harassment continues, but the struggle itself suggests that American culture is perceiving events that were not noticed twenty years ago because they were perceived differently or deemed insignificant.

We cannot even separate scientific knowledge from communication. Consider that symptoms of the HIV virus appeared and went unnoticed in 1978. By 1981, 159 official cases were registered and rumors about the disease were spreading throughout the gay community. The disease was not, however, officially named until 1982, or publicly–politically recognized until it was evident in the white, heterosexual population (Grmek, 1990). Obviously, the virus was a fact, but it was one that our interests, beliefs, and values—reinforced through daily communication—did not encourage us to see.

In one final example of how communication constructs what we know, Solomon (1985) illustrates how scientific language used in the Tuskegee research reports (1932–1972) allowed approximately one hundred black men to die in the name of scientific knowledge. Solomon argues that the Tuskegee study, which followed untreated syphilis in African-American men, continued for forty years because the language of the scientific reports dehumanized the men in the study, demonized the disease being studied, and deitized the scientists conducting the study.

Our actions, also created in communication, are an extension of who we are and what we know. As the columnist William Raspberry (1991) points out, because we talk about blacks as naturally athletic, we make it common to see a black child practicing right up to bedtime, working on his scoop lay-up, his behind-the-back dribble, his fade away jump shot. Children proudly hailed as go-getters may strive to achieve more goals than children hailed in less glowing ways. The supermom image encourages women to develop themselves professionally while raising a family. Our sociocultural identities influence the foods we eat, the occasions we celebrate, and the ways we spend our leisure. National cultures create social policies and wage war. Knowledge of past wars will shape our strategies in today's wars.

Telephones, specialized magazines, express mail, personal computers, fax machines, and satellite dishes are reconstructing time, space, and our sense of public identity, knowledge, and action. Traditional boundaries are being eradicated; we have difficulty distinguishing between public and private, political and personal, communication and identity, communication and reality, and communication and action. Without any space of its own, the public has disappeared, died, or become ignorant and powerless. Our identity and power is given to communication.

It follows that those who have power over communication have social power. Just as we struggle individually with contradictory identities, social groups struggle for dominance in the public realm. The debate over the meaning of sexual harassment illustrates the struggle. Some of the more obvious players in sociocultural power struggles are generations, races, ethnicities, sexes and genders, and social classes. A group gains social power when its meanings and ways of making meaning are assumed to be natural by the most people. Economic and cultural power are not unrelated because they fuel one another. Sociocultural groups become dominant when powerful agents of socialization, such as media, government, and education, assume their view of the world and hail all others according to that view. Being an active participant among communication power struggles is absolutely necessary to a participatory democracy.

MEETING THE CHALLENGES THROUGH CRITICAL COMMUNICATION

> The goal of critical education is to create a "public sphere of citizens who are able to exercise power over their own lives, and especially over the conditions of knowledge production and acquisition."
>
> (Freire and Giroux, 1989, p. viii)

Technological and philosophical changes in communication ask that we reconsider how to best prepare ourselves for a participatory democracy. Our overall goal is to restore public identity and facilitate social power among people through the study and practice of communication. Our solution must adapt to the shifting identities of wandering publics or audiences, the tension between our sameness and difference, and the pervasiveness of communication, particularly images. We can facilitate a participatory democracy through the practice of critical communication skills. Thinking critically about communication, a way of taking control that has been formally developed by academics, asks that we question the naturalness of our meanings. In doing so we hope to facilitate an active and intelligent public.

My suggestions for rebuilding a participatory democracy center around educating people to engage in communication critically. We should receive an education built on the framework of classical rhetoric. Then we should learn critical media-viewing skills. Finally, we should include the critical study of popular communication in our school curriculums.

A Role for Classical Rhetoric

The classical means of studying rhetoric remain a model for teaching people to use language to think through ideas and influence others in matters of politics and law. I will review the basic concepts of the classical perspective and demonstrate how a classical education might strengthen public identity and social power.[1]

The classical approach to educating the citizenry was organized into the following five canons: invention, memory, organization, style, and delivery. All the canons address themselves to thought. The canon of invention addresses thought directly by studying the reasoning processes, emotions, and character of the communicators. The canon of memory is connected to thought in at least two ways. In classical times it concerned itself with how to remember ideas. Memory is now more broadly conceived as a collective history that shapes, and is shaped by, cultures. Organization, the third canon of study, is about how we structure ideas in thought and language. Style refers to language as it reflects the world, ideas about the world, and the soul of the speaker. Delivery, the final canon, describes how a speech is physically presented. Although it includes such matters as vocal control and variation, gestures, and eye contact, it, too, reveals, presents, or delivers one person to another.

Today the canons are no longer believed to represent and influence thought and action as much as they *are* thought and action. There is also some controversy about whether they favor western, Caucasian, or male forms of thought and speech (Gill, 1994; Foss, Foss, and Trapp, 1991). The canons have, nevertheless, proven themselves flexible and continue to influence the study of public communication.

Allowing for the controversy, the classical canons remain a viable system for educating democratic citizens. Significantly, educational programs that adopt a classical approach to communication have students think and talk through issues of public significance. The classical approach involves students in contemporary issues, such as international trade, immigration, human rights, capital punishment, and the federal budget, as they are learning the principles of effective communication. Through classroom dialogue, vague, mass-produced issues can be specified and localized.

The classical perspective facilitates community by bringing students together to inform and persuade one another about the events and issues that influence their collective lives. The classroom is a physical place where people (ideally, people from different sociocultural backgrounds) come together to shape their public identities. The art of informing and persuading requires a speaker to know and respect the differences within and between himself or herself and the audience. The art of effective speaking also discovers, adapts to, reinforces, and ultimately creates similarities among people.

The classical approach does empower us by accounting for how we are influenced by communication. The traditional canons implore citizens to evaluate the evidence, assumptions, emotional content, and ethical implications of ideas. A teacher of mine, Gordon Hostettler, reminds us that today or 2,500 years ago, "armed with knowledge of rhetoric we are better able to combat demagoguery and chicanery; ignorant of it we may stand powerless before them" (1980, p. 340).

A Role for Critical Viewing

> Think of Richard Nixon or Jimmy Carter or Billy Graham, or even Albert Einstein, and what will come to your mind is an image, a picture of a face, most likely a face on a television screen (in Einstein's case, a photograph of a face) of words, almost nothing will come to mind.
>
> (Postman, 1985, p. 61)

The classical approach to communication did not include the critical study of imagery, and it is clear that we must educate people to view images in a critical manner. *Critical viewing* refers to thinking critically about visual media. Scholars and teachers agree that critically engaging with mass media, especially film and video, can be a form of power.[2] We also tend to agree that several qualities characterize someone who is critically engaged in television. The critical viewer acknowledges the syntactic construction of television (how images, sounds, and editing are combined into a message), the semantic construction of television (how the syntax combines into something audiences make meaningful), and the interpretive context of the spectator (what assumptions, beliefs, or experiences the viewer brings to the meaning) (Liebes and Katz, 1989, p. 205).

These qualities of television viewing are applicable to critically engaging with most media. They are not, however, particularly useful guidelines to forming an active public voice. Critical viewing that is conducive to social power must articulate public identities, for it is within the public realm that individuals have access to the resources, such as ideas, audiences, and authority, that can change social policy (Condit, 1989). Therefore, in an attempt to link critical viewing with democratic social power, we should employ at least three additional characteristics such as the following: (1) critical viewers should recognize the social locations of their interpretations, (2) critical viewers should not oversimplify social identities into unified and discrete territories or oppositional relationships, and (3) critical viewers should consider the social origins and implications of their meanings.[3] I will briefly elaborate on these qualities of critical viewing that are conducive to participatory democracy.

Meanings and the ways we make them are linked to our social structure (Fiske, 1987), and it is this link that we must identify. It is not enough for a television viewer to realize the context of their interpretation, which might take the following form: "I did not enjoy the show because it reminded me of a difficult time in my life." A critical statement from one who realizes the role of their social positions in meaning would be the following: "I did not enjoy or agree with the program because, as a heterosexual, I find explicit references to homosexuality offensive." An equally critical statement would be the following: "I did not enjoy or agree with the program because, as a gay person, I cannot relate to the characters' relationships." In both cases the speakers identify themselves socially, thereby consciously joining themselves to the interests and values of others. It is in our connection to others within our social groups that we can come together to effect change.

However, even the socially reflexive viewer may have access to power that is not a positive force for social change. Power may imprison rather than liberate, as with viewers who essentialize themselves and the meanings they construct. Our wandering social identities allow us a plurality of interpretations that we can put to good use. For instance, in addition to the relevance of my heterosexuality to my interpretation of a given television program about gay rights, my interpretation could also involve my identities as a woman and as a scholar. Acknowledging the plurality of my own social identities and interpretations can bring up contradictions and inconsistencies in my ideas. As a woman, I may be able to identify with the oppression of the gay character, and as a scholar I believe homosexuality is a natural fact of life only determined to be immoral by some cultures during some periods in history.

Acknowledging that there may be multiple interpretations is not the same as accepting contradictions or claiming there is no truth. The critically empowered viewer would be less likely to adopt the dogmatic view that only one way of thinking about a subject is correct by acknowledging that even his or her own meanings are sometimes false, questionable, or only partial. Viewers who see themselves as complex social beings with many identities, and who can render many intelligible interpretations of communication, gain the power of possibility and choice.

Viewers should consider possible interpretations from identities that are different from their own. For instance, how might a gay person respond to the argument presented in the film, and why? Television and other mass media make empathy with others possible by presenting "most viewers of our society with a crazy-quilt pattern of perspectives. Regardless of physical location and traditional group ties, people experience how the world looks and feels from other places and other role perspectives" (Meyrowitz, 1985, p. 144).

As viewers of mass communication, we may also probe, develop, and strengthen our social voices by reflecting upon our interpretations as part of ongoing communication processes. We must acknowledge that our meanings have a social and rhetorical history as well as implications to social policy. The heterosexual viewer's discomfort with gay relationships is not determined at a single moment of television viewing or conversation but is determined over time by communication produced by family, religion, education, medical science, economics, and so on. Viewers who realize their beliefs have been constructed by a social history are less likely to assume their meanings are natural and are more likely to participate in communication that aims to reconstruct meanings and identities.

If an individual is to deliberately and effectively influence social policy, he or she must realize that meanings have consequences. We need to think about how to make critical viewing more than an intellectual exercise. Traversing the gap between communication and social action is our greatest challenge in a world that does not often distinguish between talk and social action. An initial step is for critical viewers to realize how their meanings effect social action. The heterosexual viewers who cannot identify with the gay position in a film might consider how their "social" view realizes itself in AIDS research, military policies, and state amendments for gay rights.

We can adapt to the technological and philosophical changes in democracy and communication by developing our critical viewing skills in addition to our classical rhetorical skills. Public communication relevant to political and social action is no longer distinct in form or content. A seemingly innocuous television situation comedy will reinforce beliefs, identities, and behaviors that become relevant to policy making. Critical viewing, as presented, is a resource for a democratic and culturally diverse public life.

A Role for the Study of Popular Culture

> A successful critical pedagogy enables "people to intervene in the formation of their own subjectivities."
>
> (Giroux and Simon, 1989, p. 11)

If we are to teach people to gain power through communication, then we must study the everyday communication of everyday people. Although academics distinguish among a variety of popular cultures, I use the phrase broadly, in reference to the cultures of people in all of its forms, namely, mass culture, folk cultures, and ethnic and racial cultures.[4] I urge the inclusion of a variety of popular cultures in the classroom, crossing genders, social classes, ethnicities, and geographies. The reasons for integrating popular culture into our curriculums relate directly to our lack of public identity and social power.

Henry Giroux recalls his own education in the following explanation of the importance of popular culture to identity:

My friends and I collected and traded comic books, learned about desire through the rock and roll of Little Richard and Bill Haley and the Comets, and drank to the blues of Fats Domino. We hated Pat Boone and didn't know the suburbs even existed. We felt rather than know what was really useful knowledge. . . . Then we went to school.

Something happened to us in school. For me it was like being sent to a strange planet. . . . The language we learned and had to speak was different, strange, and unusually verbose. . . . This is not to suggest that we didn't learn anything, but what we learned had little to do with where we came from, who we were, or where we thought, at least, we were going. (1994, p. x)

The critical study of our own cultural forms brings the social history, and the often arbitrary creation, of our ideas and identities to the foreground. The recent film, *Clueless*, serves as a good example. This movie articulates the position of the white, upper-class adolescents living in the western United States today. A critical discussion of the film would explore issues of family, sex, gender, and community as they are presented in the film and potentially made sense of by different audiences (gender, age, and social class seem to be especially relevant to the film). A full-blown, critical study of the film would ask where these issues have come from and how they have been shaped by a history of communication. The study could include the works of Aesop, Shakespeare, Jane Austen, and J. D. Salinger. A full-blown, critical study of the film would also ask how the ideas and identities shaped in the film might influence our social action. This could include policies on homelessness, crime, welfare, and equal rights.

The critical study of popular culture should help us to better define ourselves in relation to others. *Clueless*, as all instances of popular communication, is produced and consumed within a particular social context. African-Americans, Asian-Indians, and wealthy Americans might make very different sense of the film's middle-class ironic view of wealthy America, and it is important to think about alternative interpretations of the same communication text. We can imagine how "others" might make sense of our music or films, but we must also critically engage with the communication texts of cultures other than our own. This process is important to understanding the similarities and differences among the many social groups that must come together to debate, decide, persuade, and act in the public interest.

I am not suggesting that we abandon the great works. After all, I strongly support the classical approach to rhetoric which is rooted in what some not-so-fondly refer to as "old, dead, white men." But speeches are primarily experienced via the television and edited into audio–visual or written news bites and headlines. Emma Thompson's contemporary film version of *Sense and Sensibility* is probably more familiar to us than Jane Austen's original novel. History is learned, in large part, through mass media. The young adults in my college classrooms know about the 1960s (Kennedy, Nixon, Vietnam, and the Doors) from the filmmaker Oliver Stone. In order to have choice in their conceptions of themselves and the way they live their lives, they must learn to identify these places where their ideas and identities are formed, how they are being formed, and with what effects.

SUMMARY

In this chapter, I assess the role of public communication in democracy. I review the practice and study of public communication through western civilization. I argue that the study of public communication is necessary to democracy, in so far as it helps the public to identify itself and exert power over itself. We can find the public and its power in critical thinking and viewing rooted in classical rhetorical skills. The culture of everyday life is where we must learn to exercise this power.

NOTES

1. Aside from the original sources noted in the previous paragraph, the following sources provide an introduction to the study of rhetoric in western civilization: Brummett (1994, Chapter 2); Gill (1994); Golden, Berquist, and Coleman (1997).

2. The ways that audiences gain power is the focus of much interdisciplinary work that falls under the rubric of cultural studies. Becker (1984) and Fiske (1987) provide informative introductions to the cultural studies perspective.

3. I developed these characteristics in a previously published essay; see Cohen, 1994.

4. For a brief discussion and bibliography on the term *popular culture*, see Grossberg, 1986.

REFERENCES

Agard, W. (1960). *What democracy meant to the Greeks*. Madison: University of Wisconsin Press.

Aristotle. (1954). *Rhetoric*. Translated by W. Rhys Roberts. New York: Random House.

Becker, S. (1984). Marxist approaches to media studies: The British experience. *Critical studies in mass communication* 1: 66–80.

Brummett, B. (1994). *Rhetoric in popular culture*. New York: St. Martin's Press.

Burke, K. (1969). *A rhetoric of motives*. Berkeley and Los Angeles: University of California Press.

Campbell, G. (1963). In *The philosophy of rhetoric*, ed. L. Bitzer. Carbondale: Southern Illinois University Press.

Cohen, J. R. (1994). Critical viewing and participatory democracy. *Journal of communication* 44: 98–113.

Condit, C. M. (1989). The rhetorical limits of polysemy. *Critical studies in mass communication* 6: 103–122.

Dewey, J. (1954). *The public and its problems*. Chicago: The Swallow Press.

Fiske, J. (1987). British cultural studies and television. In *Channels of discourse*, ed. R. C. Allen, pp. 254–290. Chapel Hill: University of North Carolina Press.

Fiske, J. (1989). *Reading the popular*. Boston: Unwin Hyman.

Foss, S. K., K. A. Foss, and R. Trapp. (1991). *Contemporary perspectives on rhetoric*. Prospect Heights, Ill.: Waveland Press.

Foucault, M. (1972). *The archaeology of knowledge*. Translated by A. M. Sheridan Smith. New York: Harper & Row.

Freire, P., and H. Giroux. (1989). Pedagogy, popular culture and public life: An introduction. In *Popular culture: Schooling and everyday life*, ed. H. Giroux and R. Simon, pp. vii–xii. New York: Bergin & Garvey.

Gergen, K. J. (1991). *The saturated self*. New York: Basic Books.

Gill, A. (1994). *Rhetoric and human understanding*. Prospect Heights, Ill.: Waveland Press.

56

Part II: Education

Giroux, H. (1994). *Disturbing pleasures: Learning popular culture*. New York: Routledge.
Giroux, H., and R. Simon. (1989). Popular culture as pedagogy of pleasure and meaning. In *Popular culture: Schooling and everyday life*, ed. H. Giroux and R. Simon, pp. 1–29. New York: Bergin & Garvey.
Golden, J. L., G. F. Berquist, and W. E. Coleman. (1997). *The rhetoric of western thought*. 6th ed. Dubuque: Kendall Hunt.
Grmek, M. D. (1990). *History of AIDS*. Translated by R. C. Maulitz and J. Duffin. Princeton: Princeton University Press.
Grossberg, L. (1986). Teaching the popular. In *Theory in the Classroom*, ed. C. Nelson, pp. 177–200. Urbana: University of Illinois Press.
Gumpert, G., and R. Cathcart. (1986). *Intermedia: Interpersonal communication in a media world*. 3rd ed. New York: Oxford University Press.
Habermas, J. (1975). *Legitimation crisis*. Translated by T. McCarthy. Boston: Beacon Press.
Habermas, J. (1979). *Communication and the evolution of society*. Translated by T. McCarthey. Boston: Beacon Press.
Hostettler, G. (1980). Speech as a liberal study II. *Communication education* 29: 332–347.
Isocrates. (1956). *Antidosis*. Translated by G. Norlin. Cambridge: Harvard University Press.
Lasch, C. (1984). *The minimal self*. New York: W. W. Norton.
Liebes, T., and E. Katz. (1989). On the critical abilities of television viewers. In *Remote control: Television, audiences and cultural power*, ed. Ellen Seiger, Hans Barchers, Gabriele Kreutzner, and Eva-Maria Warth, pp. 204–222. London: Routledge.
Lindlof, T. (1988). Media audiences as interpretive communities. In *Communication yearbook*, ed. J. Anderson, pp. 81–107. Newbury Park, Calif.: Sage.
Meyrowitz, J. (1985). *No sense of place*. New York: Oxford University Press.
Postman, N. (1985). *Amusing ourselves to death*. New York: Penguin.
Raspberry, W. (1991). The role of racism in black poverty is exaggerated. In *Racism in America*, ed. W. Dudley, pp. 85–92. San Diego: Greenhaven Press.
Richards, I. A. (1936). *The philosophy of rhetoric*. New York: Oxford University Press.
Sennett, R. (1976). *The fall of public man*. New York: Vintage Books.
Solomon, M. (1985). The rhetoric of dehumanization: An analysis of medical reports of the Tuskegee syphilis project. *Western journal of speech communication* 49: 233–247.
Vico, G. (1968). *The new science*. Translated by T. Bergin and M. Fisch. Ithaca: Cornell University Press.
Weaver, R. (1948). *Ideas have consequences*. Chicago: University of Chicago Press.
Williams, P. J. (1991). *The alchemy of race and rights*. Cambridge: Harvard University Press.
Zarefsky, D. (1995). The roots of American community. The Carroll C. Arnold distinguished lecture presented at the annual convention of the Speech Communication Association. Boston: Allyn & Bacon.

Chapter 5

Building Citizenship Skills through Media Literacy Education

Renee Hobbs

A thirteen-year-old boy is studying the cover of a *Time* magazine issue featuring the furrowed face of Bob Dole. "This photo," he says, "seems to suggest a negative attitude toward the candidate. It's in black-and-white, and this makes Dole look older, and meaner, and notice how his face has deep lines and his eyes are not looking at the camera. This image was chosen to cast doubt on the candidate."

Jeremy England, a freshman at Oyster River High School, has been part of "View Smart to Vote Smart," a media literacy program developed by Continental Cablevision that features lesson plans, print, and video resources designed for use in the classroom (Splaine, 1996). With his classmates, Jeremy has explored the ways that political advertising shapes the campaign process, and he has identified the techniques that are used to attract the attention of audiences and manipulate their emotions. He has tracked a candidate's slogan and sound bites and looked at how the media has picked up on these messages. He has monitored the enormous amount of time that the media spends telling us who is ahead in the polls as opposed to information on the issues. He has looked at differences between different media in the way they cover politics, and he has examined how television production techniques can alter images and evoke powerful feelings without the public even knowing it. Jeremy England is deeply engaged in politics and was selected to write a newspaper column sharing the teen perspective on the political campaign. He recognizes the power of the democratic process and the power of the individual to communicate a point of view. He is deeply sensitive to the media's role in shaping the public's perception of politicians and politics. Jeremy England has discovered the power of being literate in a media age.

• • •

How can citizens be best prepared to participate in a democracy? The complaints about spectator democracy emerged in potent form during the 1996 election. More and more citizens are alienated from the political process. Recent studies suggest that many Americans are confused by politics because they simply do not know enough basic facts to follow a substantive political debate. The evidence is startling: 46 percent of Americans cannot identify Newt Gingrich as the Speaker of the House, and fewer than one-third can identify the name of their representative in Congress (Morin, 1995).

Today's conflict-oriented coverage of politics makes it possible to tune in to the fireworks and miss the substance, and the media circus around political campaigns is especially distracting to less educated citizens. "[Voters] see and hear the conflict but miss the content," as reporters are "increasingly drawn to reporting strategy and partisan skirmishes surrounding major policy debates but not their substance" (Morin, 1995). According to political scientists, the information gap— differences between the most well-informed and the least well-informed citizens—is affecting how politics is practiced, dumbing down democracy and making political campaigns increasingly negative, simplistic, and character based.

What kinds of knowledge, attitudes, and skills are essential for being a citizen in a media age? How do we create opportunities for young people to develop their interests in democracy? What role can the media, teachers, and parents play?

In more and more classrooms in the United States, educators are beginning to help students acquire the skills they need to manage in a media-saturated environment, recognizing that in its broadest sense, literacy must include the ability to skillfully read and write in a wide range of message forms, especially considering the dominance of image-based electronic media. In fact, the powerful concept of literacy was the driving force that led leaders in the media literacy movement to adopt a comprehensive definition of media literacy as "the ability to access, analyze, evaluate and produce communication in a variety of forms" in a conference sponsored by the Aspen Institute (Aufderheide, 1992). Put simply, media literacy includes the skills of literacy extended through the wide variety of messages that we are exposed to in contemporary society. Media literacy includes reading and writing, speaking and listening, accessing new technologies, critical viewing, and the ability to make your own messages using a wide range of technologies, including cameras, camcorders, and computers. Media literacy is not a new subject area and it is not just about television. It is literacy for the information age.

Proponents and practitioners of media literacy often fail to identify the distinct components of media literacy, and as a result, media literacy practices vary widely, as many different approaches to building media literacy skills are proliferating. But these different practices can be conceptualized along a continuum with four phases, as articulated by Thoman (1996).

Awareness of time and choice in media consumption. This phase of media literacy involves gaining consciousness and sensitivity regarding the extent and magnitude of individuals' exposure to different kinds of media messages, from billboards to tee-shirts and from newspapers and television to video games and the Internet. Activities often involve counting and measuring one's use of media, exploring different pleasures and satisfactions people receive from a range of media messages, and learning strategies for managing media use in the home.

Critical reading and viewing skills and media production activities. This phase of media literacy involves developing skills for analyzing and producing media messages, explicitly extending the traditional skills of literacy to include critical reading and writing for the mass media. Producing media messages has long been understood as one of the most valuable methods to gain insight into how messages are constructed. Critical analysis examines specific techniques involved in constructing messages by looking inside the frame of media messages to study specific patterns in the representation of social reality in a range of genres, such as books, magazines, sitcoms, ads, public service announcements, Web sites, documentaries, films, newsletters, comics, and editorial columns. The process of looking inside the frame includes examining the range of choices made by the author about the text, including asking questions about the author's motives, purpose, and point of view; the techniques used to attract attention; the use of image, sound, and language to convey meaning; and the range of different interpretations possible.

Analysis of political, economic, social, and cultural contexts of the media environment. This phase of media literacy involves gaining knowledge about the ways that media institutions are shaped by historical, political, economic, and social forces. For example, students can learn about the historical and economic conditions which, during the nineteenth and early part of the twentieth century, led to the concept of "journalistic objectivity." They can examine the economic relationships between advertising and a consumer culture; study the patterns of representation of masculinity, power, and violence in sports reporting; examine how advertiser preferences shape television programming; understand government's role in subsidizing the technologies which comprise the

Internet; or learn about the historical dimensions of broadcast deregulation, reform, and advocacy initiatives.

Media advocacy, media action, and social change. This phase of media literacy involves active participation in efforts to mobilize public opinion toward a specific policy of media reform, or in using specific media strategies to attract press interest, build coalitions, shape policy decision making, and change offensive or problematic practices on a number of social issues. For example, students can write letters to advertisers about programs they dislike, or they can support campaigns which raise awareness of the need to protect First Amendment rights in cyberspace. They can create their own media campaigns to promote a particular social health issue, such as violence, alcohol abuse, or smoking. As an example, 2,500 teachers and students in the community of Billerica, Massachusetts, organized a comprehensive antismoking media campaign as part of their school-wide "Ad Lab" project in 1994.

What determines how educators come to enter into one or more of these practices? Teachers' concerns about the intersection of youth, media, and culture shape their practices in the classroom. Why are some teachers attracted to media literacy? Some see media literacy as a tool to build relevance into contemporary education, building links between the classroom and the culture so that students see how themes and issues resonate in popular culture as they do in the study of literature, history, or social studies. Some see media literacy as a citizenship survival skill, necessary to be a thoughtful consumer and an effective citizen in a superhighway-driven media age. Some see media literacy as a kind of protection for children against the dangers and evils engendered by the excesses of television, and see media literacy as an antidote to manipulation and propaganda. Some see media literacy as a new kind of English education, learning to appreciate and analyze ads, sitcoms, and films—some of which are destined to become the classics of the next century—with the same tools used to study the traditional genres of poetry, short story, and the novel. Some see media literacy as a way to give children the opportunity to tell their own stories and better understand the power of those who shape the stories of our culture and our times.

But there are other visions of media literacy, more narrow and more problematic. Unfortunately, some see media literacy as an option for low-performing, underachieving students whose interest can be piqued by television and nothing else. Some see it as a kind of vocational education where children can learn to make Web sites or television shows and head for careers like the grownups. Some see it as a chance to play with sophisticated electronic tools, such as servers, graphics packages, scanners, character generators, video toasters, and wave-form monitors. Still others see media literacy as a way to make children aware of the web of "false consciousness" that capitalism has woven into our psyches, moving them to advocate revolutionary change. Some think media literacy is just about making good choices about what to watch or read. And many simply think the curriculum is already too crowded and teachers already too incompetent, burned out, or overburdened to make room for media literacy. It is because American educators have so many diverse perspectives on the benefits and value of media literacy and the best strategies for implementation that its practitioners and advocates often fail to distinguish the differences between the four distinct phases. Such a wide range of divergent motives can be a sign of the media literacy movement's vitality but can also generate confused, inarticulate, and occasionally adversarial positions relative to the varying practices which fall under the umbrella term, "media literacy" (Hobbs, 1996).

Media literacy has gained some measure of official status within Great Britain, Canada, Australia, Scotland, Spain, and other nations, where it is required as part of the language arts program in grades seven through twelve. Most of the training American teachers now receive is strongly patterned after models provided by British scholars, including Len Masterman, David Buckingham, David Lusted, and Cary Bazalgette, as well as British and Canadian teachers who have written about their experiences teaching media analysis and media production to young people.

With this nation's renewed interest in children and education in the 1990s, there have been significant signs of recent growth in the emerging media literacy movement. Support from the education establishment is emerging as the drive to rewrite curriculum and develop standards and framework for kindergarten through twelfth-grade education expands. At least fifteen states have language in their state curriculum frameworks that support media literacy. In North Carolina, for example, media literacy is included in both the communication skills (English) curriculum and in the information skills curriculum. In Massachusetts, media literacy is explicitly emphasized in all of the curriculum frameworks recently developed by the state education department. New Mexico requires students to take a media literacy course in order to graduate from high school. In Texas, the language arts curriculum is being rewritten to include media analysis and production activities (Considine, 1995).

In many communities, educators have begun the process of thinking seriously about expanding the concept of literacy to systematically include media and technology. There was only one teacher-training program in media literacy in 1993 at the program developed at Harvard Graduate School of Education. In 1994, there were twelve different programs held across the United States. By 1995, many communities were developing their own staff development programs for groups of educators. However, in most communities, media literacy exists because of the energy and initiative of a single teacher, not because of a coordinated, community-wide, programmatic plan of implementation. At present, only a few communities are aiming toward district-wide implementation of media literacy concepts where all students in the school system are expected to engage in a coordinated set of media literacy activities. These include Billerica, Massachusetts, Cold Spring, Minnesota, and the Dennis Yarmouth Public Schools in Massachusetts. More long-term investment in teacher education, site-based coordination of innovative, district-level programs, and support for evaluation and assessment is needed if media literacy skills are to be recognized not as an enrichment experience for a privileged few but a basic skill that all students must master.

MEDIA LITERACY AND BUILDING CITIZENSHIP SKILLS

Elihu Katz reminds us of the organic connection between communication, education, and democracy. "Democracy is meaningless without multiple voices . . . it is simply impossible to talk about citizenship training in modern society without reference to mass communication" (1993, p. 37).

There are three major ways in which media literacy can contribute to strengthening the future of American democracy through outreach to the 52 million students in our nation's schools.

First, media literacy practices help strengthen students' information access, analysis, and communication skills, and build an appreciation for why monitoring the world is important. Media literacy can inform students about how the press functions in a democracy, why it matters that citizens gain information and exposure to diverse opinions, and how people can participate in policy decision making at the community, state, and federal levels.

Second, media literacy can support and foster educational environments where students can practice the skills of leadership, free and responsible self-expression, and conflict resolution and consensus building. Without these skills, young people will not be able to effectively engage with others in the challenges of cooperative problem solving that participation in a democratic society demands.

Finally, media literacy skills can inspire young people to become more interested in increasing their access to diverse sources of information. The trend toward increased centralization of ownership of mass media and technologies industries may promote an "illusion of diversity" that limits people's access to ideas different from their own. In a multicultural society, people need to increase their comfort levels and tolerance with a wide range of different people. Media literacy can raise awareness of the vital role of exposure to a rich array of diverse opinions and ideas. In this chapter, I examine the challenges and opportunities that accompany the pragmatic incorporation of these goals as they relate to the lives of contemporary American teachers, students, and school administrators.

Strengthening Information Skills

One of the most potent crises which face the future of American public schools is a problem that few educators address. It is the power relationship that Postman (1985) has called the struggle between "first curriculum" of the mass media and the "second curriculum" of the schools. When Sizer recently identified this issue as one of the great silences in public education, he addressed an issue that media literacy educators hold dear:

All of us know that the minds and heart of our children are influenced in ever increasing ways by information and attitudes gathered far outside the schoolhouse walls, from an insistent media and the commerce that depends on it. In our policy discussions, we barely mention that fact, much less address it. . . . How the schools do, do not, or should connect with the newly insistent media world is rarely mentioned. We live in an information-rich culture, one controlled by commerce, but we plan the reform of our educational system as though the schoolhouses were still wholly encapsulated units. . . . These are some of the silences. They need to be filled. (1995, p. 83)

Students come to class with plenty of ideas and information about how the world works and about lifestyles, relationships, and social norms, and most of the information they receive does not originate from the students' families or neighbors, their pastors, or their community leaders. As Gerbner (1993) puts it, most of the stories we tell our children are told by a few global conglomerates who have something to sell.

Yet in many classrooms, the practices of American educators are guided by the assumption that information primarily flows in one direction—from teacher to student and from textbook to student. Teachers' control over access to information has been the defining quality of their authority, from kindergarten to graduate school. According to Freire and Giroux, "The language of educational theory and practice is organized around a claim to authority that is primarily procedural and technical . . . a language that in its quest for control, certainty and objectivity . . . removes schools from their most vital connections to public life" (1989, p. 8). Ceding the role of information provider to institutions outside the classroom threatens the role of the teacher and usurps the dominance of the academy-defined canon of things worth learning. Many teachers are still in denial about this already well-entrenched shift, and as a result, they may reject media and information technology as a tool for teaching and learning precisely because it alters the authority relationship between teachers and students.

When educational leaders do come together to talk about strengthening information skills, the conversation inevitably comes around to computer technology because educators are well aware of the role that information technology plays in the workplace and are regularly exposed to the marketing messages that equate computers with superior learning and teaching. Since the early 1980s, school administrators have been eager to bring schools into the twenty-first century by giving students access to CD-ROMs, on-line databases, computer applications, and Internet access.

Although computers can be found in almost every American school, most are so old that there is limited software which can run on them. In most communities, students have limited opportunities to use them at all. As predicted, the pattern of access to technology has reproduced the inequalities in the larger social framework of public education, with huge discrepancies between schools. Information-poor schools have teachers and students with no technology access at all, and in some troubled urban schools, it is routine to see hopelessly inadequate access to even the media of books and periodicals.

By contrast, students in information-rich schools have access to a well-stocked library with books, periodicals, and audio–visual resources, computers for word processing, art and graphic design, and science activities, plus computers to support library research and information retrieval. "Whether schools are public or private, the social class of the students has been and continues to be the single most significant factor in determining how a school works and the intellectual values it promotes" (Meier, 1995, p. 97).

Media hype about the Internet has energized the frenzy once again, as California recently mandated a computer Internet connection in every school in the state but devoted no attention to the challenge of providing teachers with the ongoing training and support needed to develop effective uses of the technology within the curriculum. Such efforts to put technology in schools will do little to strengthen the information skills of students. This phenomenon merely reflects the classic American myth of "technology as savior," a belief deeply embedded in the culture and particularly troublesome in education, where limited funding and the competitive upgrading of technology has led to a "catch-22" for educators—they can never be saved by the technology because they do not have the latest, fastest, and most powerful tools that are necessary for "redemption."

To build students' information skills, many education reformers recognize that the idea of teaching as "delivering content" needs to be challenged and replaced with the idea of teaching as cultivating "habits of mind," approaches to dealing with new information in ways that promote active engagement from the learner. Meier (1995) identifies this pedagogy in terms of the following five questions which should be at the heart of all learning:

1. *The Question of Evidence*: How do we know what we know?
2. *The Question of Viewpoint*: Who's speaking?
3. *The Search for Connections and Patterns*: What causes what?
4. *The Act of Supposition*: How might things have been different?
5. *The Determination of Relevance*: Who cares?

Compare these "habits of mind" as they relate to some of the following key questions used to analyze mass media messages:

- Who is the author and what is the purpose of the message?
- What values, lifestyles, or points of view are represented by this message?
- What techniques are used to attract your attention?
- What techniques are used to enhance the authority or authenticity of this message?
- How might different people interpret this message differently?
- What was omitted from this message?
- Who makes money from this message?

These types of questions invite the learner to take an active stance toward information. One example of the application of these skills in the secondary grades can be found in the curriculum resource, KNOW-TV, developed in collaboration with The Learning Channel. This program consists of a three-hour workshop for teachers of language arts, social studies, and science in grades seven through twelve. KNOW-TV builds media literacy skills within a collection of activities, videotape, and print support materials that introduce nine critical questions for analyzing nonfiction or documentary television. Instead of simply using a documentary to "deliver" content, teachers use the documentary in a more active, engaged fashion by inviting students to analyze the choices made by the producer in deciding what information to include and what to omit, what techniques to keep and hold viewer attention, and how information was shaped to seem most believable. By learning to "ask questions about what you watch, see, and read," the fundamental premise of media literacy is about "questioning authority," and as such, can be recognized as empowering student autonomy (Hobbs, 1994).

Another critically important dimension of media literacy for citizenship is in helping students understand the crucial role of the press in a democracy. Few public school teachers are prepared to teach any meaningful analysis of the functions of journalism as a result of their own limited education. Research on television use in political education classes reveals that when teachers use newspapers and television news in the classroom, they encourage students to be critical of the issues and events depicted but tend to treat the media's depiction of those issues and events as unproblematic (Masterman, 1985). When teachers do demonstrate to students the constructed nature of the media message, they sometimes bring their own cynicism and distrust of journalists into the classroom, risking the possibility that students become even further alienated and disenfranchised from the political process.

In a media literacy program designed in Israel by Tamar Liebes to strengthen students' understanding of the legitimacy of opposing voices within a democracy, students spend three full days in a series of activities, simulations, and discussions that introduce them to the problem of reliable observations and the psychology of selective perception. Students work in groups to document a school issue and are forced to select only a limited number of items as a result of time and deadline pressure. Some groups of students receive informal pressure from the school principal to present the school in what the administration deems a "good light." After experiencing the way news is shaped, students explore national television news and learn to identify the patterns of coverage. Such activities can promote students' understanding of education for democracy and the importance of taking turns, rules of order, and rational discourse that supports the legitimacy of oppositional voices in a public space (Katz, 1993). A number of similar programs have been implemented in the United States, including a notable program designed by Karen Webster and Joshua Meyrowitz to introduce fourth graders to the making of news in a Durham, New Hampshire, school.

If one of the fundamental purposes of schools is to teach students the responsibility of living in a democratic society, then building students' tolerance for diverse opinions and the ability to critically analyze information is essential. Schools should not be in the business of preparing "docile, unquestioning workers who will go blindly into the roles assigned them in the great struggle to dominate the world economy. To be human in a democratic society is to be free and to be capable of making conscious, responsible choices. A democratic society requires that the people shall judge; schools must teach them to judge wisely" (Soder, 1995, p. 168).

Providing Opportunity to Practice Leadership and Self-Expression

The institution of public schooling works in powerful ways to re-produce the existing power relations in society, and as a result, schools can be among the most repressive and antidemocratic of social institutions. Meier writes of a dramatic example of the "petty humiliations imposed to remind teachers and children of who's the boss," remembering her first visit to a New York City school where she witnessed the principal scolding students for crossing over a line painted down the middle of the corridor (1995, p. 8). The unprofessional working conditions teachers experience, where they have little control or influence over their work, often encourages teachers to withdraw intellectually and emotionally from the enterprise. Schools can promote the kind of apathy and alienation that "are not only one of the main agencies of distributing an effective dominant culture . . . they help create people . . . who see no other serious possibility to the economic and cultural assemblage now extant" (Apple, 1990, p. 6).

What does it take to create a environment where democratic values are built into the culture of the school? Meier describes her efforts to invent a school environment that would make it possible for teachers and students to have high expectations of themselves, "where all kids can experience the power of their ideas" (1995, p. 4). Central Park East is considered one of the most remarkable public schools in the nation, where 90 percent of the students graduate from high school and 90 percent of those go on to college, in a city where the average graduation rate is 50 percent. Meier's commitment to reforming public schools is fueled by her understanding of the relationship between public education and democracy. "Public schools can train us for . . . political conversations across divisions of race, class, religion and ideology. . . . Dealing with the complicated is what training for good citizenship is all about" (pp. 7, 22). Her following perspective on the possibility that schools can be reshaped by democratic principles reflects the complexity of this issue:

We also saw schools as examples of the possibilities of democratic community, and what we meant by this was continuously under debate and review. It wasn't simply a question of governance structures, and certainly not a matter of extending the vote to four-year-olds. Although classroom life could certainly include more participation by children in decisions that traditional schools allowed, we saw it as even more critical that the school life of adults be democratic. It seemed unlikely that we could foster values of community in our classrooms unless the adults in the school had significant rights over their own workplace. For us, democracy implied that people should have a voice not only in their own individual work but in the work of others as well.

Finally, we saw collaboration and mutual respect among staff, parents, students and the larger community as part of what we mean by calling our experience democratic. (p. 22)

Meier and her colleagues created a school environment based on breaking up huge schools into small schools for the purpose of having the following: choice within the public school system; respect between teachers, parents, and students; teaching that connects learning to real-world activities; and creating a new ideal of being well educated based on the development of the skills of keen observation, playfulness, and the possession of a skeptical and open mind; the habit of imagining how others think, feel, and see the world; the ability to be respectful of evidence; the ability to be able to evaluate the quality of information; the ability to value hard work; and the ability to know how to communicate effectively. Why focus on skills and not subject matter? "Academia has no monopoly on the habits of mind that underlie good practice in all vocations of a democratic society, including the first and foremost of vocations, that of citizen" (Meier, 1995, p. 171). Broadening the definition of an educated person beyond the mastery of specific facts to promote strong intellectual habits of mind has as its consequence in the promotion of curiosity, creativity, and theory building.

How best should educators promote student leadership skills and responsible self-expression? When *Captive Voices* (Nelson, 1974) was published, it identified the range of powerful opportunities that scholastic journalism could provide to students, as the school newspaper can create a public voice to share perspectives and viewpoints, to build coalitions, and to change policies through engaging the community in issues of public concern. Commissioned by the Robert Kennedy Memorial Foundation, *Captive Voices* also identified the problems limiting the effectiveness of student journalism. The report was the single largest national inquiry into American high school journalism, and at the time, the findings represented a formidable indictment of the public schools. Censorship and harsh limits on journalistic freedom were routine practices by administrators and teachers. According to the report, most high school publications were bland and often served as a public relations tool for the school. Yet, according to the report, where a free, vigorous student press did exist, there was a healthy ferment of ideas and opinions with no indication of disruption or negative side effects on the educational experience of the school. In the 1970s, high school journalism was given second-class status in the school's curriculum. This was reflected in the elective nature of journalism courses since journalism courses did not fulfill academic requirements needed for graduation. Twenty years later, this phenomenon is largely unchanged, and the legal landscape which had protected students' First Amendment rights has deteriorated even further.

When the Supreme Court ruled on *Hazelwood v. Kuhlmeier* in 1988 in a five to three decision, the status of high school journalism was changed significantly by giving school administrators the power to censor student newspapers. In this case, a principal censored a high school student newspaper in Hazelwood, Missouri because of two stories produced by students about teen pregnancy and the effects of divorce on teenagers. In this decision, the court limited the scope of an earlier ruling, *Tinker v. Des Moines School District*, which made the basic argument that "students do not shed their constitutional rights to freedom of speech or expression at the schoolhouse gate" (1969, 393 US 503). The Supreme Court called upon a 1986 decision, *Bethel v. Fraser*, which stated that schools do not need to tolerate student speech that is contrary to its educational mission. In the Hazelwood case, the court concluded the following: "Educators do not offend the First Amendment by exercising editorial control over the style and content of student speech in school-sponsored expressive activities so long as their actions are reasonably related to legitimate pedagogical concerns."

In his dissent, Justice William Brennan wrote that a high school newspaper was a public forum "established to give students an opportunity to express their views," and he recognized that the loose phrasing of "legitimate pedagogical concerns" could easily serve as a smoke screen for administrators to void student newspapers of unwanted controversy. The Hazelwood decision "aptly illustrates how readily school officials (and courts) can camouflage viewpoint discrimination as the 'mere' protection of students from sensitive topics." More important, Brennan noted the hypocrisy of a decision that allows school officials to censor controversial ideas while purporting to teach students how to live in a democratic society where government officials cannot legally engage in such practices (*Hazelwood v. Kuhlmeier*, 1988, 484 US 260).

In response to the ruling, the professional press almost seemed to mock the students for their arrogance in believing they should be allowed to cover what was important to them. A principal is no different from an editor, claimed newspaper editorials. Most newspapers avoided noting the role of public school principals as public officials and indirect agents of the government (Freedom Forum, 1994).

The Hazelwood decision had an effect on high schools across the nation and the examples of how school administrators have applied the ruling are chilling. In Manchester, New Hampshire, a principal shut down the student newspaper after an editorial criticized a teacher for withholding the vote totals in a school election. In Fort Wayne, Indiana, a principal censored a report that documented how a tennis coach improperly charged students for court time. In Ohio, paramedics were called to the school when a student who had been drinking alcohol that morning passed out from alcohol poisoning. The school newspaper was forbidden to write about the event. In Nashville, Tennessee, nineteen students were arrested on the first day of school in 1990. The principal refused to let students report the incident and the journalism adviser was replaced by someone with no previous newspaper experience.

According to Paul McMasters of the First Amendment Center, self-censorship is on the rise, with student journalists trying to avoid conflicts and reprisals from school administrators and their peers. "Sometimes the biggest proponents of censorship are fellow students harassing students journalists. [These students] haven't been taught in their classrooms the benefits and the absolute necessity of a free and open debate and dialogue in our society" (Freedom Forum, 1994, p. 100).

Robert Trager and Joseph Russomanno make the following powerful point about the long-term impact of Hazelwood on students' socialization:

When free expression is limited in order to instill majoritarian societal values in their schools, this turns the First Amendment on its head. Rather . . . students' expressive rights should be at the core of the societal values that public schools teach—and that should allow students to practice . . . A school environment devoid of free expression is not likely to produce an adult ready to support the sentiment attributed to Voltaire: "I disapprove of what you say, but I will defend to the death your right to say it." (Freedom Forum, 1994, p. 101)

When video technology is available, the pattern of practices involving student communication becomes more complex. Edwin Posey teaches a video production class at Paul Robeson High School on the south side of Chicago. Students produce documentaries, public service announcements, and a morning news show, and they tape football games and school plays. Student-produced television programs often operate without an organized curriculum and are of widely uneven quality. In most schools, television and print journalism operate separately with little overlap between the two. Because of the instantaneous and nonpermanent character of video messages, they seem to be less subject to oversight and scrutiny from school officials. In many schools, administrators do not regard student video productions as the official voice of the school.

At Educational Video Center (EVC) in New York City, young people gain the skills to make their own media messages and are able to gain extensive training working with media professionals. Steve Goodman, the director of EVC, believes that video documentaries present rich possibilities for learning because they involve research, reporting, writing, using a camera, and editing. At EVC, young people have produced a range of documentaries on issues in their own communities, from AIDS and homelessness to stereotypes in the media and gangs. One of the most well-known works produced by youths involved in EVC's outreach program was entitled, "Unequal Education: Failing our Children," and it was broadcast as part of Bill Moyers' "Listening to America" on public television. The program profiled two seventh-grade students in two different schools in New York City, showing the broad differences between rich schools and poor schools in the community. Goodman sees video production as one central dimension to building students' media literacy skills. Electronic journalism holds out the hope that large numbers of young people can develop a different relationship with television. Transforming the nature of young people's relationship with media messages through opportunities for self-expression and communication is at the heart of media literacy.

Promoting Access to Diverse Sources of Information

A major challenge facing citizens and their access to diverse sources of information revolves around an inherent structural characteristic of the mass media—its reliance on advertising. The advertising subsidy serves as the most powerful limit on the content of information we receive from news and entertainment, since, as Baker (1994) notes, the incentive of advertising revenue encourages the media to tailor their message content by treating advertisers' products and their broader interests charitably in both news reports and editorials, by reducing partisanship and often reducing controversial elements in order to increase the size of the audience, and by favoring younger and middle- to high-income audiences who are considered more desirable by advertisers. Baker notes, "Advertisers 'pay' the media to obtain the audience they desire, providing strong incentive for the media to shape content to appeal to the 'desired' audience. . . . Since newspapers are under particular pressure to sell more affluent audiences to advertisers, newspapers sometimes purposefully limit or reduce circulation in areas or among groups of people that advertisers do not value" (1994, pp. 66–67).

Efforts on the part of independent producers and notable production companies, including the Children's Television Workshop, to create a television news program for children have been stymied by the lack of interest in buying advertising time in a serious news program for children ages eight to fifteen (Lesser, 1994). The only contemporary news program for children, *Nick News*, produced by Lucky Duck Productions, does not take as its goal the task of providing information to children about local, national, or world events but consists exclusively of soft news stories that flatter the child audience with an assortment of feature stories revolving around children's creative and community accomplishments. Some newspapers have spearheaded efforts to create a children's section for their younger readers ages nine to seventeen, and most of these efforts have failed to survive past an initial trial because of the difficulty in attracting audiences who want to "buy" children via the newspaper (Blum, 1996).

One resource used by some teachers to introduce the issue of the advertising subsidy and its impact on the commodification of culture to students at the high school level has been the quarterly magazine, *Adbusters*. Produced by the Media Foundation in Vancouver, British Columbia, *Adbusters* has a special section designed for teens ages twelve to nineteen, with articles and reviews designed to introduce the spirit of media advocacy around a challenge to consumer culture. Because the magazine is only available through large news retailers in urban centers who maintain a healthy collection of independent distributors, possession of *Adbusters* is often viewed as a prized commodity itself among teachers, who typically have had little access to nonmainstream or alternative information sources.

Since its inception, public broadcasting has offered citizens access to a wider range of messages than available via commercial media, but they have faced renewed political challenges from conservative congressmen with easy access to the talk-radio airwaves who reject the argument that public television requires federal subsidies. Such congressmen argue that "the federal government has 'no mandate' to keep funding public broadcasting; that noncommercial educational broadcasting is 'not essential' to the nation . . . that public broadcasting is elitist, a 'sandbox for the rich'" (Duggan, 1995, p. 25). Leaders in public television generally reference the numbers that show their audiences to be small but diverse and point to icons like "Big Bird" as proof of public television's vitality and worthiness. Proposals to support public television via a tax on advertising revenues or by eliminating the exemption from state sales tax generally given to advertising have uniformly received such little attention in the press that the public is largely unaware of either the problem of the corrosive censorship that results from advertising or some of the potential corrections available to improve the freedom of the press.

The power of large, vertically integrated companies to control the content of the mass media has been clearly evident in the shifting patterns of entertainment available for children and young people. The last bastion of diversity in children's media has been in the area of children's literature, which has been rapidly fading as a result of "Disney-ification." As Meyrowitz (1987) has explained, because of the new patterns of information access available to both children and adults, children's access to a wide range of adult content has blurred some of the distinctions between children and adults. Adult discomfort with children's changing status is a theme that is widely found in contemporary film and television programming. Disney merchandising has served to smooth over this tension in our culture, as De Cordova has noted: "The merchandising of Mickey Mouse toys was important in making sacred Disney's address to children . . . because that merchandising worked more assuredly than the movies to push the image of the child back into traditional categories of childhood" (1994, p. 213). At the same time that children and young people have more and more easy access to the complexities of adult relationships via prime-time television, sports programming, and the surrounding celebrity culture, the Disney mythology has served to frame childhood in ways that provide a sense of comforting tradition to parents. The huge global reach of Disney has served to displace the wider, more diverse, and authentic works of literature and art produced by authors and illustrators working in the genre of children's literature and film.

The dominance of a few, widely distributed and ubiquitous types of entertainment and information creates an appetite, as young people's expectations are shaped by the range (or lack of range) of messages available to them. Some teachers have been frustrated by students' lack of interest in noncommercial, alternative messages produced in literature, music, and the arts and available on video and computer software. A teacher at the 1995 National Media Literacy Conference in Boone, North Carolina, who had just moved from teaching at a private school to teaching at a public school, was struggling with students' lack of interest as she used a wide range of alternative media in the classroom. These materials worked well, she noted, among the children of the well educated and affluent who were accustomed to a wider range of information and entertainment. She complained about her new students' impatience and resistance to messages that did not fit their expectations of what storytelling or video should be. How can educators build their students' capacity to manage messages that do not fit comfortably within the existing commercial paradigms?

The growing community of media literacy educators has as its explicit aim the nurturance and the support for the alternative media arts. In 1990 when the media literacy movement was in its initial emergence in the United States after a prolonged hiatus, independent artists and educators met at a conference in Austin, Texas, in an event supported by the National Endowment for the Arts (NEA) and the National Alliance for Media Arts and Culture (NAMAC). By exploring the intersections of independent media arts and public education, participants recognized a critical mutual goal—to stretch young people's appreciation and understanding of the wide range of forms available for self-expression and communication. In a democracy, it is the explicit goal of education to build students' tolerance for complexity.

But such work is challenging when teachers perceive they are engaging in the task alone, without the support of the culture and often as an act of resistance against the culture. In the isolation of the classroom, alone with one hundred or more children and teenagers for six hours a day, the task is daunting. Andy Garrison is an independent filmmaker and a high school teacher who produces materials that help teachers incorporate the study of alternative media in the classroom. His film, *Night Ride*, provides a rich, multilayered, visual and auditory dramatic experience, and the creative array of activities, discussion formats, and writing assignments which accompany the film permit a teacher to engage in the kind of close analysis that builds critical thinking skills.

There is a serious need for initiatives that provide teachers with the opportunity to access, screen, and evaluate noncommercial "texts" and to provide teachers with experiences that build their own awareness, knowledge, and skills of the values of independent, noncommercial media arts. One example of this is the program, "Diverse Images and Perspectives," a workshop designed by Karon Sherarts in which teachers learn methods of integrating the work of alternative media artists into the existing curriculum. ALIVE-TV, a national public television series produced at KTCA-Minneapolis, sponsored the workshop in collaboration with the Minnesota Film Board and Independent Television Service (ITVS), an organization created by Congress to address the needs of underserved audiences, particularly minorities and children.

Teachers, of course, are the ones who shape the 1,000 hours of instruction received by the 52 million children in our nation's schools. Treated for too long as factory workers and not as professionals, it is clear that a critical focus of the media literacy movement aims to enhance the knowledge, skills, and practices of the 2.1 million teachers in the United States, better preparing them to create opportunities that stretch and enrich their students' ability to access, analyze, and communicate information, engage with their students in practices that promote leadership and problem solving, and increase students' exposure to a diverse array of opinions and ideas.

SUMMARY

It is impossible to have a healthy democracy unless there are healthy, competent, and engaged citizens. American youths, however, are using drugs and alcohol at earlier ages, are engaging in sexual behavior and getting pregnant earlier, and are causing pain and being hurt by the dramatically increased levels of violence among twelve- to seventeen-year-olds (Carnegie Council on Adolescent Development, 1995). The shifting knowledge economy now requires that people acquire sophisticated reasoning, communication, and problem-solving skills, and yet 44 million adults in the United States lack even basic literacy skills (National Center for Education Statistics, 1993). For adolescents to thrive, it is essential to improve the quality of our nation's communities, schools, and families if we are to take on the task of improving the health of American democracy.

Within this broad context, media literacy has an important role to play. As Eco claims, "A democratic civilization will save itself only if it makes the language of the image into a stimulus for critical reflection, not an invitation to hypnosis" (1979, p. 15). As a result of modern communication technology, we have become so thoroughly enmeshed in a sign system that the system has become invisible to us. As media literacy techniques help refresh our vision, we are invited to "revision" ourselves, our families, our neighbors, our communities, and all our social institutions in ways that reflect the spirit of democratic problem solving through mutual respect, rational discourse, and critical inquiry.

REFERENCES

Apple, M. W. (1990). *Ideology and curriculum.* 2nd ed. New York: Routledge.

Aufderheide, P. (1992). *Media literacy: A report of the national leadership conference on media literacy.* Washington, D.C.: The Aspen Institute.

Baker, C. E. (1994). *Advertising and the democratic process.* Princeton: Princeton University Press.

Blum, A. (1996). Personal communication, April 10, Cambridge, Mass.

Broderick, P. (1996). Independents in cyberspace. *NVR? Reports* 19: 1–2.

Carnegie Council on Adolescent Development. (1995). *Great transitions: Preparing adolescents for a new century.* New York: Carnegie Corporation.

Considine, D. (1995). Personal communication, September 20, Boone, N.C.

Continental Cablevision. (1996). *View smart to vote smart.* Boston: Continental Cablevision.

Daressa, L. (1996). Television for a change: To help us change ourselves. *Current*, February 12: 11.

De Cordova, R. (1994). The Mickey in Macy's window. Childhood, consumerism, and Disney animation. In *Disney discourse: Producing the magic kingdom*, ed. E. Smoodin. New York: Routledge.

Duggan, E. S. (1995). Spare that living tree. *Current*, February 6: 24–25.

Eco, U. (1979). Can television teach? *Screen education* 31: 12.

Freedom Forum. (1994). *Death by cheeseburger: High school journalism in the 1990s and beyond.* Arlington, Va.: Freedom Forum.

Freire, P., and H. Giroux. (1989). Pedagogy, popular culture and public life: An introduction. In *Popular culture: Schooling and everyday life*, ed. H. Giroux and R. I. Simon. New York: Bergin & Garvey.

Gerbner, G. (1993). Who tells all the stories? In *Media competency as a challenge to school and education.* Gutersloh, Germany: Bertelsmann Foundation Press.

Hobbs, R. (1994). *KNOW TV. Analyzing non-fiction television*. Bethesda, Md.: The Learning Channel.

Hobbs, R. (1995). Yo! Are you hip to this? Teaching media literacy. *Media studies journal* 8(4): 135–145.

Hobbs, R. (1996). The seven great divides in the media literacy movement. Paper presented at Media Education Colloquium, April 29, at Clark University.

Katz, E. (1993). The legitimacy of opposition: On teaching media and democracy. In *Media competency as a challenge to school and education.* Gutersloh, Germany: Bertelsmann Foundation Press.

Lesser, G. (1994). Personal communication.

Masterman, L. (1985). *Teaching the media*. London: Routledge.

Meier, D. (1995). The *power of their ideas: Lessons for America from a small school in Harlem*. Boston: Beacon Press.

Meyrowitz, J. (1987). *No sense of place*. New York: Oxford University Press.

Morin, R. (1995). Tuned out, turned off. *Washington Post National Weekly Edition*, February 5, p. 11.

National Center for Education Statistics. (1993). *Adult literacy in America*. Washington, D.C.: U.S. Department of Education.

Nelson, J. (1974). *Captive voices: The commission of inquiry into high school journalism report*. New York: Schocken.

Neuparth, B. (Ed.). (1993). *Media competency as a challenge to school and education*. Gutersloh, Germany: Bertelsmann Foundation Press.

Postman, N. (1985). *Amusing ourselves to death*. New York: Basic Books.

Sizer, T. (1995). Silences. *Daedelus* 124(4): 77–84.

Soder, R. (1995). American education: Facing up to unspoken assumptions. *Daedelus* 124(4): 163–168.

Splaine, J. (1996). Elections in the TV age. *Better viewing* (March/April): 13–14.

Thoman, E. (1996). Personal communication, March 18, at founding convention of Cultural Environment Movement.

Chapter 6

Citizenship: The Forgotten Trust That Puts Democracy at Risk

John S. Burns

> Where every man is a sharer in the direction of his ward republic, or of some of the higher ones, and feels that he is a participator in the government of affairs not merely at an election, one day in the year, but every day; when there shall not be a man in the state who will not be a member of some one of its councils, great or small, he will let the heart be torn out of his body, sooner than his power be wrested from him by a Caesar or a Bonaparte.
>
> Thomas Jefferson in a Letter to Joseph C. Cabell, February 2, 1816 (Conant, 1962, p. 119)

This chapter provides a discussion about citizenship development. Traditionally, the community, primarily through the institutions of the family, church, and schools, fulfilled the responsibility for developing citizens. Our communities have become less distinct as the institutions that used to delimit them have degenerated in contemporary American society. Schools have the potential to arrest the erosion of civic responsibility in our communities through reestablishing the traditional role of transmitting a core of values associated with citizenship and community. In contemporary society, the media are perhaps the most influential of all social institutions, a fact advertisers discovered long ago. The media need to examine their responsibility to join the schools, and for that matter families and churches, in their efforts to rediscover effective ways to transmit the values and moral trust associated with citizenship to subsequent generations.

OUR DEMOCRACY IS AT RISK

The Eisenhower Leadership Group (ELG), in its May 1996 Report to the U.S. Secretary of Education, boldly declared, "American democracy is at risk. Too many of us—either from complacency or despair, inertia or ignorance—are leaving the work of civic engagement to others. Too many of us are expecting someone else to carry the water" (ELG, 1996, p. 1). The truth is that throughout the history of the United States, American democracy has always been at risk.

Our democracy has always been at risk because we have always excluded people from effective participation in the political process. This risk to our democracy stems from the desire of the few power holders to control as much of the mechanism of government and other institutions as possible. American history is the story of the conflict and struggle by those who have had little or no power wresting it from those who do (DeMott, 1995). The real story of America reaches beyond our mythology to uncover the ongoing power struggle that has shrouded the nation since before its inception. The founders who wrote so boldly about equality and liberty were actually engaged in a narrow debate regarding those for whom liberty and equality was really being discussed, namely, which white males ought to be allowed to vote, only those with substantial property or men with little or no property. Women and people of color in the society, including the American Indians who "owned" the land in the first place, were simply excluded from consideration. And so the struggle began and has continued to the present, the assumption always being that those who participate in the governing will control who reaps the greatest benefits from society.

Democracy is at risk even though voting rights have been extended broadly to most segments of American society. Today, democracy is threatened by the lack of effective citizen participation, participation well beyond the mere act of voting. If one listens to the politicians in the media, it becomes clear that they pander to voters, not citizens. Politicians cry out to voters about the ills of society and shamelessly promote themselves as the problem solvers and the leaders who can get us going in the right direction again. Voters "buy" the message and elect the politician. Having no more of a plan to solve problems than can be contained in a short sound bite, the politician is off the hook when it comes to accountability. Indeed, the most important accountability for many politicians is gaining and continuing favor from lobbyists, special interest groups, and political action committees (PACs) who provide essential capital for future election campaigns. The best a voter can hope for is that crucial problems are managed—put under wraps, out of sight, and out of mind—instead of resolved.

Democracy is at risk today because as voters we have not developed into effective citizens. Instead, we have given up our power, and as Thomas Jefferson put it, allowed our "hearts to be plucked out of our bodies" (Conant, 1962, p. 119). We gave up our power as real participants in the governance of our communities to become consumers of entitlements from our communities and government, just as we are consumers of cheeseburgers, athletic shoes, and automobiles. As consumers of entitlements, if we participate in the governing process at all, we engage in transactions in which we exchange our votes with politicians who make us promises. Political quick fixes are sent out as press releases by the public affairs officers that every government agency and significant politician employs. The media pick them up, seldom questioning the efficacy of these slickly packaged solutions. If questions are raised at all, they usually are not offered in a way that encourages citizens to engage in a constructive debate or opportunities for personal involvement to bring about the solution to the issue. So the real problems remain, covered with fluff that appeals to reporters, editors, and the general public.

Politicians point to the fluff and tell voters that things are really getting turned around now. Election after election we willingly buy this political rhetoric in exchange for our vote. Our vote is the payment we offer to remove ourselves from meaningful (sacrificial) involvement in producing the changes our society so desperately needs. Burns (1978) calls this kind of exchange *transactional leadership*.

If a politician is serious about solving difficult problems and appropriately turns the resolution of the problem back to the people to work out through concentrated effort and sacrifice, we voters are usually outraged. We simply expect to collect what we believe we are entitled to because we have given our vote. Turning problems back to us for resolution is viewed as a failure on the part of the politician. As consumers of government, we no more expect to have problems turned back to us by our politicians than we expect a fast-food worker to tell us to step behind the counter and cook our own cheeseburgers after we have ordered them. The media is as eager to report these apparent political failures as they are to report sound-bite promises, and thus perpetuate the myth that the role of politicians is to painlessly deliver solutions to society's ills.

Barber suggests that economic forces fueled by media influence classifies people into markets for myriad products and produces consumers who are not citizens in the traditional sense at all. Instead of being active members of a civil community, voters are consumers in a market segment, and that is the way their transactional political leaders treat them. Barber notes in the following extract that the consumer paradigm has profound implications for the way voters view their role in society:

Markets simply are not designed to do the things democratic polities do. . . .
They advance individualistic rather than social goals, permitting us to say
one by one, "I want a new VCR" or "Buy yen and sell D-Marks!" but deter-
ring us from saying, in a voice made common by interaction and deliberation, "our inner city community needs new athletic facilities" or "there is too
much violence on TV and in the movies" or "we should rein in the World
Bank and democratize the IMF!" Markets preclude "we" thinking and "we"
action of any kind at all, trusting in the power of aggregated individual choices
(the invisible hand) to somehow secure the common good. Consumers speak
the elementary rhetoric of "me," citizens invent the common language of "we."
(1995, pp. 242–243)

Our democracy is at risk because as voters we have abdicated our responsibility as citizens to become involved in the solution of the myriad
problems that plague our society. We have not demanded the power and
resources nor have we made the personal sacrifice necessary to effect the
substantive changes our society needs. So in the spring of 1996, when gasoline prices jumped to their highest levels in years, politicians from both
parties fell all over themselves trying to reduce a recently imposed federal gasoline tax, believing that consumers (voters) would reward their
efforts to reduce economic pain—even if the relief was only to be temporary since the tax was due to be reimposed after the November election. This was a classic transactional leadership strategy: Give me your
vote because I feel your pain and can reduce it because, as a consumer
of government, you are entitled to a painless existence.

Transactional leadership is significantly different from Burns's (1978)
most significant contribution to leadership theory, *transforming leadership*: "The transforming leader looks for potential motives in followers, seeks to satisfy higher needs, and engages the full person of the
follower. The result of transforming leadership is a relationship of
mutual stimulation and elevation that converts followers into leaders
and may convert leaders into moral agents" (p. 4).

A political cartoon syndicated by Wright (1996) suggested an alternative to the typical transactional leadership relationship between politicians and voters. In the cartoon was a sign that stated, "The kind of
politician we need but can never hope to have." Next, it showed a politician saying, "Therefore, I propose a 15-cent-per-gallon increase to
encourage oil conservation, discourage gas-guzzlers, promote alternative energy research, rebuild roads and bridges, aid public transporta-
tion and ensure that never again will we be held hostage by OPEC."
The cartoon is a plea for transforming leadership.

We are not likely to find voters taking to the streets demanding increased
investment in mass transit or alternative energy sources to be paid for by

significantly higher fuel or other taxes associated with driving our cars. Instead, we have allowed ourselves to become the willing accomplices of politicians and the special interest groups who often pull their strings, choosing to believe in their simple sounding and equally worthless solutions to complex problems that will allegedly cost us not one whit. We have conveniently forgotten our elected representatives are there to help facilitate our effective involvement in the affairs of a civil society. When the problems persist, we never look to ourselves and our own failure at producing change. Instead, we become embittered at the process and the system and sometimes even the politicians.

Our democracy is at risk because we have not developed as citizens. The special interest groups and others who hold power continue to benefit from a government that meets their narrow needs supported by voter-consumers who have allowed themselves to become as effectively disenfranchised from participation in the governing of society as those who were prohibited from voting in the past.

What our democracy needs is transformation of its voter-consumers into citizens. Burns noted that "the process of leadership must be seen as part of the dynamics of conflict and of power; that leadership is nothing if not linked to collective purpose; that the effectiveness of leaders must be judged not by their press clippings but by actual social change measured by intent and by the satisfaction of human needs and expectations" (1978, p. 3). Our democracy is at risk because we have not learned what it is to engage in leadership and citizenship in ways that will transform our society, by first transforming ourselves.

WHAT SCHOOLS HAVE FORGOTTEN

Answer the following question before you continue reading: What is the fundamental purpose of education? Why have we invested billions of dollars in this society to establish schools, colleges, and universities and everything that goes with them?

What was your answer? Ask most parents, students, legislators, trustees, faculty members, and administrators—virtually anyone associated with education—what the purpose of education is, and you will get a variety of answers, including: gaining knowledge, becoming more aware of the world we live in, becoming technically proficient at some skill or in some knowledge base, to get a better job, and to contribute to society. When people are really pressed for an answer, however, a consistent vocational theme emerges as the primary purpose for education. Education is viewed as a means for achieving vocational objectives—get a good education and get a good job.

The vocational purpose for education was never more obvious than a decade ago when a blue ribbon commission issued a report to the U.S.

Secretary of Education entitled, *A Nation at Risk*. This report focused primarily on kindergarten through secondary school (K–12) education in
the United States, although it also made minor recommendations for
colleges and universities as well (i.e., increasing admission standards
based on performance on standardized exams). The focus of the report
was to assail our educational system's ability to provide adequate preparation for our youth so that the future workforce would enable the
United States to compete favorably in world markets. The result of
that report was a redoubling of our efforts as a society to reform K–12
education. There has been a ripple effect in higher education as some
legislatures and trustees (and the ever-responsive higher education
administrators who listen closely to legislators and trustees) craft and
implement reforms in higher education like graduate outcomes assessment policies and guaranteed four-year undergraduate degrees.

No one should devalue sincere reasoned attempts to transform our
educational processes to make them as effective as any in the world.
However, the dominant purpose for reform, vocationalism, deserves
close scrutiny. Among higher education scholars the discussion about
the purpose for education is often focused on a debate over liberal arts
versus professional (vocational) preparation. Over the decades we have
consistently moved our educational systems away from their liberal
arts roots. What do we lose as a society because of this ever-increasing
emphasis on vocational preparation as the purpose of education?
Etzioni commented as follows regarding one of the major shortfalls of
today's public education:

Once schools transmitted the moral and social values of previous generations to the young. Granted, these values were complacent, a bit authoritarian, and rather discriminatory. Did we shake them up! But this was the easy
part, as destruction often is. Now we are too often left with educational rubble.
Schools are so overwhelmed simply by maintaining order and passing on
elementary knowledge and skills that they have neither the time nor the in-
clination to attend to their most important mission: transmitting a core of
values to the next generation. (1993, p. 12)

Thomas Jefferson would have never discounted the importance of
vocational preparation as one of the important purposes of education.
Yet, Jefferson had a completely different notion of the primary purpose of education at all levels, namely, to prepare citizens to fully and
responsibly participate in a democracy. He warned the following:

In every government on earth is some trace of human weakness, some germ
of corruption and degeneracy, which cunning will discover, and wickedness
insensibly open, cultivate and improve. Every government degenerates when

trusted to the rulers of the people alone. The people themselves therefore are its only safe depositories. And to render even them safe, their minds must be improved to a certain degree. (Conant, 1962, p. 96)

Jefferson's purpose, affirmed by John Dewey in this century, cannot be identified as a significant priority in education in the United States today. Civics education is at best a marginalized subject area. The highly publicized Goals 2000 plan, a joint project developed in collaboration by the nation's governors and the federal government, devotes little attention to citizenship education. The topic is as follows, buried in Goal Three:

By the year 2000, American students will leave grades four, eight and twelve having demonstrated competency in challenging subject matter, including English, mathematics, science, history and geography; and every school in America will ensure that all students learn to use their minds well, so they may be prepared for responsible citizenship, further learning, and productive employment in our modern economy. (National Educational Goals Panel, 1993, p. x)

There is an underlying assumption that if the nation's schools, colleges, and universities produce students who perform well on standardized achievement tests, they will become productive, globally competitive workers who will also somehow become good citizens. Unfortunately, this assumption ignores the increasing evidence that active participation in our democracy at all levels of possible involvement is in decline, especially among our youngest citizens.

Typically, the curriculum for citizenship education has been relegated to a single specialized course in civics in high school or late middle school. A few schools even require students to perform some sort of community service before they graduate. When most schools use community service, however, it is as a punishment for rule infractions. What an interesting message that sends about civic responsibility! This contemporary reality is far from the vision Thomas Jefferson had for public education. While we may still believe that somehow our children are being educated to become productive, active, and involved citizens, the empirical evidence proves this is one of the greatest (and perhaps one of the most dangerous) of our society's myths. Applied civics—developing leadership and citizenship knowledge, skills, and will among students in America—requires an interdisciplinary curriculum that permeates all levels of education from kindergarten through college (Bigelow, 1994; DeMott, 1995; ELG, 1996).

When applied civics becomes an integrated part of the nation's curriculum, then courses in media literacy will have the opportunity to develop students into something more than savvy voters. Certainly these courses can teach students to recognize the influence the one-hundred corporations that sponsor 85 percent of television programming have on the media. Further, students can learn to ponder the influence the twenty-three corporations that now control most media outlets have on our ability as citizens to objectively analyze problems and to acquire the power required to effect the changes our society needs (Lappe and DuBois, 1994). Students can begin to think like citizens instead of consumers. They can critically examine the media to determine if it gives voice to the voiceless in society. They can see if the media promote community development by framing issues around tough questions, and can challenge citizens to take on the sacrificial work of positive social change (Heifetz, 1994) instead of promoting the ever-willing politician who would pretend to be "a heroic leader who, however untested or inexperienced, can lead us to the promised land, and fix what's broken without even asking us to lend a hand" (ELG, 1996, pp.1–2). Do the media even recognize the pap coming from people in authority and criticize those who would pander to voters instead of developing civic responsibility? Citizens can make demands that voter-consumers never would. Citizens can demand that the media provide a responsible vehicle for exercising the public voice instead of functioning as a commodity that produces entertainment for the purpose of delivering an audience for the sponsors.

HOW SCHOOLS CAN TRANSFORM VOTERS INTO CITIZENS

The nation's schools have not distinguished themselves by their efforts to teach democracy. Becoming familiar with the parts of the Constitution, understanding the checks and balances afforded through the various responsibilities associated with the branches of government, and studying the contributions of our foremothers and forefathers to the establishment of the government is usually pretty dry stuff. Even when the civics curriculum allows a field trip to the courthouse or state capitol, most students do not have the opportunity to connect the things they are learning in the formal curriculum with the realities in their lives. Few civics classes teach the truth about leadership, power, influence, and how citizens are personally and individually responsible for the growth and development of the nation. The ELG called for a reinvigoration of the civics curriculum in American schools by first telling the truth about America:

The truth is that the American experiment has always been riddled with tensions among groups competing with each other for some of or more of the American dream. The truth is that all our struggles—from the Revolution to the Civil War, from the battles for workers' rights to the civil rights movement—there have been winners and losers. The truth is that this is the model of power—the model of leadership—to which we have been trained since the beginning of the Republic. But the truth is that this zero sum model of power is proving to be increasingly ineffective. (ELG, 1996, p. 3)

Enlivening Civics Education through Leadership Studies

Leadership studies is an emerging academic discipline. It opens the door to developing both citizens and leaders. Schools and colleges across the country have discovered it is possible to develop the citizenship and leadership skills of students through participative learning strategies. From kindergarten to graduate school, these strategies have been successful. Students gain knowledge about leadership and citizenship through classroom instruction and through opportunities to apply theories and skills they have learned in their own communities. These examples often have an indelible impact on the students, and on those who are the recipients of the students' attention. They are not necessarily complicated, expensive, or out of the reach of virtually every classroom situation in America. Consider some examples extracted from the working papers discussed by the ELG.

An elementary school develops a team approach to the study of social studies and science to achieve a variety of instructional outcomes in addition to solving a neighborhood problem. The science teacher teaches a fifth-grade class about the ecosystem, and in particular, the hydraulic cycle as it affects the Chesapeake Bay. The students take pictures, organize clean-up projects involving the whole school, and learn how to take water samples and detect certain harmful pollutants. In social studies class, students learn about the various segments of society that can impact the health of the stream like the local community council, state legislature, U.S. Congress, Environmental Protection Agency, local industries, and a local volunteer environmental network. The students visit the stream regularly and decide to interview officials from the listed organizations to get their opinions and ideas about the stream. They learn how to arrange and conduct interviews, videotape them, and eventually how to produce a documentary about their stream using the interviews.

In one of their water sampling trips, they become concerned about the high levels of chlorine in the water. They are ready for action based on the things they have learned. They contact the county agency responsible for water resources, as well as the local newspaper. They trace the problem to overflow from upstream swimming pools. The problem is immediately addressed (Kretman, 1996). A group of children learn how to make a substantive impact on their local community—applied civics.

At a small, midwestern, private liberal arts college, during an undergraduate senate meeting, an elected, four-person student government executive team faces an insurrectionary (and probably racist and sexist) group determined to eject them. At the height of the crisis the elected officers, who are members of traditionally disenfranchised minority groups, flounder for a brief time because the threats are real, and their collective tradition regarding such threats suggests surrender to traditional majority groups. Gradually they remember important information about parliamentary procedure learned in a leadership workshop they attended the previous summer. During a short recess, they develop a strategy, and when the meeting is reconvened, they are able to make the rules of order prevail. Over the next few days these leaders are able to rally support from a more representative group of students who join in the discussion and forge a new coalition of students concerned with fair, representative student government. A small group of formerly disenfranchised people learn how to make diversity count, standing up and taking their place in their community by making the rules work for everyone—applied civics (DeMott, 1995).

A requirement in a leadership studies course at a university located in the Pacific Northwest is for each student to develop a project that will have a significant community impact. After studying Heifetz's book, *Leadership Without Easy Answers* (1994), a senior undergraduate student learns about leadership even if you are not in a formal position in an organization. He develops a written proposal and polishes an oral presentation of the proposal. He carries it from university office to university office, including that of the president. Impressed with his proposal, and willing to provide some funding for the idea, the president asks at the end of the meeting, "Tell me again, which organization do you represent?" The student's reply is that he was just a student with an idea. Soon after that, the student, and his idea—to develop an alumni mentor leadership conference—are adopted by the student activities office where full-time and part-time staff and an eventual budget of more than $10,000 are assigned to the student and his project. The conference is now an annual event valued by both undergraduate students and alumni who apply for the opportunity to participate. A student learns that an individual can make a difference if they have some skills to support their good intentions—applied civics (Burns, 1996).

At a summer enrichment program for Latinos, students find themselves overwhelmed by their academic demands. They realize that as individuals they are hopelessly behind. They also realize that they are against either quitting or pleading for lighter workloads. The students invent ways to work together to successfully meet the demands of the program. Through their collaboration, they stick up for themselves, come together as a community, and develop the synergy needed to succeed where individually some or all might have failed. Students learn that none of us is better than all of us. Through collaboration and mutual support, a community can grow and accomplish difficult goals—applied civics (DeMott, 1995).

A requirement of a mid-level leadership course at a public land-grant university is to have an impact on third-world hunger by the end of the academic term. The residential campus, located in a vast rural agricultural region, is home to mostly traditional eighteen- to twenty-two-year-old students from urban and suburban communities in another part of the state. Third-world hunger is not an issue these middle-class students often think about. For their class project, they decide to enlist the help of the student architecture club and have them build a "shelter" made from cardboard, newspaper, loading dock pallets, and plastic. To raise campus awareness about hunger issues and at the same time raise money, they choose to occupy the shelter for a week and live on a diet similar to that of a village in Mexico where they want to send two of their own people to work at a summer-long hunger project.

The weather that November week is stormy and cold and the students begin to grumble about how uncomfortable and hungry they are, and how tempted they are to just give up. A student then shares a revelation he had while sitting alone in the shelter one afternoon. He caught himself thinking about the future and when he was going to be able to get out of the situation—the things he would eat, the comforts he would seek. Then it dawned on him that the people with whom he was trying to identify in the Mexican village were afforded no such luxury—they had no foreseeable escape from their plight.

That realization, and sharing it with his classmates, serves as a catalyst that elevates the students' understanding of their experience to a transformed personal and corporate commitment to finishing the project. The original goal of raising campus awareness suddenly pales in comparison to the self-awareness each student gains. Cognitive exposure to material about the global community in the classroom becomes an affective reality when students are given the opportunity to reflect about a significant shared experience—applied civics (Burns, 1996).

DeMott (1993) was an early critic of the U.S. Department of Education's Eisenhower Leadership Program. He reviewed the funding proposals for many of the projects and subsequently studied what was happening at several of the project sites. Through his research, he became the leading authority on what the Eisenhower projects were accomplishing and one of the project's greatest supporters. He summarized his findings as follows:

Mutuality, choice, and collaboration are central in descriptions of satisfactions derived by students and faculty in successful applied civics courses.

Absent is the hackneyed hierarchical model of leaders and followers and the teaching of manipulation and power games (called leadership skills) that dominate traditional civics and leadership education. Instead, the favored pedagogics are those that place students in situations where the pertinent acts—the acts of choosing, of trusting and being trusted, and of making collaborative efforts for a common cause for common good—aren't easily avoided. The conventional term for education on this model is, of course, experiential. One clear result of such education is the abatement of self-absorption, as the "me generation" gives way to the birth of the "we generation." (DeMott, 1995, pp.15–16)

RECOMMENDATIONS FOR DEVELOPING A NEW GENERATION OF CITIZENS

The ELG has developed five recommendations every school and college in the country should seriously consider. The recommendations are based on contributions from scholars and community leaders from across the nation who were interviewed during the fall of 1995 and the spring of 1996. In addition, information was collected from the various Eisenhower Leadership projects, as well as from other sources that surfaced during the group's research. The resulting recommendations are significant yet practical. Before discussing the specific recommendations, it is important to present the general principles about leadership and citizenship education that the ELG discovered through their research.

GENERAL PRINCIPLES

Democratic Schools and Classrooms

Unfortunately, schools are traditionally very undemocratic places. It is difficult to teach about collaboration and participation in an environment that demands order and uses power to enforce an agenda established at the top. This is the model of most educational administrators for instruction in the United States. More collaborative and experiential instructional opportunities can help to address the undemocratic environment found in many classrooms.

Part of the school restructuring movement spawned by *A Nation At Risk* was to move toward more collaborative and democratic administrative practices in the schools. This move has been met with great resistance. In a recent publication by the National Policy Board for Educational Administration (Crow and Slater, 1996), the need for further efforts at democratization was underscored. This publication, as follows, identified one of the major problems collaborative democratic processes have brought to public school administration:

Democratization poses one of the most formidable challenges ever to confront organizational life and leadership. When leaders broaden participation and decision making, they inevitably invite instability into their organizations. If they do so without first educating people to tolerate conflict and to understand the imbalances of this type of governance, they permit democracy to slide into chaos and self-destruction. (p. 4)

Educational administrators must learn the skills of leadership and followership. They must learn to give up power and not seek to reorient it to themselves in other ways. If schools and school districts can model collaborative democratic administrative practices, teachers and students will be empowered to do the same in the learning process. Collaboration connotes transforming participation and ownership rather than transactional consumerism. The ideal school will model an ideal democracy where position-holders work together with constituents to accomplish mutual educational goals. Position-holders become facilitators of the learning process that is ultimately the responsibility of the students. The lessons learned from this democratic model are transferable to the larger society where students learn to be citizens who become responsible for the resolution of problems in their communities, just as they have taken the responsibility for their own education.

Critical Thinking

Voter-consumers are not necessarily critical thinkers. Citizens need to learn critical thinking skills to analyze problems with the intent of taking the responsibility of solving them instead of blaming someone else for their existence, or worse, buying simple solutions that are not solutions at all. When citizens realize that government and politicians can do little else than facilitate citizen action to resolve problems, and only elect those politicians who share that realization, they are looking at real ways to transform society. When people think deeply, they have the opportunity to examine how they can make a personal investment in making changes necessary to resolve problems. Critical thinking skills bring to the table accountability for those in a position of authority and the media that report about them.

Collaboration

Students need to learn a new paradigm of leadership. In this new paradigm, people celebrate what groups can accomplish together to transform their communities instead of what "pseudo-savior-leaders" say they will accomplish, or what their public relations spin doctors pass off as accomplishments. Real leadership helps the people do their own transforming community work and helps them feel good about what they are accomplishing together. Collaboration skills need to be taught early and continuously in the schools. Collaboration must be modeled in the way that the schools are administered as well.

Experience

Citizenship skills cannot be learned in the abstract. Sound leadership and followership theories must be taught, but lessons in theory must be reinforced with practice. Students from kindergarten through graduate school must be challenged with real opportunities to test the theories they learn against the real problems they face in their communities. The "real world" provides a tremendous civics laboratory where students can apply their citizenship skills through every other academic discipline. Teachers, administrators, and students must be supported by each other and their community as the cloistered environment of the schools is transformed into the laboratory of the community where learning opportunities that will promote the affective acquisition of knowledge can be created.

Reflection

Students must be given the opportunity for guided reflection about the things they experience and learn. Reflection is the means by which students cognitively internalize their affective learning experiences. Reflection itself brings about more affective experience which in turn needs even more reflection. It is a matter of teaching students who will be future citizens how to think and feel about the problems that face their communities. Citizens who think deeply are not readily susceptible to simple sounding solutions offered by those who only want to hold offices or obtain power.

RECOMMENDATIONS

The five principles discussed are the foundation for the five recommendations that the ELG has forwarded. Following is a listing of those recommendations and annotations about each one. Drawing from the group's report, being a former member of the ELG, I have in some cases provided my own interpretations of the annotations for each recommendation.

Recommendation One: Promote the New Model

The basic paradigm of leadership that needs to be taught in our schools and colleges has to be one that will be workable in the twenty-first century, not one that may have been workable in the twentieth century but which, by the end of that century, may be the cause of much that has put our democracy at risk. Teachers and professors can no longer espouse and teach the industrial, twentieth-century notion of leadership if they want to help revitalize our democracy and if they want their students to be engaged citizens in the new millennium.

The emerging, twenty-first-century paradigm of leadership has three basic notions. The first is that leadership is a collaborative process. It is an influence (meaning noncoercive) relationship among leaders and collabo-rators (followers) who decide to work together to do something. Leader-ship is not what one person—a leader—does. Instead, leadership is an interactive process involving lots of people who collaborate with one another to do something significant for their community (Rost, 1991).

The second notion is that leadership is not the exclusive province of presidents, governors, mayors, superintendents, chief executive officers, and other executives. Leadership can be done by people at the bottom, in the middle, and at the top of a hierarchy. Indeed, leadership can be done by people outside the organizational structure. Leadership in a democ-racy is done by citizens, employees, farmers, neighbors, children, and un-derprivileged people—all the people who make up a community who are called together to do something for the common good (Burns, 1996).

The third notion is that something the people do in a collaborative rela-tionship called leadership is make a change, solve a problem, or initiate a different approach. The reason people get together in a leadership rela-tionship is to institute some change that will improve and better the com-munity or the organization and will cause transformation. Because leadership is collaborative, the change must be agreed to by the lead-ers and collaborators in the relationship. The change must reflect their mutual purposes, their collective will, and their consensus. Collabora-tion, then, is at the heart of both the process of leadership (the way leaders and collaborators make collective decisions) and the mutual vision of change to which the leaders and collaborators agree.

Students must transform their ideas about leadership to engage them-selves and others in their twenty-first-century democratic world. Any-thing else puts us back into the world that leaders dominate and to which followers acquiesce and ultimately are relegated to the position of con-sumers. A collaborative view of leadership is essential to revitalizing citi-zenship in the twenty-first century, and teachers and professors need to start teaching this emerging paradigm of leadership now to energize stu-dents to put their citizenship skills to work in the twenty-first century.

Recommendation Two: Cross-Pollinate

It is unacceptable to relegate the curriculum for citizenship educa-tion to a single specialized course in civics in high school or late middle school. Applied civics—developing leadership and citizenship knowledge, skills, and will among students in America—requires an interdisciplinary curriculum that permeates all levels of education from kindergarten through college.

The content and practices embodied in applied civics are just as powerful in teaching environmental science to fifth graders as they are to the college professor trying to enliven an introductory course in American government. Applied civics not only bridges subject boundaries; its content is anchored in themes that connect the past to the present and future, local to national and international, and most of all, students' knowledge to their real life experiences. Powerfully integrated citizenship and leadership teaching helps students make those important connections, not just between subject matter but between themselves and the world around them. It empowers students to ask questions about how their government responds to the need to transform society historically and in the present. It allows students to explore their own visions of civic life and gives them the opportunity to apply their knowledge and decision-making skills in meaningful ways.

Applied civics can, and should, begin with our youngest students, and it must be consistently taught throughout schooling. All teachers, regardless of grade or discipline, have a critical role to play in developing a community of citizen learners and leaders. Ultimately, the goal of all education is to promote our young people's understanding of efficacy in civic life. By teaching skills within the context of applying knowledge, interdisciplinary and integrative teaching and learning are powerful means toward that end.

Recommendation Three: Reach Out

Schools must reach out to form partnerships with businesses, agencies, universities, and virtually every entity that has power in the community. Democracy is and has always been fundamentally concerned with power and fairness (DeMott, 1995). Every society must determine who will have power and how fairly that power will be distributed. In a democracy, society has the unique and usually unrealized potential to distribute power fairly among all its citizens.

Through partnerships in the community, students must learn and make judgments about the real versus the ideal evolution of the distribution of power in the United States. Simply teaching and reteaching the tired theoretical underpinnings of the traditional hierarchy of the industrial paradigm and the resulting concentration of power into the hands of the elite that paradigm supports will not serve our democracy in the twenty-first century. The curriculum should instead emphasize partnership opportunities that reinforce emerging social theory, structures, and practices that expand and nurture civil participation, collaboration, and personal investment in the development of community by both the students and the schools' partners.

Recommendation Four: Build Houses

It is no longer valid to limit the definition of leadership to the things people in positions of authority do and the traits that describe those individuals. Our society is racing toward a new post-industrial paradigm where the feudal notion of rigid social hierarchy found in the industrial paradigm has no utility. In the post-industrial paradigm, leadership is the process of influencing corporate and personal transformation (adaptive action) to significant social and environmental problems (Heifetz, 1994). Successful adaptive action to solve problems requires energized, involved, and empowered citizens working in collaboration. Adaptive action often produces conflict and stress. When, because of conflict or other reasons, a group is unable to concentrate its energy to effect necessary adaptive actions on its own, a leader must emerge who can serve as a catalyst to facilitate the group's progress toward the needed changes.

These lessons must be learned both in the classroom and in the community. You cannot learn how to build a house from a book. A book is a helpful tool, but you have to get out and pound nails, make mistakes, forge on, and achieve success. You cannot learn to be an effective citizen simply by reading about it or engaging in classroom citizenship simulations. Students must go into the community and work on real problems. Effective citizens will learn that real leadership does not happen unless everyone learns to take up and excel in their role as a follower. Effective citizens will learn that it is fruitless to simply blame others for society's ills, just as it is fruitless to dump our problems at the feet of bureaucrats and politicians and walk away from them. Effective citizens will learn long-term substantive change in society occurs through the cumulative effect of myriad small, meaningful changes at the grassroots level. Students need to learn how to have an impact on local issues and problems by actually getting out of the classroom and working on them as part of the curriculum.

Recommendation Five: Borrow Shamelessly

Teachers around the country have, in isolation, developed interdisciplinary curricula and various kinds of projects that promote civic involvement. These isolated programs must be identified and shared so all schools and all teachers can benefit from these models. This identification and sharing is an awesome opportunity for the media to help develop the citizens of the nation, instead of merely entertaining voter-consumers.

The ELG's report (1996) identifies many examples of how schools all over the nation have developed marvelous civics projects in all kinds of disciplines and at all grade levels. These need public exposure and support as they are tried and tested in new environments. In most cases, these experiences and projects can be introduced with minimal cost and huge benefits. The ELG lists several resources to help schools get started thinking about implementing an applied civics program. These examples should be borrowed, copied, adapted, and reported broadly.

SUMMARY

Our democracy is at risk. Citizens have abdicated the trust given to them to take care of their communities and the nation as they have been replaced by voter-consumers who expect entitlements. As consumers of our communities, we have become alienated from the real processes that can help bring about the transforming adaptive changes our society desperately needs. The media are caught up in perpetuating this voter-consumer paradigm and have been largely ineffective in helping us develop as responsible, contributing citizens. Also, the schools have lost their way and become wholly involved in preparing workers and consumers, virtually ignoring their responsibility to consistently and continuously transmit the values and skills necessary for citizenship development. A democracy can never survive if it is dependent on a *demos* concerned primarily with "me," a *demos* that does not value "we," the community.

Consumers of communities make poor community servants. Learning about and taking up the trust to develop and promote the community is the business of citizenship in a democracy. Rugged individualism and isolationism (me vs. we) is sometimes forwarded as the real meaning of freedom in a democracy such as ours. This is a myth and leads to tyranny. Alexis de Tocqueville, in *Democracy in America*, warned, "The despot will lightly forgive his subjects for not loving him, provided they do not love one another. . . . He calls those who try to unite their efforts to create a general prosperity 'turbulent and restless spirits,' and twisting the natural meaning of the words, he calls those 'good citizens' who care for none but themselves" (Crow and Slater, 1996, p. 12).

The schools, the media, families, and churches are all social institutions that have responsibility for transmitting the values associated with the trust of citizenship. The schools and the media have a unique and powerful presence in today's society. Because of that presence, it is imperative that these institutions take the lead in teaching and promoting citizenship to keep our democracy from remaining at risk.

REFERENCES

Barber, B. (1995). *Jihad vs. McWorld*. New York: Times Books.

Bigelow, D. L. (1994). Jefferson and higher education. Invited address, October 7, Marietta College.

Burns, J. M. (1978). *Leadership*. New York: Harper & Row.

Burns, J. S. (1996). Defining leadership: Can we see the forest for the trees? *Journal of leadership studies* 3(2): 148–157.

Commission on Excellence in Education. (1983). *A nation at risk: A report to the U.S. Secretary of Education*. Washington, D.C.: U.S. Government Printing Office.

Conant, J. B. (1962). *Thomas Jefferson and the development of American public education*. Berkeley and Los Angeles: University of California Press.

Crow, G. M., and R. O. Slater. (1996). *Educating democracy: The role of systemic leadership*. National Policy Board for Educational Administration.

DeMott, B. (1993). Choice academic pork. *Harper's* (December): 61–77.

DeMott, B. (1995). On leadership education. Report to the U.S. Secretary of Education from the Eisenhower Leadership Project.

Eisenhower Leadership Group. (1996). Democracy at risk: How schools can lead. Unpublished report to the U.S. Secretary of Education, March. College Park: University of Maryland.

Etzioni, A. (1993). *The spirit of community*. New York: Touchstone.

Heifetz, R. A. (1994). *Leadership without easy answers*. Cambridge: Harvard University Press.

Kretman, K. P. (1996). Personal telephone conversation, February.

Lappe, F. M., and P. M. DuBois. (1994). *The quickening of America*. San Francisco: Jossey-Bass.

National Educational Goals Panel. (1993). The National Education Goals Report, Vol. 2: State Reports.

Rost, J. C. (1991). *Leadership for the twenty-first century*. New York: Praeger.

Wright, D. (1996). The kind of politician we need but can never hope to have. Political cartoon, syndicated and published by the *Palm Beach Post*.

PART III

COLLABORATIONS

Chapter 7

Collaborating to Hear Public Voices

Karlyn Kohrs Campbell

None of them can do it alone—not the public, the news media, nor the politicians. They will all have to collaborate if ordinary citizens are to be empowered to speak and if they are to feel their voices matter. In my mind, that is the real challenge. Can such collaboration occur?

In *The Phantom Public*, Lippmann concluded that even in a democracy, elites rule; that we cannot expect it to be otherwise; and that journalism cannot reform itself to change that. In his view, the public generally participates politically by supporting or opposing those who govern. On rare occasions, however, the public will emerge and intervene (1924, pp. 61–62).

In the same period, an alternative perspective emerged in the work of Dewey (1925), who argued that unless the citizenry was actively involved in political decision making, the results of the decisions would be flawed because those affected by them would not be committed to their implementation. Accordingly, Dewey argued that government, education, and the press needed to bend their efforts to involve the public in decision making. Although many decades have passed since Lippmann (1924) and Dewey published their views, and despite major changes in technology, these competing views of public political participation represent the issue underlying this project (Fallows, 1996, p. 238). I tend to take the side of Dewey, but even if Lippmann was right that democratic governance occurs primarily through expert elites, the current levels of cynicism and distrust of the government and of the news media suggest a dire need for changes if the political system itself is not to be imperiled.

I first consider an instance in which, through a confluence of events and news coverage, political judgment was facilitated, and public opinion about an important issue was treated. I use that example to indicate what I believe the public needs and wants as well as to define the limits of the role of the news media. Subsequently, I focus on the discrepancy between the news agenda and the public's agenda as it emerges in presidential election campaigns and the attitudes that sustain that divergence. Finally, I consider ways in which the public's voices might be heard more frequently, including ways in which the news media and politicians and political candidates can facilitate their emergence.

During three days in mid-October 1991, the nation was mesmerized ("Hearings," 1991)[1] by Senate Judiciary Committee hearings on the nomination of Clarence Thomas to be Associate Justice of the Supreme Court (Nomination, 1993). What made these hearings so electrifying was the testimony of law professor Anita Hill that Thomas had behaved toward her in ways that seemed to fit the legal definition of sexual harassment. Those hearings and the response of the news media to them are a significant example of the processes by which publics are energized and public opinion is created. The hearings and their aftermath are a case study of democracy in action, facilitated by the news media.

The hearings had all the hallmarks of an event made to order for news coverage. The hearings were personalized as a struggle between two individuals, Hill and Thomas, as well as between groups of newsworthy U.S. Senators and involving the nation's most newsworthy person, the president. It was a dramatic conflict involving sexual behavior with exciting, prurient overtones. The event was discrete and could be televised and photographed for maximum impact, and it was novel, even extraordinary—the first time such a charge had been leveled against a nominee for the Supreme Court and probably the first time that sexually explicit language had been broadcast or printed. In one respect, however, it deviated from news norms—the subject of sexual harassment had not been an issue of ongoing interest in the public media. No reporters had been assigned to that beat, and there had been little or no news coverage of incidents or allegations. Accordingly, no standard or conventional ways of covering the issue had developed.

As documented by MacKinnon (1979), however, sexual harassment had begun to be recognized by the courts as sex discrimination as early as 1976, although it was only in 1983 that "verbal sexual abuse" was recognized as a form of sexual harassment. In 1981, when Hill's alleged harassment occurred, the uncorroborated word of a victim was not sufficient to make a legal case (Phelps and Winternitz, 1992, p. 383). Despite legal developments, there had been little or no public discussion of it or reports of women's experiences with harassment in news or in entertainment programming. In other words, most people simply had not thought about it and had not made a judgment about what it was or how serious it might be. By the time Clarence Thomas was narrowly approved as an Associate Supreme Court Justice by a Senate vote of 58 to 42, public opinion was forming or had formed. A public had been mobilized.

In response to Hill's charges, her testimony, and the testimony of Thomas, newspapers, radio, and television were filled with discussion of the issue. Interviews with experts and with women who had experienced harassment were on the front pages of newspapers. Experts, such as MacKinnon (1979), were interviewed in breaks during the televised hearings. In other words, the news media did an extraordinary job of providing expert and lay opinion on and experience with this behavior, indicating its scope and discussing its nature and its impact on the lives of women. Public deliberation about this topic filled the news media, and the public came to have an understanding of the concept and of the significance of harassment in the lives of working women. For example, despite Hill's treatment by the committee, there was a 50 percent increase (to nearly 5,000) in complaints of sexual harassment to the Equal Employment Opportunity Commission (EEOC) during the first six months of 1992 (Mayer and Abramson, 1994, p. 352).

In contrast, the Senate Judicial Committee hearings did little or nothing to inform viewers about sexual harassment. No expert witnesses were called, and the senators who questioned Hill, Thomas, and their supporters betrayed an ignorance of sexual harassment so vast that women, especially working and professional women with feminist leanings, were galvanized into action. The phrase, "They just don't get it," became a shorthand to describe the stereotyping and ignorance that were reflected in committee members' questions and comments.

That outrage was heightened because Hill was treated in ways that facilitated wide identification. In an incredible symbolic transformation, Hill's ethnicity and background were ignored; she was castigated in the most extreme terms as what one commentator summarized as "an erotomaniacal spinster who fantasized abuse at the hands of a dark-skinned man out of the depths of her experiences of rejection and sexual frustration" (Fraser, 1992, p. 605). These attacks echoed nineteenth-century attitudes, when it was believed that marriage and motherhood were essential for a woman to be healthy and sane; single women, particularly women's rights advocates and suffragists, were seen as man haters (in the hearings, Hill was described as a woman scorned and as having "proclivities," a code word that implied lesbianism) or unstable (in the hearings, Hill was characterized as prone to fantasizing, as schizophrenic, and as emotionally disturbed).

Hill refused to act as women are conventionally expected to behave. On several occasions, senators prompted her to express her feelings, to play damsel in distress, by asking, How did you feel? or How do you feel today? (Nomination, 1991, pp. 56–57, 76). Unlike Clarence Thomas, who manifested his feelings visually and vocally, Hill resolutely stuck to descriptions. She said she had been embarrassed, humiliated, and had felt helpless, depressed, and threatened. Now she was hurt and angry but she appeared composed and controlled. Her factual, descriptive, and unemotional testimony could easily be reframed to suggest she was cold and unfeeling, hence, not a real or a true woman.

Hill's inability or unwillingness to display her pain before the committee was reframed in testimony by a panel of women supporting Thomas. In an opening statement, J. C. Alvarez, a former assistant to Senator John Danforth, Thomas's chief supporter, and who had been a special assistant at the EEOC, described Hill as "opinionated, arrogant, not to be messed with, ambitious, [and] nobody's victim" (Nomination, 1991, pp. 338, 340). Once she had made these charges, the senators who supported Thomas could and did amplify them.

I do not wish to belabor the details but they are important to explain how and why a public was aroused by the hearings. By ignoring Hill's ethnicity and background, and by leveling these charges against her, Hill came to represent every woman who had been criticized for not adhering to conventional feminine roles. Because there was no expert testimony, an alternative framework had to be developed by Hill's supporters, but their explanations of Hill's behavior as consistent with a professional woman's need for recommendations from her most important supervisor were not supported or developed by democratic senators on the committee, nor were opposing witnesses impeached (Ogletree, 1995, pp. 154, 162, 168).[2]

Finally, omission became commission. Late in the evening of the last day of the hearings, Senator Alan Simpson (R-Wyo.) and Senator Hank Brown (R-Colo.) engaged in a bit of humorous byplay. In ironic tones, Simpson explained that while in law school he had read *Playboy* for its editorials, and Brown laughingly recalled that a law student in Colorado had placed pictures out of *Playboy* in his torts exam and had received the highest grade.

Much more could be said about these hearings, but two points are significant here. First, the hearings showed the news media at their best, playing a nearly ideal role in a democracy. In response to an extraordinary event, journalists not only reported the facts but they also used all the techniques at their disposal to create understanding and interpret these events and the issues they involved. Second, the contrast between the public deliberation facilitated by news coverage and the lack of informed deliberation in the hearings was an important factor in mobilizing a public to action, in this case, the decision by outraged women to run for political office and by male and female feminists to support those who did so.

Because it is unusual, this example highlights the conditions under which the news media fulfill their roles of gathering and interpreting information and of providing a venue for deliberation. They do so in response to events of national significance whose characteristics fit most traditional news norms—they can be personalized, are filled with conflict, and are deviant and discrete. Because there was no conventional framework through which to view this event, journalists mobilized to gather the information and expertise necessary to understand and interpret it. That kind of coverage facilitated public deliberation and enabled public opinion to be created and a public to form and mobilize.

This example also highlights the special difficulties that women, in general, and African-American women, in particular, face in gaining a public voice. Issues of special salience for them are often pushed to the margins as if they were the pleadings of a special interest that do not concern all Americans. That dynamic affected this case. Until Timothy Phelps and Nina Tottenberg revealed Hill's allegations, the Senate Judiciary Committee did not plan to hold hearings to consider them (Phelps and Winternitz, 1992, pp. 213, 219, 224–225, 233, 266–267). This case suggests that only when an event such as this occurs is it likely that similar issues will be discussed. Although a dramatic case can call attention to an issue of concern to women, the case may be atypical and distort the problem. For example, the Francine Hughes case called attention to the problem of domestic abuse, but it focused attention not on those who batter but on the women who kill their batterers. Made into a television movie, *The Burning Bed*, starring Farrah Fawcett, it created a distorted picture of women who kill their batterers, which included Hughes's acquittal on the grounds of temporary insanity rather than a battered woman's defense (Ewing, 1987; Schneider, 1986).

Still another problem arises when dramatic instances are easily categorized into conventional perspectives. For example, the gang rape of a white investment banker in Central Park in New York City received wide news coverage, but because the young men involved in the rape were African-American, the rape was treated as an example of racial conflict, not as an example of gang rape. In Benedict's recent survey, only one of some thirty reporters who routinely covered sex crimes had ever read a book on rape and few had made any effort to consult experts. In explaining the *New York Times*'s selective coverage of the Central Park rape, the metropolitan editor acknowledged, "I can't imagine the range of reaction to the sexual aspect of the crime would be very strong" (Benedict, forthcoming, p. 2). During the week of the highly publicized rape of a white investment banker in Central Park by a non-white gang, twenty-eight other women in New York also reported rapes. Nearly all these were women of color, and their assaults, including at least one of comparable brutality, went largely unreported by the press

(Benedict, 1992; Terry, 1993). Similarly, the rape trials of heavyweight boxer Mike Tyson and of William Kennedy Smith are additional examples of the difficulties involved in using newsworthy events as an occasion for public deliberation about such an important, controversial issue as rape, given the overwhelming impact of conventional perspectives (Lawrence, 1995, pp. 108–109).

As these examples suggest, if the concerns of groups of ordinary people, including women, are to find a voice in news coverage, several problems must be addressed. First, coverage of such issues cannot wait for dramatic events; occasions and venues must be created that encourage discussions of issues of importance to the public. Also, coverage must occur in such a way that public deliberation occurs, which means an effort must be made to question conventional perspectives on such issues. Finally, special efforts must be made to produce coverage of and deliberation about issues that resist news norms, issues that are complex or involve processes and that are simplified inappropriately by being dramatized or personalized. In these cases as in others, I believe the responsibility for such efforts must be shared equally by political leaders, the news media, and the public.

One conventional way for individuals and groups to attract news coverage on an issue is to create pseudoevents with the sorts of dramatic, agonistic, personal features that attract journalists, or to bring to press attention an instance of a particular problem that has features attractive to news people. Some of the limitations of that strategy were evident in the National Issues Forum held January 18–21,1996, in Austin, Texas. The brainchild of Professor of Government James Fishkin, the forum attracted 459 randomly selected and statistically representative U.S. citizens who came together to discuss those issues participants saw as central to the 1996 elections. In some ways, the forum was a smashing success. Parts of it were televised on the Public Broadcasting Service (PBS), and in many cases, delegates were able to report back to their local communities in columns in local newspapers. Although all the presidential candidates were invited to attend, only Richard Lugar and Vice President Al Gore, representing Clinton, actually did so. Phil Gramm, Lamar Alexander, and Steve Forbes participated by satellite, but Pat Buchanan and Robert Dole, two of the most important Republican candidates, disregarded it. Worst of all, the forum was ignored by leading reporters and columnists for the networks and major newspapers.

The absence of major candidates and the limited coverage of the forum constitute a vicious circle. If reporters and columnists for national newspapers and networks do not cover events, major candidates will not attend them. If major candidates do not attend them, then leading journalists will not cover them. Writing in *The Nation*, New York University professor Jay Rosen assigns primary responsibility to the news media (1996b, p. 10). If they had chosen to cover the event, he argues, the candidates would have attended. That argument can be reversed, however; it is equally plausible that if the major candidates had decided that this was an important event and had chosen to attend, major news media coverage would have followed.

Why did Dole and Buchanan not attend the forum? Quite simply, the forum offered them no advantages or benefits. Its structure was suited to exploring the complexities of issues, and participants reported that their views were modified and qualified as the result of discussions with others directly affected by proposed policies. Because primary campaigns, particularly as covered in brief sound bites and disseminated through political advertisements, reward what former Vice President Spiro Agnew called "bits of red meat" that energize targeted supporters and attract television and newspaper coverage, the forum with its complexity could only bring them grief. Deliberation on issues in all their complexity is perceived by newspeople as boring, and nuanced positions on these issues are condemned as wishy-washy. At present, campaigning has nothing to do with deliberation, which was the focus of the forum. Why should any candidate bother?

Why did the major news media choose to disregard it? Some of the reasons are the same as those for politicians. A format emphasizing the complexity of issues that led many participants toward more qualified positions on key issues is the antithesis of the conflict and deviance that attract media coverage. In the sound-bite world of most television, that kind of deliberation and those kinds of conclusions are unlikely to attract television cameras, and they are hard to treat within the space limits of newspaper columns.

More important, however, is that fewer than half of the journalists who were queried in a recent survey believed that giving ordinary people a chance to express their views is important (Weaver and Wilhoit, 1992). In other words, only the views of newsworthy people—celebrities, politicians, and television and print pundits—merit coverage. Such attitudes constitute a significant barrier to journalism that gives the public a voice.

Recent critiques of the electronic media, particularly those adopting the perspectives of cultural or critical studies, have argued that both news and entertainment programming contribute to the perpetuating and reinforcing of the interests of the privileged. As the Weaver and Wilhoit (1992) survey demonstrates, one need not adopt those perspectives to conclude that the news media are, generally speaking, supporters of the status quo and adopt conventional, official frameworks in interpreting information. As Schudson comments, "Every social scientific study of the press of the past ten or fifteen years has found that the press overrepresents the views of government officials" (1995, p. 214).

The findings of Weaver and Wilhoit's survey are mirrored in public attitudes toward the news media as well as in instances that highlight the differences between what interests the public and what interests journalists. As survey after survey attests, public trust in and approval of the news media has declined, as has public support for their role in society. In a 1993 Yankelovich Associates poll, only 20 percent of those surveyed had a great deal of confidence in what they read in newspapers, and only 25 percent held that view of television news. These figures represent declines from 51 and 55 percent, respectively, from the findings of a similar 1988 poll (Black, 1996). In a survey by The Times-Mirror Center for the People and the Press (1994), 71 percent of respondents agreed with the statement, "The news media gets in the way of society solving its problems;" only 25 percent thought the news media help (p. 121). In a survey by the Pew Research Center for the People and the Press in March 1995, 57 percent agreed that the media hinder rather than help society solve its problems, and in October 1995, 65 percent of Minnesotans queried in a *Star Tribune*/WCCO-TV Minnesota poll agreed with the statement that "the media destroy candidates' effectiveness before they have a chance to prove themselves" (Black, 1996, p. A10).

What qualities of news coverage might lead to such negative evaluations? The interests of ordinary citizens are significantly different from those of journalists. Those differences were dramatized in the 1992 presidential debate held in Richmond, Virginia, in which ordinary citizens not strongly committed to any of the three presidential candidates questioned George Bush, Bill Clinton, and H. Ross Perot. The questions they asked were about issues and about policies that affected ordinary individuals. There was no overlap with questions asked in other debates by journalists.

Reactions to President Clinton's 1995 State-of-the-Union Address are a more recent illustration. Clinton's eighty-one-minute speech was panned by television and print journalists, but many ordinary citizens responded differently. Nielsen ratings recorded that the longer the speech went on, the larger the number of people who tuned in to watch (Fallows, 1996). Commenting on this discrepancy, Fallows argues that the positive responses of citizens arose because they had access to the speech unmediated by expert analysis. I think there is an additional reason. Clinton's 1995 State-of-the-Union Address was one of the most coherent of its type (Campbell and Jamieson, 1990), an instance of deliberation that enunciated values, described initiatives that were needed to implement them, and tallied how far such initiatives had gone. It presented argument about issues that helped listeners understand what needed to be done if shared goals were to be achieved. In other words, it was a speech that helped listeners to make judgments and to form opinions about policies. Admittedly, there was partisanship as well as challenges to the Republican majorities in Congress to act in ways consistent with what Clinton presented as shared goals, but of more importance is that this speech was one of the few times Americans could hear one of their political leaders reason about public issues. In recent years, they have had relatively few such opportunities.[3]

What interests journalists? The evidence is overwhelming—strategy. On March 11, 1996, the *New York Times* (Peterson, 1996) published the results of an analysis by the Center for Media and Public Affairs, a nonprofit research group in Washington, of 315 campaign news reports on ABC, CBS, and NBC—a total of ten hours, thirty minutes of airtime from January 1 to February 19, 1996. They found that the amount of time devoted to the horse race aspects of the Republican primary campaign had tripled from 1992, an increase "that is all the more striking," a center report said, "because both parties had contested primaries in 1992." In fact, horse race stories accounted for 56 percent of network campaign coverage, twice that devoted to the candidates' ideas and proposals. My observation of CNN coverage leads me to believe that adding their coverage to this survey would only have underscored the emphasis on strategy. What is even more disturbing about such results is that after the 1992 campaign, journalists recognized that coverage needed to be driven more by issues and less by preoccupation with horse race reporting and strategy.

Why this emphasis? It fits news norms that emphasize drama and conflict, but there is another reason—strategy is an area in which journalists have expertise, which is not usually the case when talk turns to issues. If welfare reform, free trade, or the declines in U.S. manufacturing are the subjects, most reporters must turn to outside experts. It is a quite natural tendency to emphasize topics on which one has expertise. In my view, however, that is a self-defined limitation. If economic reporters like Hobart Rowan or legal affairs' reporters like Linda Greenhouse can emerge, clearly other journalists can develop expertise in important subject areas. If that is to happen more often, however, editors and journalists will have to reexamine the presupposition that expertise on an issue compromises objectivity.

If the voice of the public is to be heard more clearly and more frequently, journalists will have to establish procedures that ensure greater emphasis on issues; as the comparison between 1992 and 1996 coverage shows, they cannot assume that because they recognize a problem, changes will happen. Also, there needs to be greater recognition of the importance of the views of ordinary people. Again, procedures are needed, and some are already in place. For example, nearly fifty newspapers have reader representatives or ombudsmen whose function is to respond to the public and to take their concerns into account

(Peterson, 1996); some news outlets have set up World Wide Web pages that allow readers or viewers to talk back to editors and reporters. But more is required, and the solutions are not easy or obvious. For example, interviewing voters is not enough if the questions and answers are in the service of strategic punditry. As Rosen (1996b) points out, on January 7, 1996, Richard Berke of the *New York Times* reported that the paper had interviewed more than 1,000 voters, but Berke used the results to claim that the central question of the forthcoming campaign is whether the "electorate will be able to resolve the conflict that it created by electing Mr. Clinton in 1992 and sending Mr. Gingrich to the Speaker's chair in 1994." As Rosen comments, that is a pundit's, not a citizen's, issue.

What is variously referred to as public, civic, or community journalism is an effort to alter relationships between the public and the news media. It seeks to create an environment in which public judgment becomes possible. As defined by Yankelovich, *public judgment* is "the state of highly developed public opinion that exists once people have engaged an issue, considered it from all sides, understood the choices it leads to, and accepted the full consequences of the choices they make" (1991, p. 6). Ideally, voters should go to the polls having made such judgments in relation to the stands of candidates, but unless issues are deliberated during the campaign and discussed in news coverage, that cannot occur.

Some news media are experimenting with ways to make that happen. For example, the *Minneapolis Star Tribune*, in conjunction with KTCA-TV, a PBS outlet, plans an experiment in public journalism called, "Minnesota 400," that will convene 400 Minnesotans in June to identify issues they want candidates to address in this year's U.S. Senate and presidential races. The *Star Tribune* will use these issues to develop its campaign coverage (Black, 1996). Fallows (1996, p. 254) reports that by 1995, more than 170 newspapers, sometimes in conjunction with broadcast stations, had taken part in some similar effort.

The cooperation of political leaders and candidates is also needed if public judgments related to voting are to be facilitated. The decision by two major candidates not to participate in the forum in Austin is an indicator of the problem. As revealed in their advertising and in CNN and C-SPAN coverage of rallies, the Republican candidates have followed a strategy of energizing subgroups of Republicans on a few issues or even a single issue. More complex treatment of issues is strategically necessary in a general election when the candidates need to attract independents and voters from other parties. Ironically, the narrow appeals of the primaries threatened to produce a nominee whose ability to attract an activist Republican party subgroup would make it difficult for the nominee to appeal to independents or previously Democratic voters. Obviously, it would be better for the citizenry if all primary candidates were pressed to deal with issues in more complex, less-simplistic ways.

On some occasions, the news media have created opportunities for candidates to present their views in a more deliberate and complex way. On Sunday, March 3, 1996, for example, Tim Russert interviewed Patrick Buchanan for forty-five minutes on "Meet the Press." In contrast to the rally speeches I had listened to on CNN, Buchanan developed his positions as arguments with evidence and linked his stands to historical analogs. Russert pushed him on many points, but only in ways that forced Buchanan to offer reasons and provide evidence and respond to important counterarguments. The format—a single interviewer and a single interviewee—facilitated that kind of presentation. A Republican primary voter who tuned in had an excellent basis for making a choice about Buchanan, but given Sunday morning viewership, it is likely that few of them were exposed to this reasoned and developed statement of his views.

Similarly, in response to issues about jobs, trade, and layoffs raised by Patrick Buchanan in the New Hampshire primary, the *New York Times* published a week-long series of stories titled, "The Downsizing of America," between March 3 and March 9, 1996. A reader of the series would have had a good basis for understanding the scope of the problem, the impact on individuals and communities, and possible alternatives to layoffs as a way of reducing costs in industry.

That news media create such opportunities for candidates or develop extended analyses of issues should be praised and encouraged, and credit should be given for the democratic contributions such programming and coverage make. What has to be acknowledged is that most of the campaigning in primary elections takes the form of photo opportunities with sound bite one-liners or rally speeches aimed at energizing small, targeted groups of potential supporters. In these venues, no voter will hear candidates deliberating or presenting the arguments and evidence that have led them to adopt particular policy positions. In the damning words of Dionne on most of our political campaigning, "Debate on issues is carried out by liberals and conservatives in a frame of false choices mired in ideology" (1991, p. 21).

That comment perfectly describes the treatment of issues on such television programs as "Crossfire" or "The McLaughlin Group." Based on these examples, it is clear that programming designed primarily to be entertaining does not allow deliberation about serious issues. Can the serious discussion of issues attract mass audiences? The 1992 campaign seemed to answer affirmatively, given the viewership of the presidential debates and of Perot's half-hour infomercials. Candidates, however, must be willing to debate in formats that do not replicate the sound bites of rallies or the quick interchanges that characterize "Crossfire," something they have rarely been willing to do. Photo-opportunity, sound-bite campaigning at brief rallies does not prepare candidates to deliberate about issues, which is one reason they avoid the risks involved in formats that require it. The 1992 presidential debate in Richmond was a creative effort to privilege the concerns of ordinary voters. It should be repeated, but the formats of other debate should be changed to facilitate more extended policy statements and deliberations. Also, confronting candidates with their own advertisements, as was done in the South Carolina Republican primary debate, is an effective way to compel candidates to take responsibility for the charges and claims made in them.

Finally, the public also has responsibilities. As Americans, we tend to believe that in former times, there must have been an ideal public sphere through which the public participated more fully in politics. In *The Power of News*, Schudson (1995) addresses the question of whether this golden age ever existed. The criteria he uses were the level of participation (of those eligible, who and how many participate) and the extent to which participation was carried out through rational and critical discourse. Based on analysis of historical records, he concludes that there was no time when such a public sphere existed in the United States. He also concludes that the news media are ill-equipped to facilitate its creation because their commercial character, targeted at the mass audiences they seek to deliver to advertisers, is the antithesis of association and community. His views echo those of Lippmann (1924) (Schudson, 1995, p. 189). In other words, under ordinary conditions, the citizenry participates indirectly through supporting or opposing governing elites, with only rare moments at which the public will intervenes.

If Schudson and Lippmann are right, the links connecting the government and the citizenry are those groups known as intermediary associations. In the past, these consisted primarily of political parties, labor unions, churches, and civic associations. At present, political parties and labor unions as well as many civic associations are in decline, and they do not perform this function well. Accordingly, for many Americans, the primary or only link to government is a member of Congress and a state representative. Yet, if citizens wish to have their voices heard, intermediary associations are a vital means to that end. The voices of citizens who are not associated with others of like mind will find it more difficult to be heard; the decline in community and voluntary associations diminishes the ability of publics to have their views heeded. Here, the public has full responsibility.

That the public acknowledges a responsibility for news content is evident in recent studies investigating what viewers see as ways to improve television news. When respondents evaluate methods of controlling news content, a substantial number believe that individual viewers have a responsibility to take action to control television news content (86 of 99 respondents) in one study, and that citizen groups have a similar responsibility (58 of 102 respondents) in another study (Lind, 1995, p. 364). When viewers evaluate the efficacy of these controls, however, in the first study, of 99 respondents, 20 said individual viewer action would not work and 13 said few will take action; similarly in evaluating citizen group action, of 102 respondents, 27 said controls will not work and 13 said few will take action (pp. 366–367). These findings are an acknowledgment of public responsibility, but they suggest substantial doubt that individual or group action will be effective, one of the most important deterrents to action. Unless members of the public believe that what they say will make a difference, there is small likelihood they will try to make an effort to be heard.

Those results are supported by research on political disaffection by Austin and Pinkleton who found surprisingly that "apathy was associated with voter behavioral intentions only via its relationship with voter efficacy." They concluded that "political disaffection is related to voter efficacy" and found that perceptions of efficacy were positively related to intent to vote (1995, p. 231). In other words, if they are to act even by voting, citizens must believe that their actions will make a difference.

If a public voice is to emerge, citizens must put a high priority both on acquiring information and seeking out ways to interpret it, a priority that was reflected in high viewership of the 1992 presidential debates. It is of even greater importance that they must believe their opinions and concerns matter. Ideally, they will become linked to intermediary associations that will turn up the volume on matters of importance to them. However, media outlets must make an effort to facilitate their participation through readers' representatives, World Wide Web pages, and experiments in public journalism that convince members of the public that their views count. Finally, political candidates must show a willingness to deliberate, whether in extended interviews on programs like "Meet the Press," in forums in which the questioners are ordinary voters, and in debates whose formats require an extended presentation of policy positions with reasons and evidence.

Each of these entities can put pressure on the others. Through its feedback, the public can influence news media coverage and formats. As they did in 1992, voters can continue to use sources outside mainstream news media for information to pressure changes in the mainstream news media. The news media can undertake public journalism initiatives, like that of the *Minneapolis Star Tribune*, to create mechanisms that ensure that the issues of concern to many voters receive priority and to pressure candidates to address these issues at length. They also must implement procedures to prevent the continued emphasis on strategy that has emerged in the 1996 Republican primary campaign, so their coverage matches their initiatives on issues and does not reward conventional sound-bite campaigning. Finally, as they did in 1992, political candidates can choose to appear in media settings that expose them to ordinary citizens and the issues they care about rather than appear in mainstream news outlets where pundits emphasize strategy. Unless all these entities collaborate, however, change will not occur. The public alone cannot make these changes happen.

NOTES

1. According to the A. C. Nielsen Company, over the weekend of October 10–12, 1991, 90 percent of the households in the United States tuned in to some part of these hearings. Nationwide, the hearings drew a larger viewership than college football, the baseball playoffs, or pro football. On Saturday, for example, NBC and ABC carried the hearings and achieved ratings of 26.5, compared to a rating of 9 for CBS, which broadcast the fifth game of the Atlanta–Pittsburgh baseball playoffs.

2. Ogletree points out that because "the Democrats on the committee had known about Professor Hill's charges and had sat on them, the more serious her accusations looked, the more serious the misconduct with which the Democrats could be charged" (1995, p. 154). In other words, the democrats had reasons not to be too supportive of her accusations.

3. The Senate debate on the Gulf War in 1991 was an extended instance of such deliberation.

REFERENCES

Austin, E. W., and B. E. Pinkleton. (1995). Positive and negative effects of political disaffection on the less experienced voter. *Journal of broadcasting media* 39(2): 215–235.

Benedict, H. (forthcoming). Covering rape without feminism. In *Women and law in the media*, ed. Martha Fineman. New York: Routledge.

Benedict, H. (1992). *Virgin or vamp: How the press cover sex crimes*. New York: Oxford University Press.

Black, E. (1996). Media's new status: Public's enemy No. 1. *Tribune*, January 28, pp. A1, A10.

Campbell, K. K., and K. H. Jamieson. (1990). *Deeds done in words: Presidential rhetoric and the genres of governance*. Chicago: University of Chicago Press.

Dewey, J. (1925). *Experience and nature*. Chicago: Open Court.

Dionne, E. J. (1991). *Why Americans hate politics*. New York: Simon & Schuster.

Ewing, C. P. (1987). *Battered women who kill*. Lexington, Mass.: Lexington Books.

Fallows, J. (1996). *Breaking the news: How the media undermine American democracy*. New York: Pantheon.

Fraser, N. (1992). Sex, lies, and the public sphere: Some reflections on the confirmation of Clarence Thomas. *Critical inquiry* 18: 595–612.

Hearings capture big audience. (1991). *New York Times*, October 13, p. A20.

Hill, A. F., and E. C. Jordan. (Eds.). (1995). *Race, gender and power in America: The legacy of the Hill–Thomas hearings*. New York: Oxford University Press.

Lawrence, C. R., III. (1995). The message of the verdict: A three-act morality play starring Clarence Thomas, Willie Smith, and Mike Tyson. In *Race, gender and power in America: The legacy of the Hill–Thomas hearings*, ed. A. F. Hill and E. C. Jordan. New York: Oxford University Press.

Lind, R. A. (1995). How can TV news be improved?: Viewer perceptions of quality and responsibility. *Journal of broadcasting* 39: 360–375.

Lippmann, W. (1922). *Public opinion*. New York: Harcourt, Brace.

Lippmann, W. (1924). *The phantom public*. New York: Harcourt, Brace.

MacKinnon, C. A. (1979). *Sexual harassment*. New Haven and London: Yale University Press.

Mayer, J., and J. Abramson. (1994). *Strange justice*. Boston: Houghton Mifflin.

Merritt, D. (1995). *Public journalism and public life: Why telling the news is not enough*. Hillsdale, N.J.: Lawrence Erlbaum Associates.

Nomination of Judge Clarence Thomas to Be Associate Justice of the Supreme Court of the United States. (1991). *Hearings before the Committee on the Judiciary United States Senate*, Part 4, October 11–13.

Ogletree, C. J. (1995). The people vs. Anita Hill: A case for client-centered advocacy. In *Race, gender and power in America: The legacy of the Hill–Thomas hearings*, ed. A. F. Hill and E. C. Jordan. New York: Oxford University Press.

Peterson, I. (1996). Media. *New York Times*, March 11, p. C5.

Phelps, T. M., and H. Winternitz. (1992). *Capitol games*. New York: Hyperion.

Rosen, J. (1996a). Take back the campaign. *Nation*, February 19, p. 10.

Rosen. J. (1996b). Scoring the idea race. *Nation*, March 4, p. 10.

Schneider, E. (1986). Describing and changing: Women's self-defense work and the problem of expert testimony on battering. *Woman's right's law reporter* 9: 195–222.

Schudson, M. (1995). *The power of news*. Cambridge: Harvard University Press.

Terry, D. (1993). In the week of an infamous rape, 28 other victims suffer. In *Gender and public policy*, ed. K. Winston and M. J. Bane. Boulder, Colo.: Westview.

Times-Mirror Center for the People and the Press. (1994). *The people, the press and politics: The new political landscape*. Washington, D.C.: Times-Mirror.

Weaver, D., and G. Wilhoit. (1992). *The American journalist in the 1990's*. Arlington,Va.: Freedom Forum.

Yankelovich, D. (1991). *Coming to public judgment: Making democracy work in a complex world*. Syracuse, N.Y.: Syracuse University Press.

Chapter 8

Does Civic Journalism Have a Future?

Edmund B. Lambeth

Will the waning years of the twentieth century pass without a full and fair test of "civic journalism"—arguably, the most promising yet controversial experiment in the recent history of the American press? For those of us with a lifetime appreciation of the role—if not always the reality—of the press as a steward of free expression, the answer, sadly, is probably so. Were these journalistic initiatives aimed at something less fundamental than improving the press's contribution to the quality of public life, the sadness could be dismissed as little more than the private disappointment of Arthurian believers in a once and future "Fourth Estate."

Civic journalism, often called "public journalism," is the term used to describe the widely varying experiments in which 200 or more news organizations attempted in the early 1990s to connect more effectively with the public not only as readers and viewers but as citizens. Their aim, at its most genuine, was to stimulate more and more informed citizen participation in public business and raise the quality of public deliberation on how best to respond to some of the most pressing issues in American communities, such as youth crime, family decay, race relations, and lagging local economies.

Several major foundations have been instrumental in the growth of the civic journalism movement. In 1993, the John S. and James L. Knight Foundation made grants that helped launch the Project on Public Life and the Press (PPLP). Directed by Professor Jay Rosen of New York University (NYU), PPLP's partners, in addition to the Knight Foundation and NYU, are the Kettering Foundation, with its long experience in developing community dialogues, and the American Press Institute, a mid-career training center. PPLP has convened editors, reporters, intellectuals, and foundation staff to help conceptualize, stimulate, and encourage the experiments.

Shortly after the birth of PPLP, the Pew Charitable Trusts created the Pew Center for Civic Journalism, led by executive director and former CBS correspondent Edward M. Fouhy and deputy director Jan Schaffer, formerly a reporter for the *Philadelphia Inquirer*. Its influential partners are the Radio and Television News Directors Foundation, Knight-Ridder, Inc., and the Poynter Institute for Media Studies. The Pew Center made grants to encourage, and later to evaluate, its initiatives, particularly joint projects by newspapers and television stations.

Nonetheless, civic journalism experiments across the country have drawn the editorial scorn and negative news coverage of influential journalists at the *New York Times* (Frankel, 1995), *The Washington Post* (Case, 1994), *Newsday,*[1] the *Philadelphia Inquirer* (Eisner, 1994), and the *New Yorker* (Remnick, 1996), and critical reviews in the *Columbia Journalism Review* (Hoyt, 1995) and *American Journalism Review* (Shepard, 1994). In most of these critiques, a liberal press elite warns against the likely loss of editorial independence by media corporations that are said to use news coverage to market themselves as "the community's pal" (Hoyt, 1995, p. 29).

Despite the disapproval of many American journalism's elite, civic journalism has burgeoned—from Huntington, West Virginia, to Dayton, Ohio, and Wichita, Kansas, in the heartland, to Spokane, Washington, and San Jose, California, in the West. The experiments have focused chiefly in small- and medium-sized cities. Only occasionally have they been tried in major urban areas, such as Boston and Seattle. The pattern held in the East, too, where typical civic journalism sites include Portland, Maine; Norfolk, Virginia; and Charlotte, North Carolina. To identify, develop, and fine-tune coverage of issues most relevant to their communities, newspapers, television newsrooms, and, increasingly, public radio stations asked their reporters to listen more systematically and carefully to citizens in polls, public forums, focus groups, and community and neighborhood conversations.

Systematic "public listening," usually conducted before but sometimes after major series of in-depth articles and public issue broadcasts, came to typify the civic journalism experiment. It may be the most widely accepted feature of the movement. Less frequently, the experiments brought print and electronic newsrooms together in partnerships. Controversially, some news media cooperated with nonmedia organizations or institutions, usually in matters of logistics but, in some cases, accepting grants or help from philanthropic foundations to test innovations in community coverage. In general, the public journalism projects that gained the most favorable recognition—those at the *Wichita Eagle*, the *Charlotte Observer*, and the *Norfolk Virginian Pilot*—excelled in creative combinations of public listening, "shoe-leather" reporting at the grassroots, computer-assisted research, and analytical public polling. Even these particular experiments, however, came under some fire (Hoyt, 1995; Remnick, 1996).

The *Wichita Eagle*, led by soft-spoken editor Davis Merritt, began holding Kansas politicians to closer account after deep reflection on his newspaper's coverage of the 1988 election. His epiphany came in identifying how acutely Kansas voters were turned off by the negative effects of daily journalism's horse race style of election reporting. The latter, he realized, too often left the agenda almost entirely up to politicians with only modest input from voters. More explicit issue-oriented election coverage followed in 1990, highlighted by weekly issue summaries that persuaded candidates to spell out their views in more detail. Merritt later reflected, "There were two substantive results: Voter turnout was up across the state but more so in areas where our coverage was available; voter cognizance of issues was strongly higher in our readership area than elsewhere in the state" (1995, p. 82).

The *Eagle* also broke new ground with "The People Project: Solving It Ourselves," a ten-week effort to engage Wichita citizens in thinking about major issues of crime, education, government gridlock, and family breakdown. Key features of the project were success stories, tips on alternative ways citizens could get involved in the search for solutions, and invitations from sundry quarters to discuss solutions, in print and in person. Especially innovative were "core values graphics"—exercises to help readers identify those overriding values that come into play as difficult public choices are made among competing courses of action. The *Eagle* gave their readers an opportunity to experience the sometimes painful process of making tradeoffs among values in its coverage of health care. Impressively, 5,000 people completed questionnaires on health care and returned them to the newspaper.

None of the public journalism initiatives at the *Eagle* has caused any dramatic improvement in the economic fortunes of the newspaper. However, it is Merritt's belief, and apparently Knight-Ridder management's belief, that civic vitality and newspaper readership are intimately linked. "Although journalism is only one of the forces at work in our society today, it, almost uniquely, has the potential to become the glue of a healthy public life" (1995, p. 124).

The *Eagle*'s sister Knight-Ridder newspaper, the *Observer* in Charlotte, took the issues emphasis even further. Joined by the Poynter Institute for Media Studies, the *Observer* polled throughout the state to identify the major concerns of voters and took pains to see that those were covered as extensively as issues raised by the campaigns of the candidates (Merritt, 1995, p. 83). Systematic issue polling of the electorate also allowed reporters to identify citizen volunteers who agreed to be quoted during continuing state and local campaign coverage.

But the *Observer* became as or more widely known for the public journalism approach it took to an anticrime series, "Taking Back Our Neighborhoods." The eighteen-month effort generated citizen introspection, discussion, and grassroots participation in projects to combat a soaring crime rate. The series also triggered extensive municipal and private donations of time, money, equipment, and support for corrective action. It was a finalist for the Pulitzer prize.

In some ways, the most highly organized, varied, and enduring public journalism project is the five-partner enterprise, "We the People," headquartered in Madison, Wisconsin. It began in 1991 as the *Wisconsin State Journal* joined Wisconsin Public Television and, in an unorthodox mating, Wood Communications Group, a public relations firm. That trio first joined with Minnesota colleagues to present interviews with democratic presidential candidates in 1992. Citizen town hall meetings with Wisconsin senatorial candidates followed that same year.

Subsequent print and electronic coverage in Wisconsin consistently included civic journalism-style coverage of a state superintendent of schools race, a proposed state property tax freeze, the federal deficit, a gubernatorial election, the state budget, and a state Supreme Court election. Organizers of the coverage assembled and prepared diverse groups of citizen participants who discussed issues with public officials and candidates and developed questions, positions, or proposals of their own during novel meeting formats, such as a grand jury or Supreme Court hearing.

The eleven-station Wisconsin Public Radio network and CBS affiliate, WISC-TV3, joined "We the People" in 1994. One of the most significant results is that the media appear to be leveraging more attention collectively than any one of them could generate on their own (Denton, Thorson, and Coyle, 1995). Another byproduct has been the consulting requests that have come in for "We the People" from other news organizations wanting to begin their own civic journalism projects. The continued presence of a public relations firm would be a red flag, or a white one, for most journalists. But its presence is said to have provided a logistical consistency the lack of which has doomed many cooperative public journalism projects. The three founding partners are described as having established a relationship of trust (Schaffer and Miller, 1995).

In Norfolk, the Landmark-owned *Virginian Pilot* has steered a different course. Rather than the major project approach characteristic of many civic journalism initiatives, it has emphasized reform in the daily framing of stories and issues. More than most news organizations, it has imported academic specialists and consultants to confer intensively with the public affairs reporting team it created to lead its public journalism work.

This mid-career training effort is reflected in news coverage designed to stimulate public dialogue and "possibility thinking" on tough issues such as race relations, capital punishment, and prisoner rehabilitation (Charity, 1995). Significantly, editor Cole C. Campbell, of the *Virginian Pilot*, has sought to stimulate the staff's creativity in search of new concepts to guide its news coverage. A new vocabulary is emerging to describe, focus, and stimulate the staff to engage readers as citizens at different levels of complexity.

Literacy is a term for stories written in a way that allows citizens to converse adequately with others about a topic and pursue related information on their own initiative. *Utility* stories help readers navigate their daily lives as citizens, family members, investors, or employees. *Mastery* stories prepare citizens to grasp, assimilate, and evaluate not only their own stake in public issues but the stakes of other citizens, lobbies, and civic organizations (Campbell, 1996; Hartig, 1996). But what difference do the new techniques used by civic journalists make in an election?

In 1994, Wisconsin's "We the People" project surveyed voters before and after the 1994 elections for governor and U.S. senator. One purpose of the study, sponsored by the Pew Center, was to assess the impact, if any, of "We the People" discussion sessions among citizens. At the meetings, citizens talked about issues important to them and learned more about how to watch political debates and analyze negative campaign advertising.

About half of those who responded to the survey had heard of the project. Before the election, 26 percent said the project had increased their interest in public affairs. After the election, 32 percent reported increased interest—a rise of 6 percent. Those who said that the "We the People" project had increased their knowledge rose from 51 to 56 percent.

Reporting these results, *New York Times* reporter Ivar Peterson (1996) began his summary of the study by suggesting that a 5 to 6 percent increase in knowledge and interest would seem to be "minimal at best." Left unremarked was the fact that such percentages, if translated into new voting, is more than enough to make a difference in elections. My colleague, Esther Thorson, associate dean for graduate studies at the University of Missouri School of Journalism, was allowed by Peterson the following "printed sound bite":

The question is, can civic journalism fight back against all the negative advertising that people see in a campaign? You may look at these results and say the changes are small, but my guess is we have a shot at it. It (the "We the

People" program) does not increase cynicism; it does increase knowledge, and it probably increases the likelihood of voting. (1996, p. C5)

Earlier, a study team at the University of Missouri in Columbia concluded that a key feature of the civic journalism movement—cross-media partnerships—has the potential to significantly gain attention of the public, increase knowledge of content, and improve consumers' evaluation of media performance. The study, in May 1994, focused on reader, viewer, and listener reactions to carefully coordinated coverage of health care. Faculty researchers worked in tandem with the editors and reporters of the daily and Sunday *Missourian* of Columbia, NBC-affiliate KOMU-TV, and public radio KBIA. These are the teaching newsrooms of the Missouri journalism school.

Stories in the three media showed how the interplay of cost, quality, and access to health care affected the experience of patients as well as the nature of the proposals made to correct problems in the system. Although there were some important differences among the media in the approaches taken and material used in the stories reported, there also was planned overlap in much of the content.

Survey findings were based on 397 random digit-dialed interviews conducted in Boone County after an intensive week of carefully coordinated health care coverage. In general, we found that strong awareness of the health care stories, knowledge of their content, and positive evaluations of them increased significantly among people who encounter the stories in more than one medium (Thorson and Lambeth, 1995). We found most of these increases held up even when statistical controls were introduced to account for the possibility that the changes were caused by demographics; that is, by differences in the ages, income, education, gender, and employment of survey respondents.

The synergy resulting from coordinated, cross-media news coverage can be illustrated briefly by showing the results for one of the major variables—the knowledge of story content. The following represents the percentage of respondents answering correctly the questions asked about the content of stories in coordinated, multimedia coverage of health care:

	This medium alone	With one other medium	With two other media
Newspaper	58	64	71
Television	30	33	63
Radio	12	35	46

Among leaders of the movement, there is a keen sense that the naysayers of civic journalism have often made superficial and uninformed criticisms. Merritt (1995), known as a soft-spoken and philosophical editor, said the movement is still maturing. He said that he becomes "upset when I hear others unfairly and ignorantly trashing" the enterprise (p. 2). Yet, he acknowledged that "some public journalism efforts" reflect an adolescence of "self-absorption . . . self-promotion . . . superficialities . . . an anxiety to make an impact . . . and a dangerous over-romanticizing of the citizen" (pp. 6–7). To Merritt, that simply adds the sin of hypocrisy to the arrogance of the traditional journalistic view of citizens. He adds, "There is no useful difference between the traditional journalists' dismissive view of citizens and the new, superficial view of, 'Look at all those citizens. Aren't they cute?' Putting uninformed citizen views in the newspaper and calling it public journalism has the same value as talk radio. That is, none" (p. 8).

Critics raise legitimate questions about civic journalism. Arguably, much of the energy to launch the experiments came not only from newsrooms, foundations, and university intellectuals but also from corporate board rooms. Particularly influential were executives such as the late James K. Batten of Knight-Ridder, Inc., and corporate strategies, such as the Gannett Company's, that make commitment to community central to news coverage. It is no secret that newspaper readership has been declining in recent years and that well-led newspaper companies are both alarmed and actively attempting to combat the trend. Civic and public journalism projects are part of that attempt.

Optimists, such as social scientist Leo Bogart (1995), who believes printed news will continue to play an important economic and social role in the future, are concerned, nonetheless, about the commercial culture that has come to dominate the media and the direction their leaders are taking. This concern is well founded and ought to be part of the debate over public journalism. Merritt (1995), for example, notes that the excessive self-promotion accompanying some public journalism projects lends credence to the criticism that public journalism is simply another marketing ploy (Campbell, 1996; Hartig, 1996).

Fundamentally, commercialism damages journalism at its roots when corporate leaders require profit margins so high that not enough resources are available to conduct either investigative reporting or civic journalism at a level of excellence. Unless there is a continuing healthy investment in both, corporate leaders who helped their newsrooms pioneer public journalism run the risk of being accused of having reneged on an important commitment. The short-term profit mentality of American business is especially acute among the corporate management of both print and electronic media.

However, it is one thing to be alert to the penurious tendencies of corporate media and quite another to argue that civic journalism—whether in projects or in daily coverage—is incapable of preserving its integrity with readers, listeners, and viewers. Ethical issues confront reporters and editors whether they work within investigative, expository, narrative, or new journalism traditions. The ethical questions civic journalists face are not different in kind or degree. They, too, need to face and publicly work through the issues they face, whether they be conflicts of interest or risks to their independence (Lambeth and Craig, 1995).

The suspicions critics have of civic journalism are often unfounded. Howard Schneider, managing editor of *Newsday*, predicted that the *Charlotte Observer* would not be able to separate itself from solutions proposed by the crime-prone areas to which it paid special attention in its "Taking Back our Neighborhoods" series.[2] "I don't think they will be able to probe whether those solutions are inclusive or whether they are well done," he said. Yet, before the eighteen-month project was over, *Observer* reporters John Hechinger and Gary L. Wright exposed "Fighting Back," an antidrug and neighborhood uplift organization that had sought to benefit by donations associated with the *Observer* project. Their story disclosed mismanagement and misuse of moneys donated to "Fighting Back" (Hechinger and Wright, 1995).

Mark Jurkowitz (1996), ombudsman for the *Boston Globe*, made important distinctions between the quality of civic journalism initiatives after studies he conducted of projects at the *Mercury News* in San Jose, California, the *Herald* in Grand Forks, North Dakota, the *Spokesman Review* in Spokane, Washington, and the *Charlotte Observer*.

The *Mercury News* conducted a classic investigation of state lobbying, "Legislature for Sale," but erred, in Jurkowitz's (1996) view, by then organizing and training a civic activist group that risked becoming too political. The *Herald*, legitimately concerned about the region's economy, crossed a conflict-of-interest line by loaning an editor to the local chamber of commerce for a project parallel to the newspaper's community conversation on the economy. The *Spokesman Review* convened "pizza party" conversations in the community on how best to manage regional growth, and then hired an outside consultant, Neal Peirce, to write an in-depth report. Essentially, Jurkowitz (1996) observed, the *Spokesman Review* substituted imported talent for the work of its own staff.

But of the *Charlotte Observer*'s "Taking Back Our Neighborhoods" project, Jurkowitz wrote the following:

By combining sensitive, stellar reporting with a program to mobilize local agencies and institutions, "Taking Back Our Neighborhoods" galvanized an entire city and fueled the effort to improve blighted urban areas. More importantly from the standpoint of public journalism, a single newspaper inspired citizens to effect these changes, and it did so without threatening traditional journalistic standards. (1996, p. 82)

Reflecting on his four case studies, Jurkowitz concluded:

The mixed record of these projects suggests why partisans on both sides of the argument over public journalism have it wrong. Public journalism is neither inherently evil nor a panacea for the woes of the news media or democracy. It's all in the execution. (1996, p. 83)

Minimized or largely ignored by critics, yet central to civic journalism, is its search for ways to reframe stories on public affairs to actively engage citizens. The *Virginian Pilot* has done this in its daily coverage of controversy. It does so not by ignoring conflict stories—as some critics allege civic journalism inherently does—but by consistently showing the middle ranges of many issues and how citizens can explore them. The *Eagle* framed education, crime, government, and family stories in terms of values. In doing so, the *Eagle* acted not as an advocate but as a sophisticated interpreter aware that social science research has shown that applying values is central to how readers process the news (Neuman, Just, and Crigler, 1992).

Why did the *Charlotte Observer* hire a coordinator to organize solution-seeking activity within neighborhoods as part of its eighteen-month crime series? What was the justification of such an extensive project? In 1993, Charlotte, North Carolina, thirty-fourth among major cities in population, ranked eighteenth in the prevalence of violent crime. The 66,000 people in the central city neighborhoods represented 16 percent of the population but suffered 54 percent of the crime (Chandler, Mellnick, and Wright, 1994). The *Observer*'s judgment was that the community needed the newspaper to frame the problem so government officials and citizens could begin to reclaim the most seriously affected neighborhoods. Civic journalism, at its best and most genuine, seeks new ways to enhance the news media's historic role of helping citizens interact effectively with their government and community leaders.

But the public no longer trusts the press. The extent of the public's disaffection was crystallized dramatically in a survey by the Times-Mirror Center for the People and the Press (1994). It found that 71 percent of the citizens agreed that the news media inhibit society solving its problems. The degree of disaffection also was reflected in a major shift in public opinion between 1988 and 1993 when Daniel Yankelovich and colleagues (*Yankelovich Monitor*, 1993) asked citizens, "In which of these do you find that you have great confidence?" A representative sample (in percentages) answered as follows:

	1988	1993
Doctors	71	63
Religious leaders	38	26
Federal government	18	12
State government	12	9
Local government	15	10
News reports on television	55	25
News reports in newspapers	50	20
News in magazines	38	12

A similar poll, conducted by the Kaiser Foundation for *The Washington Post* in 1996, showed that only one in five Americans has "a great deal" or "quite a lot" of confidence in the news media (Washington Post/Kaiser Family Foundation/Harvard University Survey Project, 1996).

Rosen, intrepid intellectual, puts well the question asked by those active in the movement when repeatedly told their activities risk loss of credibility: "What makes you think you have credibility now? After all the challenge is not to remain, it is to become credible in an environment where no institution, least of all the press, seems to be addressing people's deepest concerns" (1995, p. 8).

Civic journalism makes a greater effort than traditional journalism to identify those concerns, report them with fidelity, and link them to questions of public policy. Its search is for ways to help stimulate public deliberation and help maximize the likelihood that citizens will generate the will to inform themselves and act in their own and in the public's interest.

An intellectual foundation for civic journalism has begun to be laid by contemporary scholars and journalists.[3] The distinctions Yankelovich (1991) makes between the role of information and judgment in the formation of public opinion are central to the techniques civic journalists are attempting to develop and perfect. So is his three-stage model in which the public first has its consciousness raised, then confronts needed change, and finally, comes to judgment. In a real sense, civic journalism's challenge is to figure out how the competencies it already has or can develop can be used to help the public emotionally, cognitively, and morally work through issues. It would be better still if that challenge were assumed by the field of journalism as a whole.

Some progress has been made by social science in understanding the dynamics by which journalists frame and audiences attempt to assimilate the news. Neuman, Just, and Crigler (1992) have richly documented the similarities and, particularly, the differences in the way media and citizens frame issues and the potentially negative impact of those differences on the public's attitude toward public affairs. They have also helped explain how it is likely that print and electronic media can be deployed synergistically, thereby increasing public knowledge and understanding of issues.

Practitioners in Madison, Wisconsin; Wichita, Kansas; Charlotte, North Carolina; Norfolk, Virginia; and Columbia, Missouri have contributed directly and indirectly to scholarly research and reflection on civic journalism. More work needs to be done, however, to fully test the implications of the insights of scholars such as Yankelovich (1991) and Neuman, Just, and Crigler (1992) and to assess the potential and effectiveness of the innovations already launched by editors such as Merritt (1995, 1996) and Campbell (1996). However, such work will require new and sophisticated forms of cooperation between the academy, the practice of journalism, and philanthropic foundations. If such an enterprise does emerge, civic journalism may yet reach a maturity that fairly tests its promised contributions to public life.

NOTES

1. See Howard Schneider, of *Newsday,* interviewed by Walter Cronkite, "Is That the Way It Is?" broadcast on the Discovery Channel, March 22, 1995.
2. Ibid.
3. See "Rethinking Journalism: Rebuilding Civic Life," *National Civic Review,* Winter–Spring 1996, pp. 3–44, including my own summary of related literature, "A Bibliographic Review of Civic Journalism," Rosen (1994).

REFERENCES

Bogart, L. (1995). *Commercial culture: The media system and the public interest.* New York: Oxford University Press.
Campbell, Cole C. (1996). Personal communication, February 9, Columbia, Mo.
Case, T. (1994). Public journalism denounced. *Editor & publisher,* November 12, pp. 14–15.
Chandler, L., T. Mellnick, and G. L. Wright. (1994). At Charlotte's core, violence a daily threat. *Charlotte Observer,* June 5, pp. 1, 13A.
Charity, A. (1995). *Doing public journalism.* New York: Guilford Press.
Denton, F., E. Thorson, and J. Coyle. (1995). Effects of a multimedia public journalism project on political knowledge and attitudes. Paper presented to the Association for Education in Journalism and Mass Communication, August, Washington, D.C.
Eisner, J. (1994). Should journalists abandon their detachment to solve problems? *The Philadelphia Inquirer,* October 16, p. E7.
Frankel, M. (1995). Fix-it journalism. *New York Times,* May 21, p. 28.
Hartig, D. (1996). Personal communication, February 9, Columbia, Mo.

Hechinger, J., and G. L. Wright (1995). How financial mistakes derailed Fighting Back, Mecklenburg's anti-drug effort. (1995). *Charlotte Observer*, October 15, p. A1.

Hoyt, M. (1995). A civic journalist? *Columbia journalism review*, 27–33.

Jurkowitz, M. (1996). From the citizen up. *Forbes Mediacritic* (Winter): 78–81.

Lambeth, E. B., and D. Craig. (1995). Civic journalism as research. *Newspaper research journal* (16): 148–160.

Merritt, D. (1995). *Public journalism and public life: Why telling the news is not enough*. Hillsdale, N.J.: Lawrence Erlbaum Associates.

Merritt, D. (1996). Ruminations upon public journalism's adolescence. Presentation at a Civic Journalism Teach-In at the University of Missouri School of Journalism by the Civic Journalism Interest Group, March 22–24, 1996, Columbia, Missouri.

Neuman, W. R., M. R. Just, and A. M. Crigler. (1992). *Common knowledge: News and the construction of political meaning*. Chicago: University of Chicago Press.

Peterson, I. (1996). Civic-minded pursuits gain ground at newspapers. *New York Times*, March 4, p. C5.

Remnick, D. (1996). Scoop. *The New Yorker* (January 29): 38–42.

Rethinking journalism: Rebuilding civic life. (1996). *National civic review* (Winter/Spring): 3–44.

Rosen, J. (1994). Making things more public: On the political responsibility of the media intellectual. *Critical studies in mass communication* 16: 363–388.

Rosen, J. (1995). What should we be doing? *The IRE journal* (November/December): 8.

Schaffer, J., and E. D. Miller. (1995). *Civic journalism: Six case studies*. Washington, D.C.: Pew Center for Civic Journalism.

Shepard, A. (1994). The gospel of public journalism. *American journalism review* 1: 25–28.

Thorson, E., and E. B. Lambeth. (1995). An evaluation of the cognitive, attitudinal and synergistic effects of a multi-media civic journalism project. Paper presented to the annual meeting of the Association for Education in Journalism and Mass Communication, August, Washington, D.C.

Times-Mirror Center for the People and the Press. (1994). *The people, the press and politics: The new political landscape*. Washington, D.C.: Times-Mirror Center for the People and the Press.

Washington Post/Kaiser Family Foundation/Harvard University. (1996). Why don't Americans trust the government? The Washington Post/Kaiser Family Foundation/Harvard University Survey Project.

Yankelovich, D. (1991). *Coming to public judgment*. Syracuse, N.Y.: Syracuse University Press.

Yankelovich Monitor. (1993). Yankelovich Partners, p. 46.

Chapter 9

Media Critics and
Newsgroup-Embedded Newspapers:
Making Attentive Citizens Attentive

Richard A. Pride

"Americans now distrust journalists even more than they do government officials. Unless journalism changes, it will destroy itself and severely damage American democracy." That is what it says on the dust cover of James Fallows's (1996) new book, *Breaking the News*.

The blurb is not just publisher's hype for the latest American crisis of the minute, and the author is not some Johnny-come-lately academic expert. Fallows is one of America's most respected and thoughtful magazine journalists.

Moreover, Fallows has a personal history of calling us to face what we want to deny. As a young man, he wrote "What Did You Do In The Class War, Daddy?" for *The Washington Monthly* (1975). It was widely discussed. In it, he tells how he and classmates from Harvard University deliberately, even cleverly, failed their physical exams for the military draft in the late 1960s, while the boys from Chelsea routinely passed theirs, just as their daddies had in an earlier war. Fallows (1975) uses the story to illuminate why the social class inequality of those who actually fought and died in Vietnam undermined the moral legitimacy of that war.

Now, Fallows (1996) tells us journalism has serious problems that corrupt active citizenship. Once again, it is a moral problem for him: Politicians and the press today routinely exclude meaningful participation by ordinary citizens.

With Fallows's track record, we had better pay attention. Fallows says, "Deep forces in American political, social, and economic structures account for most of the frustration of today's politics, but the media's attitudes have played a surprisingly important and destructive role" (1996, p. 7). A kind of tunnel vision permeates media accounts of political life. Policy problems are reduced to mere politics, and politics are seen as the self-centered quest for power by ambitious, manipulative men and women.

Fallows also says, "What is important is different from what is urgent. What is important is often not what's new. What is important is often crowded out by what is most novel or attention-getting that day— Lorena Bobbitt, the latest earthquake, a scandal involving a movie star" (p. 131). When there is a scandal, the media goes overboard. When the media have no scandal, they hope and search for one. "All of them are too busy looking for what is 'urgent' to do the daily chore of telling us what is important, and why."

Finally, Fallows says, "Part of the press's job is to keep things in proportion. Television's natural tendency is to see the world in shards. It shows us one event with an air of utmost drama, then forgets about it and shows us the next" (p. 53). Television news presents no history, no context, just the energetic now. Even when it tries to give perspective, it subverts itself. Too often, television turns news into spectacle. When Dan Rather goes to Bosnia, the news becomes a Rather-does-Bosnia more than Bosnia speaks.

Tom Patterson (1993), a prominent political scientist, also faults the media in his book, *Out of Order*. Patterson says media, particularly television, subvert the electoral process by supplanting candidates' issues and interpretations with those of their own devising. He blames the press because candidates' messages do not get out unfettered. (It seems to me that politicians are just as manipulative as the press is misguided.) In the end, Patterson does not hope to reform the press—"The nature of news exposes the foolhardiness of the idea that the press, if it would only handle things better, could make a presidential election into a sensible affair. The press is in the news business, and the news is simply not an adequate guide to political choice" (p. 206). He argues instead that political campaigns must be shortened in order to reduce the negative effects of the media, a recommendation that seems to shortchange hope for democratic deliberation.

Fallows (1996), too, is better at illustrating what is wrong with journalism than specifying what to do about it. He does offer one new approach though—it is called "civic journalism."

Civic journalism sprang up among a few regional newspapers in the past five years, and it has provoked considerable comment among worried professionals (Hoyt, 1995).

The approach begins with the recognition that journalists have responsibility commensurate with their freedom and that the rising tide of cynicism and apathy among the American people is partly the media's fault.

Civic journalism, both in theory and practice, requires print and broadcast media to actively reawaken healthy discourse and community-oriented participation among diverse segments of society. People who do not participate in civic life have no use for news. People without information cannot and should not participate in democratic decisions.

Typically, in those communities where this has been acted upon, a newspaper will take the lead by bringing together local leaders and followers in focus groups or commissioning a public opinion poll to identify the issues that trouble people the most. Then, the media set about educating themselves and everyone else about all sides of complicated problems through in-depth studies and special reports, enough so that important decisions can be made, not just finessed.

In Seattle, as one observer said, media constructed "a veritable front porch where residents could talk to political candidates and to each other and where a poll picked up unexpected anxieties about the future of the family and affordable housing" (Schaffer and Miller, 1995, p. 48).

A media and community partnership to address local problems promises to reduce cynicism and impotence in one fell swoop. It sounds too good to be true—and it probably is.

There are dangers along this path. Since public journalism begins with publishers, senior editors, and community leaders, it can readily become a self-fulfilling pseudocampaign followed by celebratory grandstanding—leaders, whether media or community, working together are unlikely to make each other look bad. And, as newspaper and television stations develop commitments to particular policies and programs, they lose both critical perspective and may possibly even buy into the prevailing distribution of material and social goods. Public journalism can make the system's "watchdog" into a "fat cat."

In his essay about the Vietnam draft, Fallows (1975) said that the burdens of war had to be shared equally if a democracy was to fight and win. I think that is what he has in mind this time, too: We all need to do our part to bring back a robust civic life. Unlike Fallows, though, I am not sure a media and community partnership is the way.

For my part, I believe we have to create attentive citizens first. This means hands-on education in schools and around supper tables. Otherwise the media and community partnership is so unequal that powerful interests will turn civic journalism into another public relations shell game.

People distrust government for a reason. Political leaders have not dealt with the people faithfully over the course of several decades, and the press has let them down, too. People are right to be suspicious because both politicians and press have treated them as objects to be manipulated for power and profit. The recent use of negative attack ads in political campaigns is only the most vivid example of rank opportunism prevailing over informed debate (Jamieson, 1992).

Part of the way back to a more vital public life could be the following: (1) for reporters to regain the trust and respect of citizens by doing the work citizens ask of them—to tell the truths that lie behind the public relations doubletalk of contemporary politics; (2) for media criticism, both by in-house and citizen observers, to become a regular feature of newspapers and television; and, out of this, (3) for a curriculum of news media criticism to be developed and offered simultaneously as regular fare in schools for students and in the broader community for those who want to be actively engaged.

SOCIAL RESPONSIBILITY

The main function of mass media in a free society is to provide the public with information and entertainment, and in America, among theorists and practitioners alike, there have been two competing philosophies about how this could be done.

The *libertarian* camp has stressed audience appeal. News is whatever interests the public, even if it tends toward sex and violence, and it should be conveyed quickly and accurately: "Just the facts, Ma'am."

Libertarian journalism favors stenographic reporting of the doings and sayings of important people. Because officials trust the press to report them unquestioningly, officials talk freely, both on and off the record. The public gets a lot of official information that way—just as Patterson (1993) asserts—but as political leaders have learned to manipulate rather than submit to democratic oversight, stenographic reporting has increasingly come to deaden the civic mind.

Contemporary "tabloid journalism" issues from libertarian philosophy. Tabloids are not really interested in truth at all. They delight in being stenographers for the macabre assertions of whoever will talk. The most we can expect from them is that they cite some source for the stories they print. The source may be untrustworthy and the information false, but the tabloids feel free to publish it if they can "source" it at all. Tabloids revel in the notion of multiple truths, and, by example, they signal the journalistic world of the future unless new reportorial norms are set in place.

A competing journalistic philosophy, called *social responsibility*, emerged in the 1950s and required reporters not only to report the facts but to tell "the truth behind the facts." This kind of reporting began with a distrust of powerful interests, and it assumed that the public could be easily misled or duped by smooth public relations rhetoric as much as by outright deception. Social responsibility journalism asked reporters to serve as guardians of the public welfare and to use their own individual consciences to guide them in this task.

The theory of social responsibility emerged out of the experiences and critiques of the 1930s and 1940s, rose to prominence in the 1960s, and all but disappeared by the late 1970s. The recent movement toward civic or, as it has sometimes been called, public journalism picks up threads of this problematic social responsibility theory—ideas like media responsibility commensurate with its freedom—but it departs in some significant ways, too. The new civic journalism locates the ethical center of journalism in the consensus of media and community leaders, whereas the older, social responsibility theory freed the moral compasses of individual reporters.

Commercial interests today have penetrated newsrooms more fully than at any time since the 1930s. At that time, big business was often directly able to shape the news. Over the years, strong efforts were made to rid newsrooms of heavy-handed interference by publishers— the nearest agent of the economic system. While those efforts were largely successful, indirect influence has grown steadily more obvious since the 1960s, mainly as media chains have gobbled up more and more independent newspapers. Media executives now have more loyalty to corporate advancement, by generating bottom-line profits, than to the respect bestowed on them by an appreciative community. If you listen carefully to what they say, these executives justify their decisions by market research more than by prophetic vision.

By the 1940s, business had so subverted the idea of a responsible press that a Commission on Freedom of the Press (1947) was created after World War II to sort out the issues. It offered the book, *A Free and Responsible Press*. A member, William E. Hocking (1947), published *Freedom of the Press: A Framework of Principle*. Together, these and *Four Theories of the Press*, published in 1956, gave shape to the social responsibility theory of the press, a set of ideas that stimulated a whole generation of reporters coming into their own in the 1950s and 1960s. The new theory sought to balance rights and responsibilities, and its champions rallied to the cry, "The public has a right to know!"

Today, you do not hear journalists make that cry like you did back in the 1960s or early 1970s. And that is a shame. This absence is partly because journalists cannot rouse public indignation by its use. People are jaded. Too many folks already think the media want to know too much. It is true that boundaries of personal privacy are frequently breached by mercenary reporters and greedy editors willing to serve up salacious details to mindless consumers, especially if there is sex, drugs, money, or violence somewhere in the story. But in truth, the right to know was always meant to force open boardrooms not bedrooms. Not enough boardrooms have been forced open lately.

These days, we do not hear reporters spit out the challenge, "The public has a right to know," mainly because the press is not championing community interests as it once did. Perhaps reporters are too busy just surviving. Perhaps media firms themselves do not want to offend advertisers. Whatever the cause, newsroom denizens seem somewhat tentative, unsure of their proper roles. But corporate managers for Gannett and Knight-Ridder know their jobs, and right now it is to drive up stock values through downsizing and other efficiencies. Journalistic values and public interests suffer in proportion: too few reporters with too little time digging too little into the muck of postmodern American life.

In the folklore of journalism, the following three events in the 1950s gave impetus to the rise of the social responsibility perspective among reporters in the 1960s and early 1970s (Weaver, 1974):

1. Senator Joseph McCarthy (R-Wisc.) used to hold up papers that, he said, listed the names of communists and fellow travelers who worked in the U.S. government. Under libertarian norms, reporters were compelled to report what he said without comment, even if they knew he was being utterly false and demagogic.

2. In 1959, President Eisenhower announced that a weather plane had gone off course over the Soviet Union. The Soviets belied that when they showed off Gary Powers, the pilot, and the wreckage of a spy plane, Ike had lied and had gotten reporters to participate in the fabrication.

3. In 1960, the *New York Times* found out about the planned Bay of Pigs invasion months before it happened. President Kennedy asked them personally not to publish the story. The *Times* deferred. The invasion was a disaster, and Kennedy told the *Times* later he wished they had published and saved him and the country from so great a blunder.

In each case, if the press had given more than the official statements, the country would have known the truth behind the facts and been better able to cope.

I mention these happenings because journalists later came to see them as clear-cut examples of a fundamental and enduring issue—the responsibility of reporters to the community in which they live and work, indeed to the very nature of journalism itself. They remind us that events unfolding today may seem similarly significant to observers a decade hence. Indeed, I nominate three events for just such a distinction: Ruby Ridge, Waco, and Whitewater. In each instance, news media gave us culturally approved stories. It is not just that reporters and editors missed the "real" story because they depended on official sources, it is that they supplied information to us based on barely conscious narratives already fixed in our minds. With Ruby Ridge and Waco, outlaws are brought to justice by the sheriff and his posse. We have seen that one a hundred times. Whitewater was a bit different. The text there was Nixon's "Watergate," and this one just did not measure up to that standard of presidential abuse of power, so the mainstream press let Whitewater lapse. Special prosecutors, not an investigative press, refocused our attention.

Stunningly, while the major media missed the subtexts of these unfolding news stories, information and misinformation poured through various Internet newsgroups like water through a broken bucket.

Libertarian journalism asks reporters—whether at Ruby Ridge, Waco, or Whitewater—to record what official sources assert; social responsibility journalism asks reporters to dig. It was no accident that investigative journalism was vigorous in the 1960s—the social responsibility theory of the press encouraged it.

In those days, all facets of American life were challenged, but in the middle 1970s, after the Watergate scandals led to President Nixon's resignation, debates over the proper role of the media were raised to new heights. Some attacked press arrogance: "Who had appointed them as guardians?" they asked (Epstein, 1974). Editors and publishers, particularly of the newly forming media chains, sought to regain control of newsrooms from reporters and editors who had become champions of the weak and powerless in the name of the public interest.

Over time, the passive libertarian stream in journalism once again became dominant. There is far less investigative reporting in the 1980s and 1990s than in the 1960s and early 1970s.

Among reporters today, almost all that remains of that burst of journalistic energy is a cynical habit of mind. Too many reporters are prepared to disbelieve, but they are not inclined or encouraged to get to a deeper and more complex level of meaning. While political candidates are portrayed by reporters as manipulative seekers of power rather than as national problem solvers, crucial issues are ignored.

Here is a case in point. Last November, *Nashville Banner* business writer Elizabeth Pagano wrote a story about The Lee Co. closing a jeans factory in Fayetteville, Tennessee, which put 731 people out of work. In December, she wrote a "help wanted" story that said there were a thousand jobs going unfilled in Nashville's hospitality industry. She did not make the connection between the two, if one can be made, but I would like to know, Is there a pattern? Are semiskilled jobs going to China (or someplace) while American workers are made to feel guilty for not rushing to Nashville to take unskilled jobs washing dishes and making beds? Does this have anything to do with the growing income gap between the rich and the poor in this country?

In some respects, the distrust of the 1960s wounded the press as much as other social institutions. A two-track newsroom developed. Among political reporters, habits of mind, formed then, hardened into corrosive disbelief, and their habituated distrust of authority poisoned the well of good media–government relations to this day. On other beats, stenographic reporting was justified by libertarian norms of pleasing the customer. Contemporary civic journalism is, in large part, a misguided attempt to break out of the reflexive and adversarial mind-set shared by journalists and politicians using the intellectual grounding provided by the 1950s social responsibility theory of the press. But unlike social responsibility theory, civic journalism, as it is proposed today, is controlled at the top by publishers and editors, not by reporters who are at the bottom of the journalistic enterprise.

PARTICIPATORY VENUES

News media are central to our understanding of the world where we live, and yet as organizations and practices, they are remote and forbidding. Print and broadcast media shape our individual and collective agendas but we know very little about how that happens or why. Many of us have worried about our country's steadily dimming public voice—the poor quality of our public debate. It is true that too often we get public relations generated talking points and pseudoevents from our public officials, instead of the real thing.

And surveys show that distrust of news media parallels distrust of the government. Both institutions are seen by many people as unresponsive, bullying, and remote. Nevertheless, government and media are about the only places we can engage collective problems through public debate. Other institutions, those with a more human face and scale, have either disappeared or been subsumed into mega-organizations. Once, the party caucus and union hall supported public participation, but they have all but disappeared. Our churches are too narrowly based to do the job; our business corporations are too focused on balance sheets and profitability to become effective venues for public debate. Our civic clubs have frequently become public booster clubs led by professional cheerleaders.

At one time in American life, the town square was a literal marketplace of ideas. Neighbors read newspapers, encountered strangers, and discussed schools, goods, prices, and whatever else they were interested in or troubled by, face to face. The town square has been displaced by the shopping mall, and shopping malls, as we all know, are reluctant to permit civic affairs to be debated on their premises. They should be truly ashamed. With the change in American society over recent decades, active interaction among citizens has been reduced to nodding acquaintance between passing consumers.

Where can we go? What can we do?

We must make it clear that turning eighteen does not make one a citizen; citizenship, truly grasped, is earned through sustained experience of the burdens of participation in public life. We must make it possible for people to become citizens in just this sense or democracy will become a hollow husk.

The answer lies in giving people the tools and opportunities to become active and critical participants in public life, and the innovative use of new technology may make this happen. Many of us have found vitality on the Internet, and that is what intrigues me. Although it is used by relatively few now, its potential is enormous. Hundreds of newsgroups are actively visited by tens of thousands of people every day. Comments are offered; threads are pursued.

I foresee a time when all of the literate among us will be able to engage each other in a new town square. The new electronic technology offers our best hope for stimulating a new and serious public voice because it makes possible swift, pertinent, and easy interaction among attentive citizens.

But if this interaction is to be institutionalized in an effective way, the participation of citizens has to engage news media, not just each other. One pattern that could develop in the not too distant future is that citizens would read "electronic newspapers" (which are supported largely through advertizing, just as now), and these newspapers would contain embedded newsgroups, perhaps linked to beats, to which readers have immediate access (one click of the mouse) and on which readers could write their comments for others to read and respond to. Reporters or editors would also react to the gist of newsgroup readers' comments from time to time in the daily cycle.

Such a system would establish immediate, easy, and dialogic communication about the day's news. It is a "place" where a diverse group of citizens could meet and talk about things that matter to them, stimulated and constrained by accounts of the news found in either the electronic or printed traditional newspaper.

This scheme would require new skills among journalists. They would be responsible not only for writing accounts of the day's news but also engaging readers on the affiliated newsgroup.

Also, I foresee newspapers commissioning media critics to act as interested third parties, prompting issues and responses as necessary from readers and reporters. In-house media critics would be "agents provocateur"; everything would be fair game for them. They would evaluate the news coverage, raise unasked and unanswered questions, and (initially at least) teach readers about journalism and the news business.

In my view, newspaper newsgroups could capture the interest of readers much like talk radio does now, but unlike most talk radio, their newsgroups would be constrained by the news accounts published in the newspaper—that is the information base readers would share and be continually and directly referred to.

Electronic newspapers with embedded newsgroups would become the functional equivalent of the town square displacing the present-day letter to the editor, which is, if you think about it, clearly inadequate as an interactive venue for public voice.

Alienation and apathy are understandable responses to political practices that are boring, remote, and unresponsive, and we have had too much of that. Interactive commentary, including media criticism, would be like an old town square again. News media are businesses and if the embedded newsgroups and media critics stimulate new and more readers, as I think they will, they should sell themselves to corporate executives and capitalism could serve democracy.

PERSONAL OBSERVATIONS

Propaganda has become the preferred method of ruling this country in our time because it is efficient and effective and because the news media aid in that process (Combs and Nimmo, 1993, p. 92). Powerful interests have discovered that it is far easier to persuade a credulous people of the justice of their cause than it is to be just. For example, a major paper company pollutes a river ceaselessly but blunts that asocial assault by sponsoring a recycling program in the schools for which it gets both kudos and thanks—a million tons of pollution in exchange for a few thousand dollars spent on recycling.

I have taught political communication for over twenty years and I have become both distressed at the basic ignorance of most people about our processes of political communication and hopeful about the way education can provide the implements of my students' emancipation. Last year, I wrote a media critique column, "After the News," for Nashville's afternoon newspaper. I was granted total freedom and chose to see myself as a public teacher more than as a media "referee." I was more interested in stimulating attentive citizenship than monitoring the daily successes and failures of workaday journalism.

I discovered many things in this role, including the fact that reporters and editors do not like to be criticized, whether it is fair or not. They are used to dishing it out but not taking it. I was continually amazed that the editor of Nashville's morning newspaper, *The Tennessean*, forbade any of his staff to talk to me or the other media critic in town on pain of being fired outright. He said that only he could answer questions about the internal decisions of the paper, but when you called him, he was not really helpful. The principal news-gathering organization in middle Tennessee stonewalled other journalists. By suppressing responsible criticism, some in the press make clear that they are more interested in competitive advantage, market share, and power than in the free flow of information. I was struck by how many people called to say they appreciated what I did. And what I did, basically, was teach. I wanted to help people become attentive citizens, and I wanted to provoke reporters to think actively about what they did and why.

If I am right, business incentives and democratic impulses can work together as newspapers change to utilize electronic digital communication. Readers will visit the electronic paper via computer, and they will want to respond right away. If active citizenship is to be encouraged, media will need to accommodate this need for immediate comment. Every section of the paper should have a newsgroup linked to it. A reader could click over and type out his reaction to the event itself or to the way it was covered as news. That is, citizens could engage the meaning of events as much as the objective facts of worldly happenings. Others could read those comments and react to them. Each newspaper beat would have its own electronic letter to the editor.

Reporters would be able (encouraged) to engage their critics periodically during the daily cycle. Interaction provokes readers and writers to do their homework. It is likely that this form of engagement would quickly grow into a major aspect of reporter's work—interaction with customers would stimulate more visits (hits) and therefore higher ad rates.

Media today are one way. Readers are made passive citizens by the circumstances of modern life. We barely know our real neighbors anymore, but we are intimately involved with truly unapproachable characters of television sitcoms. If we can create interaction with the news, we will have begun the process of reinvigorating our public voice. It is in critical dialogue that active citizens are made.

Newspapers will also recover readers because the news columns will be supplemented by electronically accessible databases and graphic illustrations, including video clips. Newspapers will become electronic information managers.

More important, newspapers will recreate the village marketplace once again. Viewpoints, interests, prices, and products—everything will be electronically proximate.

The key to it all, of course, is an active citizenry. Some few, perhaps, will master the new technology and develop the habits of mind all by themselves. Others will have to be taught. It is important that new curricula be developed for schools and interested citizens so they can develop the habits of participation. One part of the curriculum should be the nascent media critic because criticism of the messenger presently arouses as much interest as the events themselves.

SEGMENTS FROM THE CURRICULUM

A thoroughgoing curriculum, whether developed for students or offered to readers by an in-house media critic, would include how journalists define news and how they get their information, ranging from public relations press releases and press kits to confidential sources. It would be essential for the decision-making processes of news organizations to be described and the importance of standard operating procedures and bureaucratic, intramedia politics to be made clear.

The curriculum need not be appreciably different whether directed at high school students or uninformed adults. The lessons and their potential impact are the same.

I offer some examples of what a curriculum might contain. Imagine, if you will, that students would have been given a newspaper article or television news story and a media critic's reaction to that news account, just as you would find on a newsgroup embedded within an electronic newspaper of the future. The following examples are columns of media criticism that I wrote for the *Nashville Banner*, intended both to inform and provoke attentive citizens just as the formal curriculum would.

Interpretive Frames—Newspapers

Opryland recruiting expands to Ireland

by Heather Newman

Peter Clare grew up a glass-maker's son in the broad streets and spacious squares of Dublin, Ireland. He dreamed of becoming a great chef.

It was 22 years before the double-headed dragon of a depressed economy and double-digit unemployment ruined his life in that beautiful city. Last year, Clare lost his job as a hotel butcher and could not find another. Then he heard a radio commercial, enticing him to work at an American hotel.

"I couldn't find work in Dublin. I decided to give it a go."

The business on the radio was Opryland Hotel.

Hotel spokesman Tom Adkinson said the recruiting trip to Ireland and Northern Ireland was the first the company has ever made outside the U.S. territories. Clare, now 23, is the first person from Ireland to start work at the hotel. But up to 25 more people recruited with him are on the way.

The situation in his country is desperate, Clare said. Ireland's unemployment rate routinely tops 15%, compared to Nashville's 3% average.

"The world is getting really tight. It's really hard to get work. If I hadn't have come, I might never have worked again."

Three Opryland employees made the headhunting trip in early August, after a food manager here got a tip from a friend in the industry. Skilled workers in Ireland were there to be had, he was told. The group visited the Irish cities of Dublin and Limerick, and Belfast, Northern Ireland.

While the Irish class of recruits is tiny compared to the 250 people Opryland collected from Puerto Rico, Adkinson said the company is very happy with the qualifications of its newest potential employees.

"The labor market in Nashville is beyond the saturation point. If it works well, we could continue to explore and recruit there."

After the News Column

Opryland employment story misses deeper issue

by Richard A. Pride

American jobs are up for grabs, and newspapers frame our point of view.

Here is an example of what I mean. Heather Newman is a business writer for *The Tennessean*, but you could not tell that from her short, front-page piece on November 21, 1995, where she used cultural fable more than hard-headed reason to frame her story.

She began, "Peter Clare grew up a glassmaker's son in the broad streets and spacious squares of Dublin, Ireland. He dreamed of becoming a great chef." Double-digit unemployment stymied Clare's career, Newman related, until he heard a radio commercial, in Dublin, encouraging him to work at the Opryland Hotel in America. With that opening, she hooked us with the great American myth: immigrant rags to American riches.

Newman quoted the twenty-three-year-old Clare saying, "The world is getting really tight. It's really hard to get work. If I hadn't have come, I might never have worked again." America is a land of immigrants. Our forbearers came to this continent to better themselves, and Peter Clare has the necessary pluck. Okay, you might think, Welcome to America, and end of story. But not quite.

Opryland spokesman Tom Adkinson told Newman how the hotel happened to get Clare. Adkinson said three Opryland employees went to Ireland in August expressly to recruit skilled workers there. Clare was one of twenty-five hired and the first to arrive in Nashville.

Adkinson told *The Tennessean*, "The labor market in Nashville is beyond the saturation point. If this works well, we would continue to explore and recruit there."

Now that is important news stuck in the last paragraph of Newman's story! Opryland Hotel has hired foreign workers and plans to hire more! Newman seemed to me to underplay what she found out. Nashville's unemployment rate is only 3 percent, but does that justify hiring truly foreign workers?

Last year, Opryland hired workers in the southwestern states and Puerto Rico, and both *The Tennessean* and *Nashville Banner* newspapers had stories about that move. But this is the first time the company said it plans to hire skilled workers abroad. Puerto Rico is not considered foreign under our law.

Here is another frame for Newman's story: Foreign workers drive down the wages of American workers. Opryland's foreign hires signal the globalization of the labor market. From now on, it seems, Nashville's workers will get only what foreign workers are willing to work for. I wonder, how would Opryland's spokesman feel if I told him there were probably well-qualified public relations specialists in Ireland who might be willing to take his job at two-thirds of what Opryland is paying him?

Reporters are charged by readers with finding out what is happening and what it means. In this case, for example, is the meaning of Clare's coming to work at Opryland that America is still the land of opportunity or is it that Opryland Hotel will hire cheap foreign workers in order to increase its profitability?

Newman's article begins with the up-by-your-own-bootstraps American myth, which seems to justify hiring more foreign workers. This is the only interpretive theme she gives us. But when I probed, I found out that editors had cut her piece, presumably to fit a tight news hole, and that Newman was aware of a lot more than what made the paper that day.

Opryland's Adkinson was not quite as aware of how potentially controversial Clare's hiring was. For him, the issue was simple: Good workers could be gotten from Ireland when they could not be found in the United States.

Adkinson told me, "We're competing with other people in our own industry and every other industry in town." He continues, "Any given job in any given industry has only a certain value." Opryland pays the prevailing wage, and "the prevailing wage is appropriate."

"The simple observation that if you pay more, you'd have [enough Americans] is flawed. The broad market helps define what a certain task is worth. If we were paying lead cooks $50,000 a year, we'd have no problem with lead cooks. If you took that theory across the board with employees, we would have a problem with profitability. The idea of having a handful of people from another country who happen to work for us is not offensive."

Isn't it? Should the prevailing wage be set by what Americans will work for or by what the world's poor will work for? Is capitalism or nationalism more important?

There is a very significant transition in employment going on before our eyes, and we will miss the forest for the trees if the *Banner* and *Tennessean* do not focus our attention on underlying issues. So far they have not.

Interpretive Frames—Television News

The proposed curriculum needs to establish a dramatic triangle among the media's news story, the critic's critique, and the attentive citizen's active intelligence. The analysis in the foregoing column could serve equally well as part of a newsgroup embedded within the newspaper or as part of a package published for classroom use. Indeed, the process of creating active citizens might work best if parents and children learned simultaneously from the same contemporary texts.

Any plan for media literacy should involve television. This example presumes that students would view a video compiled tape from the Vanderbilt Television News Archive, something anyone could order.

In this case, the compiled tape would simply record the network television news stories that were broadcast day by day following the initial raid by the Bureau of Alcohol, Tobacco, and Firearms (ATF) on the Branch Davidian compound near Waco, Texas. An essay of media criticism, such as the following "After the News" column, could be used following the tape to provoke participation in an ongoing debate.

After the News Column

TV news often sheer melodrama

by Richard A. Pride

Do news media tell us the truth or only a story? The answer matters.

Too often, television news dissolves the line between reality and illusion. It claims to take us there live, or nearly so, and in so doing it collapses distance and time, two elements necessary for any kind of mature perspective. Sometimes television news uses false immediacy to undermine deliberative citizenship. It creates a new reality that citizens too often enter into willingly, naively, and to our discredit.

Some folks come to prefer illusion to reality because it is so much more appealing. Illusion, unlike truth, is simple, dramatic, and packaged. People are irresistibly drawn into the world created by a few dozen producers, editors, and reporters at the networks and local stations because they make a complex world into a compelling melodrama.

Look at the television news coverage of the Waco–Branch Davidian episode (episode is a loaded term. Why not "confrontation" or "tragedy?").

If you watched television, you first heard about the Waco incident on Sunday, February 28, 1993. It topped the evening news. First the anchorman, then the reporter told us: Over forty agents of the ATF, an agency of the federal government, had tried to serve three warrants on a cult at a heavily armed compound outside of Waco, Texas. The cult was led by a man who had fifteen wives and claimed to be Jesus Christ. The agents met a barrage of gunfire and had to pull back. Four agents had been killed and sixteen wounded; the standoff continued. The report had some good video, too: agents firing from behind vans, wounded being carried away, and an interview with a local newspaper reporter who was there.

Television had its script. It was clearly a movie out of the "Old West." There were good guys and bad guys. The bad guys were holed up, and the sheriff and his posse, figuratively speaking, had to get them out.

Notice, the first thing television news told us was that these Davidians were bad people; they had put themselves outside society. They were an armed and dangerous cult led by a madman, and they deserved to be attacked.

But, how did television know this? The answer is simple: The network reporter had dashed to the scene and asked federal agents what had happened and why. Then, she put it on the air for all of America to take in.

There is something fundamentally wrong about this. Agents who had really screwed up were getting their story out, but others were not being told.

Nor would they be; federal agents blocked reporters from getting into the compound continuously after the aborted raid.

What made Branch Davidians so bad? That first day, we were not told what the warrants were for, and after that it did not seem to matter. Only much later, after the fiery deaths of dozens, did someone ask the following questions: Is being in a fundamentalist religious sect against federal law? Does buying and selling guns warrant an armed raid? The answer for both is no, but at the time, television news did not seem to care.

On March 1, when asked why the raid had been so spectacularly unsuccessful, the ATF spokesperson replied that they were outgunned. Outgunned? Was the issue firepower or stupidity. We now know, of course, that government officials leading the raid were told by an infiltrator that David Koresh, the Branch Davidian leader, had been alerted to expect a raid that morning. The ATF plan was based on surprise, but government officials went ahead anyway.

All the information put into the news programs supported the basic story. Reporters interviewed some people who had left the Waco group years before. They said its leader, David Koresh, was insane and had a hit list. The ATF press spokesman was shown on the news stating the Koresh was an irrational figure who had now murdered four agents.

As days went by, the crazy outlaw story continued to be reported, but it was increasingly modified by the women-and-children-as-hostages motif. Indeed, when Attorney General Janet Reno justified the final raid on the compound, she said her decision was based on the misery that the women and children increasingly lived in. Reporters did not point out to us the irony there: It was the FBI who made their lives miserable by cutting off electricity for air conditioning, water, refrigeration, and lights; who continually bombarded the compound with buzzing helicopters and blaring loudspeakers; and who isolated the community from the outside world. When Reno said that she feared especially for the safety of the children, viewers were not directly encouraged to ask how children might be affected by tanks ripping into the building and shooting tear gas.

An alternative story that supplied meaning to the whole confrontation made its way onto television news only after it was over. After surveying the still smoldering ashes, live, from a helicopter, CBS's Dan Rather interviewed Koresh's lawyer. The lawyer, who had visited Koresh several times at the compound, claimed that the whole tragedy was caused by an out-of-control government agency. From personal observation he disputed that Koresh abused women or children; indeed, he said they seemed fond of him. Koresh did not seem crazy but intensely religious. One can only wonder why CBS did not have him on the news with this story earlier, when it could have helped to shape our view of unfolding events.

After the bombing of the federal building in Oklahoma City, underground militias got another story of Waco into the news. The story they told was about an oppressive federal government conspiring with the United Nations and all sorts of international bad guys to take away basic American freedoms. The attack on the Branch Davidians, they said, was only one sign of the conspiracy's power.

Now we have truly entered into the new age: Fantasy conflicts with fantasy on television news like episodes from a Hollywood studio rather than journalistic accounts from a professional newsroom. Television news promised us the truth up close and personal, but instead, at Waco as at other places, it showed that its real purpose was sheer melodrama.

The foregoing is heavy criticism, not unlike that found on Internet newsgroups, but it gets folks talking. The mere act of questioning is itself liberating, even engaging, but we cannot permit its product to be a cynical or apathetic habit of mind—we should instead strive for the development of a more discerning citizen. Someone has to reply to the stories as they unfold. And that takes active participation in the give-and-take of a newsgroup-embedded newspaper or a classroom.

Newspapers and television news provide interpretive frames for unfolding events, and citizens should know and contest those frames where their life experience offers countervailing bases. Sometimes, though, the issues raised will urge caution, as is the case in the following example, one where confidential sources have been used.

Sources

Imagine a world where newspapers reported only what was given to them by press information officers. I would not like it one bit because we, the public, would only know what corporate and government bosses wanted us to know.

Sometimes I think we are moving in that direction. More and more institutions are making it a matter of policy that employees funnel all reporters' questions back to their public information office.

A few years ago, the Metro-Nashville police department employed Don Aaron, a former television reporter, to intercede between officials and the press. The Metro-Nashville schools hired former Channel Five television reporter Craig Owensby for the same thing last year. Reporters told me that access to public information became more difficult after Aaron's ascendancy. How long will it be before teachers and policemen are forbidden to talk to the press? At Tennessee State University, all press calls to professors and administrative staff are routinely rerouted through the press information office.

In any case, people everywhere realistically fear that reprisals will be taken against them if they talk to the media about things that embarrass or threaten anyone more powerful than themselves, especially their bosses.

Practically speaking, this means most people would rather bite their tongues than be fired, even when doing nothing allows corruption, inefficiency, or unfairness to go unchallenged.

There is a middle way between bitter silence and public protest, though. Conscientious citizens can sometimes become confidential sources.

Journalistic conventions regulate the relationship of a reporter and her source, and it helps to know them. Once a reporter identifies herself to you, everything you say is on the record unless the two of you agree before you say anything more, often using magic words like "background" and "off-the-record," that she will not print what you are about to say.

If you, as the source, want to pass information along but also remain anonymous, you can tell the reporter that you will give her something "on background." *Background* means reporters can use the information without attributing anything directly to you. Sometimes reporters will use information gained on background in a news story, attributing it to some anonymous source, but more often they use it for guidance; it helps reporters shake the tree, so to speak, to flush out other sources who will talk on the record. On background talk is very common by savvy officials.

Off the record generally means that a source wants the reporter to file the information away and not use it even as a prod to get another source to talk because even to do that might point to who had given out the information.

Confidential sources are the lifeblood of beat journalism. Phone calls and letters alert reporters to things that just are not right, or things that are being covered up to protect someone's hindmost part.

The public depends on the press to be the watchdog of democracy, and without sources, reporters (and all of us) would be dangerously in the dark.

Bob Woodward and Carl Bernstein, the two *Washington Post* reporters who broke open the Watergate scandal, depended almost wholly on confidential sources. "Deep Throat" was only one of many.

Some folks feel that Watergate was the worst of times for us as a nation, but in some respects it was the best. Our institutions, especially the press, did not submit to an abuse of power.

One cannot help wonder if newspapers and television news would make the same stand today. They surely would not without our help.

Here is a story that appeared in the *Banner* one day and a column I wrote in response.

Secretary accuses lawmaker of harassment

by Kriste Goad

A member of the state House of Representatives has been charged by his secretary with sexual harassment, marking the first test of a new harassment policy enacted by the General Assembly in 1994.

That policy calls for full confidentiality of complaints and those involved in them.

An investigation has taken place, with the findings being forwarded today to House Speaker Jimmy Naifeh.

Naifeh, D-Covington, would not reveal the name of the representative involved.

"The legislative personnel officer has informed me a sexual harassment complaint has been made involving a legislator and an employee," Naifeh said in a prepared statement. "On the advice of our attorneys, I will await the report on the findings of the investigation before commenting further on this matter."

The official complaint was submitted last Monday to Connie Frederick, legislative personnel director, who then reported it to Naifeh. Fredcrick said she will give Naifeh her personal opinion on the findings only if he requests it.

Rep. Carol Chumney, D-Memphis, initiated adoption of the sexual harassment policy in 1993 and says she has "the utmost confidence in the Speaker of the House and his ability to handle the issue appropriately and apply the policy."

Under the policy, Naifeh can choose to give an oral or written reprimand to a legislator who violates the policy, or he can refer it to committee. It would take a two-thirds vote of the House to actually expel a member.

A legislative employee could face reprimand or termination if found to be in violation of the sexual harassment policy.

"I think the reason we passed the policy in the Legislature is because all businesses and governmental bodies today have them," Chumney said. "So when questions or problems arrive there is a set procedure that can be followed to help make sure all the rights are protected in evaluating the allegations.

"I think the whole process of passing that legislation was awareness training," Chumney said. "We discussed the issues, and information was distributed to legislators. This was about evaluating our responsibilities in our own offices and the way we conduct our business. I really have had no contact with the allegations so, really, I have no idea what's happening in that process.

"I really have no reason to know about that at this point," Chumney said. "It's really not appropriate for legislators to comment on that at this point."

This is the first time the Tennessee Legislature has had to deal with such a complaint.

Once Naifeh reviews Frederick's findings he will decide whether the charges are valid and whether they are serious enough to warrant further scrutiny by the House Ethics Committee. The committee could recommend expulsion of the member by the full House, but so far members of the body are treading lightly on the subject and refuse to discuss it on the record.

The policy itself states that sexual harassment is the violation of Title VII of the Civil Rights Act of 1964 and that it is against the policy of the Tennessee General Assembly for any employee, male or female, to sexually harass another employee by:

- Making unwelcome sexual advances or requests for sexual favors or other verbal or physical conduct of a sexual nature as a condition of employment or continued employment.
- Making submission to or rejections of such conduct the basis for administrative decisions affecting employment.
- Creating an intimidating, hostile or offensive working environment by such conduct.

After the News Column

When to use anonymous sources a judgment call

By Richard A. Pride

In standard American journalism, all the information in a news story is supposed to be attributed to some specific source, either by direct quotation or paraphrase, but sometimes no one will talk on the record.

When that happens, reporters and editors have to decide whether to publish anyway, citing only confidential sources—as in "sources close to the investigation say"—or wait and risk either losing the story to another paper or letting some misdeed go unpublicized and possibly unredeemed.

That kind of decision arose recently.

People at the state capitol told reporters that a woman had filed a sexual harassment complaint against a state legislator, but none of them would say so publicly. I can see why.

Under sexual harassment policy adopted in 1993 by the legislature, complaints were to be handled in a confidential manner. The records were sealed, and anyone associated with the legislature who was directly quoted in a newspaper would be breaking that policy.

Nevertheless, there are very few secrets on capitol hill, and before long, everyone knew the particulars, including that the woman had taped an encounter.

The *Tennessean's* capitol hill reporters had a story ready to go, citing unnamed sources, but after the issues were discussed among reporters and editors, the story was held.

Issues of fairness, legal liability, competition, and the people's right to know were raised in many newsrooms that week. If they published a story without the names, then the behavior of many male legislators would be wrongfully put into question. If they published the allegation with the name of the legislator, again citing only unnamed sources, the allegations might be found to be false and the paper would have jeopardized the reputation and career of a guiltless man. If they did not publish at all and were beaten by another paper, the decision they finally decided upon, then they would have lost a round in the competitive struggle. But if no one published the story, newspapers would be letting the legislature set the news' agenda.

Over the weekend, newspapers in Knoxville and Memphis (in east and west Tennessee) ran stories about the complaint, citing unnamed sources and without using the names of the secretary or the legislator involved. Nashville and middle Tennessee were still not told of the allegations. After that, Kriste Goad, a *Nashville Banner* capitol hill reporter, wanted to publish all the particulars, citing only confidential sources, but her editor would not let her print the name, only the gist of the story. All that *Banner* readers learned that day from Goad's story was that an unnamed state legislator was alleged to have sexually harassed his secretary.

At six o'clock that same evening, though, citing anonymous sources, both the local Associated Press (AP) bureau and Jim Travis, reporter for Channel

Four, named Representative Joe Bell in their accounts. With AP leading the way, local newspapers followed.

In the world of competitive journalism, being first is a large part of being best, and by the time reporter Goad got the names into the *Banner* the next day, everybody, including the *Tennessean*, already had the story out. Goad was miffed when she was not backed up by her editors, but she stayed with the unfolding story and later got the accuser to talk on the record when other reporters could not.

AP bureau chief Kent Flanagan said he uses the following three criteria when deciding whether to publish based only on confidential sources: (1) when his reporters have tried and failed to get the information from all valid and identifiable sources; (2) when both he and the reporter are convinced that a source is both knowledgeable and reliable, usually when there has been a relationship of trust established between the source and the reporter; and (3) when he has come to respect the judgment of the reporter. All three criteria were met when AP moved the sexual harassment story.

Channel Four's Jim Travis told me he felt he had enough certainty to put out the name when he found Representative Bell meeting with his attorney in his locked office just after Speaker Naifeh had announced at a press conference that the accused legislator was meeting with his lawyer.

Arcane journalistic decisions are interesting, but what is the public's interest in all this? The answer is clear, or should be: Journalism is not mechanical, it is about making judgments.

A free flow of information makes self-government possible, but it is constrained by law, elemental fairness, and a competitive instinct.

SUMMARY

Many Americans are disenchanted with both government and news media, and they have reason to be. Too often people are simply treated as objects to be shuffled around for some government program or news package. In a democratic culture, all sides need to have some of the power, and many people now feel powerless and excluded from the real action.

Citizenship means active participation in meaningful public debate, and we have lost or destroyed the institutions that made that possible. Too often today, potential citizens are reduced to voting in secret after a negative ad-driven political campaign. Potential citizens need the following two things if they are to grow into full citizenship: (1) knowledge of the way government and media interact, and (2) a place where they can encounter the views of other citizens. Internet newsgroups already offer some of this for those who venture into cyberspace, but those adventures need to be routinized if others are to make use of the new technology.

I argue that newsgroups embedded within electronic newspapers offer one important venue for active citizenship, especially since commentators there would be constrained by unfolding news stories. I believe that process could be immeasurably strengthened if newspapers employed media critics themselves to guide and teach. With embedded newsgroups, electronic newspapers could become a functional town square: news and views and criticism all together. It would be a venue more disciplined than talk radio, quicker than letters to the editor, and more informed than banter among friends.

REFERENCES

Combs, J. E., and D. Nimmo. (1993). *The new propaganda*. New York: Longman.
Commission on Freedom of the Press. (1947). *A free and responsible press*. Chicago: University of Chicago Press.
Epstein, E. J. (1974). Journalism and truth. *Commentary* (April): 36–40.
Fallows, J. (1975). What did you do in the class war, Daddy? *The Washington monthly* 7(8): 5.
Fallows, J. (1996). *Breaking the news: How the media undermine American democracy*. New York: Pantheon Books.
Goad, K. (1995). Secretary accuses lawmaker of harassment. *Nashville banner*, June 20.
Hocking, W. E. (1947). *Freedom of the press: A framework of principle*. Chicago: University of Chicago Press.
Hoyt, M. (1995). Are you now or will you ever be, a civic journalist? *Columbia journalism review* (September–October): 27.
Jamieson, K. H. (1992). *Dirty politics: Deception, distraction, and democracy*. New York: Oxford University Press.
Newman, H. (1995). Opryland recruiting expands to Ireland. *The Tennessean*, Nov. 21.
Novack, R. D. (1974). The new journalism. In *The mass media and modern democracy*, ed. H. Clor. Chicago: Rand McNally.
Patterson, T. E. (1993). *Out of order*. New York: Knopf.
Pride, R. A. (1995a). TV news often sheer melodrama. *Nashville Banner*. June 19, A-11.
Pride, R. A. (1995b). When to use anonymous sources a judgment call. *Nashville Banner*, August 8, A-5.
Pride, R. A. (1995c). Opryland employment story misses deeper issue. *Nashville Banner*, November 28, A-9.
Schaffer, J., and E. D. Miller. (1995). *Civic journalism: Six case studies*. Joint report by the Pew Center for Civic Journalism and the Poynter Institute for Media Studies. Washington, D.C.: Pew Center for Civic Journalism.
Siebert, F., T. Peterson, and W. Schramm. (1956). *Four theories of the press*. Urbana: University of Illinois Press.
Weaver, P. (1974). The new journalism and the old—thoughts after Watergate. *Public interest* (Spring): 66–68.

PART IV

REFLECTIONS

Chapter 10

On Discursive Amnesia: Reinventing the Possibilities for Democracy through Discursive Amnesty

Wen Shu Lee and Philip C. Wander

In the 1990s in the United States, attacks on racism, classism, sexism, homonegativity, religious fundamentalism, and cultural imperialism increasingly put words under surveillance. There are correct words and there are incorrect words. On a personal level, whatever the theoretical issues involved, this can be perplexing. Maivan Lam, a Vietnamese-American woman and a law professor at the State University of New York (SUNY), tells the story of an encounter with a good friend over the use of "girl" and "woman" (1994, p. 870).

Lam and her son flew into the Denver airport an hour apart from each other to enjoy Christmas together. Lam's plane was delayed. While waiting, her son struck up an acquaintance with a young woman. It turned out she was three years older than himself and she had a baby. In Vietnamese and American cultures, a single woman with a child, especially if she is older than the man, is considered undesirable. But Lam's son was really taken with her.

Surprised by this encounter of luck, Lam (1994) was pleased with her son's novel and progressive act of friendship. A few days later, to show him support, she asked her son if he wanted to invite the woman over for dinner, and he responded, "She's not a woman, Mom, she's only a girl." Lam explained that "woman" was a more appropriate term. But he made it very clear that he could not think of her as a woman, that his age set of guys simply dated "girls." This made sense to her, given his age and his culture, and they went on with their business.

Some days later, Lam recounted this story to a friend who had known and loved her son since he was a toddler. Her friend's response surprised her. "You have," she said curtly, "to go back and tell him that he must call her a woman. . . . Allowing him to call her a girl, and calling her so yourself, simply does not square with the rest of your politics." Lam wanted to share "the novelty and progressiveness" in her son's emotional life. She was proud of him. Her white, feminist friend focused on language and Lam's political lapse. They reached an impasse—the conversation broke off.

The "right" for a mature American female to demand that others to call her a "woman" rather than a "girl" grows out of a long, difficult struggle waged by feminists in the United States. The history includes sacrifice and hard work by tens of thousands of women, most of whom never wrote a book on the topic or taught in universities. At the same time, such a right often is unwittingly exercised by white, middle, and upper-middle class, professional women. For women of color[1] or Third World women[2] (not to mention poor and uneducated white women),[3] their struggle to be free and equal almost always involves other histories—systematic opposition to racism and international imperialism—which are often forgotten by privileged white men and white bourgeois feminists.

Lam was criticized for her suspension of a feminist discursive right. She understood the point. What outraged her was her friend's absolute "right" to set her straight in no uncertain terms. She did not feel respected. She felt like a stereotyped "other," a woman of color, a Third World woman. She felt nonwhite. "Empire, it is clear," Lam concluded, "intrudes even into important friendships" (1994, p. 873).

Words used by us today are histories themselves.[4] To get beyond the impasse now pejoratively dismissed in the name of "political correctness," we need to learn to inform each other out of our own *discursive amnesia*, a concept we choose to label a constituent element firmly built into human discourse—specific acts of collective forgetting that perpetuate privilege and interest in a particular economic and political context. Let us elaborate more on this concept, which, together with the notion of *discursive amnesty*, may help engender critical discursive habits among citizens and reinvent fruitful possibilities for democracy in a world mass mediated by uncritical and naturalized discourse.

ON AMNESIA

We as humans cannot remember everything we see, say, and encounter daily. Nonetheless, we are expected to have a reasonable, if not perfect, ability to remember. Amnesia, on the other hand, denotes an abnormal state in which a loss of memory (complete or partial) is caused by physical or psychical trauma. Amnesia may be anterograde, in which events following causative trauma or disease are forgotten. Amnesia may also be retrograde, a more common form shown in the media, in which events preceding the causative event are forgotten.

In contrast to a physical trauma such as a brain injury or some chemical reaction in which memories are erased, amnesia may have to do with psychoneurotic escape from or denial of memories that might cause anxiety. As such, they become symptoms of repression or motivated forgetting. The memories are not, in this instance, actually lost. They may be recovered through methods like hypnosis, but amnesia may last for weeks, even years. During this period, one may begin to lead a completely new life. This new life, because it has been wholly detached from what went on before, is called a *fugue* state. One lives contrapuntally but without being conscious of the two melodic lines.

ON AMNESTY

An etymologically related term, amnesty, is of interest in our discussion of amnesia. *Amnesty* literally means forgetfulness, oblivion, and intentional overlooking. In a political context, a sovereign act of oblivion is called an amnesty. This process is often initiated by an agency (e.g., Amnesty International, the Human Rights Watch) embracing an ideology different from that upheld by a political entity (e.g., apartheid South Africa) that names individuals' behaviors as offenses (e.g., Nelson Mandela's political organizing). An amnesty-seeking agency is neither geographically nor nationally defined. Rather, its existence falls outside of the contested regime's discursive practices. This outsideness denaturalizes the taken-for-granted discourse smoothly circulated in daily conversations, media reports, and instructions at schools.

Through concerted efforts of information gathering, fundraising, and international appeals, amnesty-seeking agents challenge official history. Thriving on unspoken and uncontested amnesia, official histories legitimize negative labeling of certain individuals. They are "rebels," "trouble makers," or "criminals."[5] They are something that takes away their names and their history. They are something that shuts them up. An amnesty campaign affirms and publicizes alternative histories. Not all such campaigns are successful. Not all individuals accused of committing crimes should be freed. But when a revisionist view gathers enough support, amnesty may be granted. In overlooking and forgetting offenses, former rebels, like Mandela, may begin to register in public memory as heroes and heroines.[6] Their "crimes" become the stuff school children are encouraged to emulate.

ON AMNESIA AND AMNESTY AS
DISCURSIVE METAPHORS

We use amnesia and amnesty as central metaphors in this chapter. We believe that remembering and forgetting form a duality. Like a person and his or her own shadow, they never part. We also believe that remembering and forgetting are constituent mechanisms of human discursive practices. Because we are interested in social, political, and historical effects generated by this duality through human discourse, we coin the terms *discursive amnesia* and *discursive amnesty*. We also associate them with their respective shadow dualities: discursive amnesia with continuist histories, and discursive amnesty with genealogical histories.

Discursive Amnesia and Continuist History

For us, *discursive amnesia* means the collective forgetting (or writing out of history) of people and events that may make us recall catastrophes collectively experienced (e.g., the Trail of Tears; the Chinese Exclusion Act; the stories of Nat Turner and Sojourner Truth; the Operation Wetback). Discursive amnesia refers to a group's inability or unwillingness to recall certain people, events, and offenses, even though they have been the subject of public discussion—either advocated or denounced—from time to time. Just as an individual's memories are a clue to (if not the definition of) identity, so a group identifies itself not only through what it publicly or officially recalls but also through what it systematically forgets. Discursive amnesia refers to much deeper levels of forgetting, levels far beyond the need of a censor, and levels created both positively through accretions of endorsed recollection (official histories) and negatively through lack of reward (underfunded histories).

Discursive amnesia leaves unchallenged its shadow duality—a collective remembering that constructs histories to be pure, homogeneous, and devoid of shifts and discontinuities. Working off Foucault's (1993) theoretical framework, Sawicki (1991) calls such a history, *continuist or functionalist history*: Not only do continuist histories tend to legitimate rather than criticize present practices, they also obscure the conflicts and struggles in history (p. 57). When conflicts and struggles are forgotten and erased, there is no need to question the names, labels, and wisdom written into the continuist history. To challenge such a tyranny, we need to turn to a discussion of discursive amnesty and genealogical history.

Discursive Amnesty and Genealogical History

Foucault's notion of subjugated knowledge is useful for our purposes here. But what knowledge is subjugated? Where do we look for them? How do we bring them into public awareness? Sawicki offers some clues.

"Subjugated knowledge" refers not only to historical contents that are obscured within functionalist histories but also to those forms of experience that fall below the level of scientificity. The latter include the low-ranking knowledge of the psychiatric patient, the hysteric, the midwife, the housewife, and the mother, to name only a few. Because these disqualified knowledges arise out of the experience of oppression, resurrecting them serves a critical function. Through the retrieval of subjugated knowledge, one establishes a historical knowledge of resistance and struggle. (1991, p. 57)

Resurrecting knowledge that is subjugated and disqualified is central to the act of discursive amnesty. It aims to promote a collective remembering that resurrects causes and events sealed into oblivion in the name of crime or political misconduct—insubordination, rebellion, revolution, or un-Americanism.

The remembering associated with discursive amnesty we call genealogical histories. Grounded in Foucault's work, genealogy is not a theory. Rather, it suggests a grid of analysis that radically facilitates "collective remembering" of the forgotten (Sawicki, 1991, p. 53). As a starting point, a genealogist identifies a discontinuity (or shift or change) in discursive practices. Discontinuities may embody multiple and mutable forms. A case in point is when names used to label a specific group of people change over time (e.g., from "girl" to "woman"; from "nigger" to "Negro" to "colored" to "black" to "Afro-American" to "African-American"; from "lady" or "fairy" to "homosexual" to "lesbian" or "gay" to "queer"). Other kinds of discontinuities may include mutable meanings associated with a name (e.g., "whites" to mean people of white skin nowadays, or "whites" to mean "privileged" Chinese in Mississippi after the Civil Rights Movement;[7] "Eurasian" to mean children born to parents of European and Asian descent or "Eurasian" to mean Jewish in a euphemistic manner).[8]

Obviously, our project, at one level, involves definitions. It historicizes controversial terms. Our aim is to fashion a language fit for collective deliberation. One part of this project involves a recovery of historical discourse—the way issues were articulated in our forgotten past. Many of the questions dividing us as a people today were debated in the eighteenth, nineteenth, and early-twentieth centuries. Most of us do not know about these debates or what they have to tell us in the here and now of our own confusions and struggles.

Another part of this project involves enriching and thickening our current political vocabulary.[9] This means recovering the forgotten sociopolitical contexts in which these terms once worked. One of the reasons public language is dead is that it assumes a kind of effortless continuity. It has been detached from and avoids struggle—the efforts of people in the past and in the present to create a better society. It becomes ceremonial utterance. Recovery will not and cannot guarantee clear, true, and rightly defined terms, but what it will give us is the sense of difference, conflict, and debate out of which we can begin to learn again how to talk in ways that enable us to understand one another.

In the following sections, we probe the discursive amnesia enveloping color-based terms (e.g., black, brown, red, white, and yellow) commonly used in the United States. These terms are central to our social and political life. Terkel (1992) calls them the *American obsession*. Historicizing color and race and recovering their transformations and the crises associated with them enables us to confront a stumbling block in American politics—the assumption that democratic ideals work to solve problems on their own.

What we have before us is not democracy but the possibility and the glory of acting democratically—of actually deliberating and acting as a people to solve problems and doing so in ways that respect inalienable rights; respect them in ways more consistent than our founding documents which accord them to humanity ("mankind") in one section and reserve them for land-owning, white males in another. Some people have struggled against this contradiction in the past but we have forgotten their efforts. Or worse, we now find such efforts impossible. Others have failed to act accordingly in the past, using color and race as the basis for exploitation and exclusion, and we have forgotten these acts. Or even worse, we have written them off as no longer relevant. Until we can talk about color, race, poverty, and our inner cities—the political space created for such people—with a keen sense of genealogical history, we will simply repeat the past and it will again become our future.

Discursive Amnesia in the Construction of "Hispanicity"

On November 7, 1994, Proposition 187, California's illegal alien control initiative (abbreviated as SOS—Save Our State), was passed by a ratio of 3 to 2 (59% voting for it and 41% against). Mass media noted differences in support of this measure: "Exit polls done for Associated Press found that the vote was split among ethnic and racial lines. Whites favored it 3–2, blacks were split evenly and Hispanics rejected it by 3–1" (McLaughlin, 1994, p. 1EL).

This information, at first glance, seems to be objective, neutral, and, hence, nonoffensive. We can just "consume" it and then go about doing our business as usual. But if we probe further by questioning the discursive amnesia built into its discourse of race and ethnicity, we begin to wonder, Who are whites, blacks, or Hispanics? If we also focus on who is forgotten in the report, the ghosts of Native Americans and Asians, women, and gays and lesbians leap out to haunt our exclusionary practice. Because "Hispanics" were the main target of Proposition 187, we will first turn to its discursive amnesia by reviewing Kaminsky's (1994) genealogical research on "Hispanicity."[10]

The word "Hispanidad" was first deployed by the Spanish empire (between 1492 and the mid- to late-nineteenth century) to manage its racialized crises. The first crisis had to do with Spain's imprecise and ill-defined racial origins (e.g., the influence of Moors, the majority of whom were black Muslims), and the second crisis was related to the racialized impurity exacerbated by the massive and diverse peoples conquered by the empire. The imperial invention of Hispanidad absorbed all of the peoples (black, brown, red, white, and yellow) under Spain's sphere of influence. However, it homogenized the conquered peoples with an imperial will of "patriarchal whitening" which reserved many privileges (e.g., the right to receive higher education) to nonslave males of white origins ruled by Spain.

Spain's loss of colonies gave rise to the postcolonial era in Spanish America in the early nineteenth century. This was characterized by heated nationalistic fervor which deployed Hispanidad to mark the difference between newly established, independent nations and their European colonizers. However, like its imperial predecessor, the postcolonial Hispanidad also carried with it a nationalistic will of patriarchal whitening. With the affirmation of European whiteness, which was often traced to white Spanish fathers, Hispanidad, upheld by the new order (mainly composed of racially mixed people), had to ostracize their mothers of Indian blood. "When he repudiates Malinche [his Indian mother who was raped by Cortes, a white Spanish man] . . . the Mexican breaks his ties with the past, renounces his origins, and enters history alone" (Kaminsky, 1994, p. 15).

In the United States, the word "American" shares the political functions performed by the imperial and nationalistic "Hispanidad." It is used to mark the difference between the United States and its former colonizers (British, French, and Dutch). It is also used to contrast the civilized and superior and the savage and inferior (e.g., Native Americans and women). "American" also wills a patriarchal whitening. At first, this will operated in the most blatant ways via slavery, denying naturalization rights to people of nonwhite origins and suffrage to men of color and all women. Then, after the Civil War, the Civil Rights Movement, women's suffrage movement, feminist movements, and movements for gay, lesbian, and bisexual rights, such a will, more or less, goes underground, but only to haunt our discourse in ever subtler and more sophisticated forms.

In an "American" context, the English word "Hispanic" has become "an adjective signifying a form of non-whiteness, a marker of difference with implications of inferiority" (p. 8). Operating with the differentiating function of white Americans versus others, Hispanic serves to homogenize vast gendered, sexual, religious, class-based, and national differences expediently absorbed into its semantic umbrella. This racialized homogeneity becomes a function of the U.S.'s whitening desire.

Ironically, Hispanidad, an imperial and nationalistic agent of whitening, feels diminished to find Hispanic, its relative in the United States, a browned inferior. Kaminsky renders this ironic reversal more personal. "Aurora Levins Morales describes the shock of 'white' Puerto Ricans from the island who come to the mainland and find they are 'brown.' . . . The Spanish language, or its residual mark, the accent, is a determinant, now marking the outsider instead of the insider" (1994, p. 21).

The genealogical histories of Hispanicity provided by Kaminsky confront the discursive amnesia embedded in the report of Proposition 187. The resurrected discontinuities in Hispanicity across cultural boundaries and over time destabilize the labeling of Hispanic people in our discourse. We do not suggest abandoning this term at once. Rather, we become aware of its own oppressions, complicities, and victimization in different historical moments. Especially, we have to ask ourselves, Without challenging a seemingly neutral use of Hispanics, do we tacitly perpetuate forces running counter to our professed democracy? To refine such a critical question without attempting hasty responses, we explore the discursive amnesia built into our contemporary construction of "whiteness."

Discursive Amnesia in the Construction of "Whiteness"

When asked, Who are whites? most people in the United States would suggest without hesitation that, pure British, French, German, Dutch, and Scandinavian Americans are whites. This biologically based response with an emphasis on racial purity requires a racialized terminology to name "white" people's "others": blacks, Hispanics, Native Americans, Asians, and people of mixed blood. Examining this, we note a few assumptions that pervade contemporary American discourse. One is that skin-based definition of color, however imprecise, is the rule. Another is that such a rule deciphers racial differences but does not endorse a racial caste system (i.e., we are different but equal). Drawing extensively on work done by Roediger (1991) and Harris (1993), we conclude that these rules are symptoms of discursive amnesia. This becomes evident when we recover the shifting historical links between "whiteness" and "interests" shaped by classical and modern definitions of "property."

The meaning of "whiteness" shifts historically, as does the meaning of "property." Three historical moments are crucial to our discussion here: (1) the legalization of slavery, (2) the abolition of slavery and the rise of Jim Crow, and (3) the outlawing of state-endorsed racial segregation. Let us turn to the first historical moment.

The term "white" preceded British settlement in this country. It was used to distinguish European settlers from two different groups, namely, Native Americans and Africans. Between 1607 and 1800, among the lower classes, racial lines were not unambiguously maintained (Harris, 1993, p. 1716). In fact, in the early period, the contrast between blacks and whites was not so onerous. This was because slavery in colonial America could be seen to include whites as well as blacks. Indentured servants were also transported to the colonies and sold at auction. Armed men led lines of manacled, lower class, English men, women, and children through the countryside selling them off one by one at farmhouses along the way. Captured Africans sold as slaves and unfree non-Christian white servants shared similar abject socioeconomic conditions. Those who could afford servants chose from among people of every skin color. The contrast then was not between white and nonwhite but between independent workers ("free") and slaves ("unfree").

The most severe form of slavery was "chattel" slavery. Chattel slavery in this country meant that workers could be bought and sold. They could be used as collateral in loans. They could not legally marry, swear out a complaint, or learn to read and write. Their children became the property of the master and could be sold away from their parents at any time. The first slave codes, which appeared between 1680 and 1682, marked a dire turn for black people, as seen in the following observations:

Blacks were not permitted to travel without permits, to own property, to assemble publicly, or to own weapons; nor were they to be educated. Racial identity was further merged with stratified social and legal status: "Black" racial identity marked who was subject to enslavement; "white" racial identity marked who was "free" or, at minimum, not a slave. The ideological and rhetorical move from "slave" and "free" to "Black" and "white" as polar constructs marked an important step in the social construction of race. (Harris, 1993, p. 1718)

The comparison at the beginning of the nineteenth century was between "free" workers and "slaves," but faced with chattel slavery grounded in race, workers in the North reasoned that, since Blacks were slaves, maybe they were not fit to be free. Black people lacked the strength, virtue, and resolve that guarded them from enslavement and that made them a threat to the Republic.

White hirelings worked long hours (sometimes twelve to sixteen hours a day, six or seven days a week), performed mind-numbing and often dangerous tasks, had to be punctual, and in some cases had to submit to beatings by their bosses. Miners never saw the light of day. Children lost their fingers separating slag from coal on conveyor belts. If a worker lost an arm or a leg in the machinery, and this was not uncommon, he might be allowed to beg in front of the factory gates. There was no workmen's compensation, no guaranteed medical care, and no right to sue. This misery was sometimes denounced as "white slavery," but the indictment drew a sharp line between black and white slavery.

Legalized slavery changed the meaning of "property." A human being, because of his or her race, became permanently commodified. Black (human) as property was especially pronounced in the case of "blackwomen" (treated as one word to emphasize dual oppressions because of race and gender). Despite his democratic sympathies, Thomas Jefferson was still a man of property. He was able to calculate the difference between profit and loss. "I consider the labor of breeding [Negro] women," he wrote in one of his letters, "as no object, and that a child raised every 2 years is of more profit than the crop of the best laboring [Negro] man" (Harris, 1993, p. 1720). The link between whiteness and property in Jefferson's letter and in that historical moment meant that "white identity and whiteness were sources of privilege [for wealthy whites] and protection [for poor whites]; their absence meant being the object of property" (p. 1721).

The consolidation of whiteness and property also enabled early white settlers to plunder Indian land.[11] This had to do with the meaning of land possession. Indians roamed. They left their land in its natural state. However, this definition of possession was interpreted as nonuse, or "waste," in establishing the white settlers' first possession rule. Accompanying this racialized land usurpation was anti-Indian thought, which, Roediger argues in the following, played a big role in the formation of American racial Anglo-Saxonism, or the notion of white superiority:

The images developed by colonists to rationalize dispossession of Native Americans from the land had a strong connection to work and to discipline. Settler ideology held that improvident, sexually abandoned "lazy Indians" were failing to "husband" or "subdue" the resources God has provided and thus should forfeit those resources. Work and whiteness joined in the arguments for dispossession. Settlers, whether or not they worked harder or more steadily than Native Americans, came to consider themselves "hardworking whites" in counterpoint to their imagination of Indian styles of life. (1991, p. 21)

Racialized slavery (only black people were to be enslaved) and racialized land usurpation (Indians did not, could not, and therefore, should not own land) placed whiteness atop a legalized hierarchy. Whiteness marked the ability to own property (both slaves and land) or, as a consolation for propertyless white people, the right not to be treated as savages. This meant, at the very least, the right to own property in the future, the right to enter into contracts, the right to marry, and the right not to have one's children sold. This was thought to be a great advantage at the time.

We have recovered some subjugated knowledge related to whiteness. It was not God-given whiteness. It was constructed. We learned that property was intimately associated with the construction of whiteness; white workers, black slaves, and landless Indians, if the racial line had not been drawn along the property line, could have formed more effective coalitions against economic exploitation by wealthy elites. Denied the privileges enjoyed by the ruling class, white workers' identity as "not slaves" and "not blacks" deflected their attention from the unbearable nature of their own position in an economic caste system (Harris, 1993, p. 1742). Race riots in the north against blacks and the plight of Irish immigrants in the nineteenth century evidence this racialized deflection of class exploitation.

Race Riots against Blacks

By 1805, black Philadelphians were driven out of Independence Day celebrations. Roediger (1991) sketches a genealogical history of attacks on free blacks in the north. This includes gangs of people (made up of young, white, working class males) in blackface who celebrated Christmas by beating up black people, white people in Boston who made a game of running black people off the Commons, and a riot in New York in 1863 (a draft riot) in which blacks were hanged from the lampposts, cut down, and their bodies stripped and sexually mutilated. Race riots, black pogroms, and lynchings have largely been forgotten and, if remembered, used to congratulate our progress.

But what caused these? One explanation for the terrorizing of free black people from 1800 to 1860 in the United States lies in rapid industrialization. Industrialization brought with it a new culture. In contrast to Jefferson's small, independent farmer, free to stand up to tyrants, hirelings (people who worked for a salary) took their orders from a master. In this there was not much to differentiate them from slaves (the Dutch word "boss," introduced in the 1830s, took the place of "master" which was too closely associated with chattel slavery).

The Plight of Irish Immigrants

People at the time still clung to a distinction between white and black slavery. This was an especially serious matter for poverty-stricken immigrants. Millions of immigrants came to work in the factories and mines and on the railroads in the nineteenth century. Among the most wretched were Irish Catholics fleeing the potato famine. Between 1845 and 1855, two million came. Among those who stayed in Ireland, a million or more died of starvation and related diseases. Given these conditions, it might be thought that the Irish were welcomed. Leaving their families, their loved ones not knowing whether they would live or die, they came to America to create a better life, to send money back home, and perhaps to bring their families over or even to return, as many immigrants did, a wealthy man or woman.

"White" nativists in the 1850s in this country scorned the Irish. They argued that they were inferior to blacks. If not inferior, they were a great deal like them. "Ape like," "simians," and "niggers turned inside out," the Irish were reviled in both England and America. In 1885, an English physician, John Beddoe, produced an "index of nigrescence" to determine a people's racial components. He concluded that "the Irish were darker than the people of eastern and central England, and were closer to the aborigines of the British Isles, who in turn had traces of 'negro' ancestry in their appearances. The British upper classes also regarded their own working class as almost a race apart, and claimed that they had darker skin and hair than themselves" (Pieterse, 1995, p. 25).

Our amnesia about all this is profound. One of the authors studied nineteenth-century arguments over slavery (Wander, 1968; 1971; 1972) and he did not know that gangs of Irishmen worked on plantations in the south, draining swamps, clearing fields, and doing work. The masters, Roediger (1991) tells us, reasoned that such work was too dangerous for their "valuable" slaves. If a slave died, the financial loss might approach two-thousand dollars, depending on the age, sex, and condition of the slave and, of course, the market price. But if a "Paddy" (Irish person) died, what difference did that make? In 1829, blacks and Irish were covictims in a Boston race riot.

We do not even remember the Irish Catholics who opposed slavery, and there were many, especially in Ireland, where people felt they had been enslaved by the British. Frederick Douglass, the famous black abolitionist, remarked on the relative absence of racism and a sympathy for slaves in Ireland.

In 1842, 70,000 Irish in Ireland signed an antislavery address and petition that called on Irish Americans to "cling by the abolitionists" in seeking not just the end of slavery but of racial discrimination as well. The address advised the following: "Irishmen and Irishwomen! treat the colored people as your equals, as brethren" (Roediger, 1991, p. 134). The sponsor of this petition, the great Irish liberator, Daniel O'Connell, knew that it would alienate some Irish Americans and cut into financial contributions flowing from the United States, but he plunged ahead anyway, secure in his belief that the antislavery principle would serve both Irish Americans and African-Americans. William Lloyd Garrison, Wendell Phillips, and John A. Collins organized a meeting at Faneuil

Hall in Boston to receive the petition and, Roediger remarks, to pass petitions for black and Irish freedom (p. 135). Five thousand people attended, but the initiative proved a failure, with many Irish Americans eventually denouncing O'Connell as an outsider and a meddler.

For Irish Americans, the struggle was less against slavery and more for distinguishing themselves from blacks. Many Irish Americans fought to become "white" and, further, to preserve whiteness as evidence of racial superiority and property rights due to such a race. Before the Civil War in this country, Irish immigrants had been welcomed into the American Catholic Church and the Democratic party, both of which were on record in support of southern slavery, white supremacy, and in opposition to any form of amalgamation.

After the war, many Irish Americans continued their efforts to differentiate themselves from blacks and to include themselves under the ideological umbrella called "white workers." This struggle grew more desperate as hundreds of thousands of freed slaves began competing for unskilled jobs in northern cities. Out west, the Irish had to compete with immigrant Chinese.

The making of the Irish worker into a white worker was thus a two sided process. On the one hand . . . Irish immigrants won acceptance as whites among the larger American population. On the other hand, much to the chagrin of Frederick Douglass and Daniel O'Connell [the antislavery Irish leader], the Irish themselves came to insist on their own whiteness and on white supremacy. The success of the Irish in being recognized as white resulted largely from the political power of Irish and other immigrant voters. The imperative to define themselves as white came from the particular "public and psychological wages" whiteness offered to a desperate rural and often pre-industrial Irish population coming to labor in industrializing American cities. (Roediger, 1991, p. 137)

Roediger evidences the ideological consolidation of whiteness in this country through the mass popularity of minstrel shows (in which white people put on blackface and satirized both black people and the upper classes) and, later, at the turn of the twentieth century, the "coon songs." "The 'coon song' craze swept the nation, with individual racist songs selling as many as three million copies in sheet music. Probably the best known of the 'coon songs,' Ernest Hogan's 'All Coons Look Alike to Me,' bore a title that suggested how thoroughly dehumanizing racist stage stereotypes could be" (p. 98).

Summarizing the links between whiteness and property, we can say that two hundred years of legalized slavery meant that whiteness became "status-property" in a classical sense (Harris, 1993, p. 1745). The Irish case was especially poignant. While Daniel O'Connell fought to abolish racial hierarchy and challenge racialized class interests, many of his Irish

American fellows fought to consolidate whiteness as wages and as property. Let us now explore another link between whiteness and property in the second historical moment, that emerged after slavery.

After slavery, with the rise of Jim Crow (all the laws and practices that kept whites and Negroes apart), whiteness as property acquired a modern sense.[12] Through legalized segregation, blacks were denied job opportunities, access to public and private facilities, mobility in major areas, well-funded schools, and more. In this way, inequality between blacks and whites was ratified by law. Whether one was white or colored affected one's job prospects, social status, physical and economic mobility, and ability to marry and to receive education.[13] This was concealed by the rhetoric of "separate but equal."[14] Whiteness as property, in its modern sense, refers to the relative privileges guaranteed to whites over blacks, and its ability to deny discursively such a racialized parity.

With this in mind, let us turn to a third historical moment—one between desegregation and today. In 1954, the Supreme Court struck down the "separate but equal" rhetoric in *Brown v. Board of Education*. This case "condemned legalized race segregation in public schools as inherently unequal" (Harris, 1993, p. 1750). The end of segregation did not, of course, guarantee equality. Nor did it make any systematic effort to recompense peoples who had been disadvantaged socially, politically, and economically by a history of slavery and segregation.

This is important because the loss in material terms resulting from slavery and segregation cannot be wished or ordered away legally. How could one calculate such a loss? What would a court award one who was kidnapped, forced to work a lifetime, and had her child sold? What would a court award people who, by law, were to be kept illiterate, had all their lands stolen, and were not allowed to buy property? Add this up; calculate what families today were denied as their rightful inheritance based on those awards and factor in inflation and taxes, along with a compensatory success factor (potential earnings) that accompanies education, land, a fair wage, and real opportunities. However conservative our estimates, the total must be considerable.

Ending legal segregation was a great victory but it brought with it its own kind of amnesia. It could have, but did not, call for concrete political and economic actions to redress three hundred years of victimization, and this is a kind of forgetting. One may object that those were old crimes; there should be a statute of limitations. But the problem here is not unlike that associated with smoking. When a person, after thirty years of chain-smoking, announces that he or she is quitting, common sense tells us that he or she still has a long way to go. The announcement is hopeful, and we all applaud. But the difficulty lies in not lighting up again, and equally important, in treating medical problems caused by years of smoking (e.g., lung cancer) and inhaling second-hand smoke (e.g., asthma and heart problems). We cannot expect that accumulated losses owing to three hundred years of legalized "whiteness as property" can be overcome by declaring an end to segregation.

In fact, segregation did not end. Instead of redistributive (or rehabilitating) government actions, there appeared segregated real estate planning, discriminatory lending practices, white exodus from so-called polluted neighborhoods, and resistance to integrate (through terrorizing blacks). Four decades after desegregation was ordered by the federal government, another form of whiteness as property has emerged. "White privilege accorded as a legal right was rejected, but de facto white privilege not mandated by law remained unaddressed" (Harris, 1993, p. 1753).

Whiteness as property today is promoted less by law than by concrete daily practices. It has taken an informal existence. Challenged by teachers and scholars, abandoned by the courts, attacked by the federal government during the Kennedy and Johnson administrations, the superiority of the white race retreated into personal prejudice, local politics, and coded language. The assumption of superiority has been masked by remembering today that skin color is casteless. Skin color is no longer used by law to make one either a slave or a master, and skin color does not dictate whether one has the right to get on a certain train, go to a certain restaurant, and go to a specific type of school. We often mistake the abolition of slavery and segregation as racial neutrality and realized racial equality, which then paralyzes concrete distributive efforts (e.g., affirmative action and student aid). The legal, political, cultural, and social apparatus that worked over the years to allocate resources in ways favorable to "white" people has largely been forgotten, even though it continues to deliver the goods.

So much has this story been forgotten and so great is our collective amnesia that there are many "innocent" white males today who have come to believe, as their prospects have dwindled with downsizing and outsourcing, that they are the leading victims of discrimination. A color-blind and gender-blind society is an ideal that we want to and need to strive for. But such blindness should not be fought selectively. Who gets this job? and Who is granted financial aid? are just as important questions as Who is granted a home-equity loan? and Whose school is given enough funds to buy computers? We have three decades of affirmative action to help redistribute opportunities and social gains for men of minority status (suffering three hundred years of slavery and discrimination in the new world) and all women (suffering three hundred years of disenfranchisement, and in the case of minority women, a double oppression of three hundred years of slavery and discrimination). To urge an end to the affirmative action without addressing unequal lending practices and unequal pay is to mistake color and gender blindness (I no longer see it and do not support it) for color and gender equality (therefore, inequality no longer exists).

When times are hard and economic resources are shrinking, we ought to work even harder to create laws to combat poverty, to help the poor, regardless of their color, work to obtain a decent living, rather than to work to abolish the little redistributive programs we have going for ourselves. If we remain blind to the schism created by a racialized, gendered, and class-based hierarchy, albeit in informal or nondocumented social practices (e.g., bank lending practices, zoning, real estate practices, underfunded schools, unequal pay, and glass ceilings), we incapacitate ourselves. We can see, understand, or even remember the fact that white and nonwhite people together suffer from an economy that prospers in part through capital, not labor intensive, investment (e.g., investment in computer technology that eliminates even highly-skilled workers). Together, white and nonwhite, we are entering into a new, sociopolitical and economic structure that, unlike other industrialized nations, does not guarantee medical coverage or the transport of retirement benefits. It is, moreover, a structure that as yet shows no signs of guaranteeing jobs for anyone and everyone, white and nonwhite, who needs and wants to work.[15]

The point of our genealogical histories has not been to indict Irish people or white people in general as racist. Most of us are not racist in the classical sense. The Irish, Italian, German, Chinese, Native American, and African working class people have historically had to fight and scratch to make a living. This struggle now includes middle class engineers,[16] upper-middle class managers, and even older doctors and nurses, as they have become more the victims of downsizing, reorganizing, and subcontracting than the victims of affirmative action and welfare programs.

What cannot be denied, historically speaking, is that most economic, political, and social rules were established to maintain the interest of the wealthy. And when property and whiteness coincided, these rules were designed to maintain the superiority of the white race. Laws against miscegenation, and limiting the right to stake a claim, to purchase farmland, to vote in local elections, represent a system of privilege favoring "white" people. This story accounts for the disadvantage people of color still face in jobs, education, and income. It accounts for the psychological inclinations of those in a position to hire and fire. It also accounts for a tendency on the part of people of color, especially those who encountered the accumulated inequities (the hostile and uncaring looks, the miserable schools, and the drugs and violence as natural and inevitable), to question their own worth in a society that has bestowed and continues to bestow rewards on others.

What this account does not address sufficiently, the discursive amnesia that attends our recovery of the "crafting of white people," are the histories of white people who fought against whiteness—people like Daniel O'Connell, the Abolitionists, civil rights workers, and others who opposed the assertions of white superiority publicly and privately, who worked hand in hand with people of color to create a fairer, more equitable society, and who at times laid down their lives in this effort. It also downplays the efforts of people of color, such as Frederick Douglass, Harriet Tubman, Fannie Lou Hamer, the American Indian Movement (AIM), the United Farm Workers (UFW), and many others, to organize, to assert themselves, and to overcome the economic, social, political, and legal system designed to hold them back. Finally, it does not explore and document the tendency on the part of some white people and some people of color to identify the poor—the welfare recipient, the breeder, and the lazy, unwilling to work, dishonest, shifty street people—as the cause of so much economic insecurity in our time. Here, too, historical research uncovers the kind of discursive amnesia that obscures the links between whiteness and property.

SUMMARY

"Fueled by immigration and higher birth rates among Hispanic women, the United States is undergoing a profound demographic shift, and by the middle of the next century only about half of the population will be non-Hispanic whites, the Census Bureau predicted today" (Holmes, 1996, p. A8).

This appeared in the *New York Times*. It reflects a category scheme that goes back to the founding of the British colonies along the eastern seaboard. White people, unaware of the social, political, and economic benefits of whiteness over the years, are invited to look upon a shift in demographics projected by an authorized agency, the Census Bureau. Given our genealogical histories, this information can no longer be interpreted as an objective trend on racialized but equal populations in the United States. Rather, it warns white people—at least those who identify themselves as such—that they are somehow losing ground and that their vested interests, privileges, and right to exclude may be severely challenged in the near future.

Our ability to differentiate Hispanidad—a whitening marker of superiority in the old Spanish empire and postcolonial Spanish America—from Hispanic as a browned marker of homogenized inferiors in the United States helps crystallize the awkward and revealing term *non-Hispanic whites*. Hispanic Americans seem to have mustered enough power to create an uneasy feeling among "purer" whites that there is a need to draw a line between whites who are non-Hispanic and whites who are Hispanic. Maybe we can make up new terms. How about "non-black whites," or "non-Indian whites," or "non-Asian whites," or "non-black Americans"? We do not find such terms in the *Times*.

If it is all a matter of skin color in a color-blind society, why would white people be threatened by becoming a minority? Why would there be white people at all? What is at stake here—privilege, property, political control, and status? And who is responsible for this profound demographic shift? Nonwhite immigrants and Hispanic women? What of the Irish who were likened to blacks and denounced for their sexual habits in the nineteenth century? They are now safely white. They find their historic reincarnation in another group of ambiguous nonwhites, the Hispanics. Nonwhite breeders were once profitable, recalling Jefferson's letter, but now "breeder" refers to welfare mothers and inferior, or nonwhite, races who are on the verge of overwhelming "us" in "our" own country.

In a strange way, discursive amnesia plagues our mass media. People, whether black, brown, red, yellow, or white, are locked up in our inner cities with poor schools, few services, and no jobs. They are rarely shown as walled up in politically constructed spaces (films such as *Do the Right Thing* in 1989 and *Hoop Dreams* in 1994 are rare exceptions).[17] Too often, inner-city dwellers are portrayed as violent criminals or the victims of criminals (in films from *Taxi Driver* in 1976 to *New Jack City* in 1991 to *American Me* in 1992).[18] The histories we need—histories of past debates over issues relevant to us and histories of words that we take for granted in what is left of our public space—do not make the news. They rarely appear on prime-time television, though they enter into some documentaries, and sometimes they are dramatized on film (the film *Dead Man Walking* from 1995 plays out these issues with white criminals in rural America). To make sense of this and deal with the problems, we will have to confront the amnesia in our mass media and grant amnesty to these inner city dwellers from the thousands of crimes we see them committing twenty-four hours a day on film and television.[19]

Resurrecting subjugated knowledge (whiteness as property; Hispanicity as an ever-shifting term associated with the Spanish and American empires; blackness as a term designating people who could be bought and sold and kept in their place formally, then, and informally, now; Indianness as a term for people who could have their land stolen and their treaties ignored; and Asianness as a shifting term to signify individuals ranging from the ignorant "coolies" who built the railroads in the West to the high-tech, straight-A engineers who work in the Silicon Valley), perhaps we can learn to exercise our discursive amnesty by actively remembering genealogical histories. This means that "crimes" attributed to Hispanics, blacks, Native Americans, and Asians as groups or classes of people be set aside. This also means that "crimes" attributed to white people (in contrast to whiteness, which is about privilege) be set aside. Amnesty gives us a space in which to entertain alternatives that go beyond official rhetoric, naturalized ideologies, and everyday language.

We search for ways to revitalize our public space and to fashion a language fit for deliberating public issues. An option offered in this chapter lies in confronting our collective amnesia through histories that, instead of dividing the world into good and evil, make amnesty-seeking efforts plausible. In this effort, we begin to recover our critical ability to use naturalized vocabulary in ways that leave space for people of all colors (remembering that white is also a color) to live, work, and struggle for ideals together. Lam is quite right:

> Words may not be magic,
> but they most certainly are history,
> which in turn is the only light that we have
> to train on the future. (1994, p. 880)

If this effort includes many and not just the few—the wealthy, well educated, and the privileged, it may take us beyond the impasse maintained by the rhetoric of political correctness, both on the left and on the right, regardless of race and gender. Moving beyond these dualities, we may as a people once again organize ourselves to build a future. Through discursive amnesty, we can reinvent the possibilities of and for democracy in the United States.

NOTES

1. For a discussion on the thesis that gendered oppression may be shared but is never identical among women of different race, class, and sexual orientation, see hooks (1981; 1984), Moraga and Anzaldua (1981), Sievers (1989), duCille (1994), Canning (1994), and Butler (1991).

2. For ways that Western women were colonized by their gender but acted to support the cause of their colonizing countries, see Afary (1989), Burton (1991), Chaudhuri and Strobel (1992), Lee (1997), and Mohanty, Russo, and Torres (1991).

3. This unmentioned class of people is easy to forget in a story about a conflict between two professional, politically aware women.

4. For a more detailed discussion regarding discourse and history, see Foucault (1993, pp. 126–131).

5. The conflict over terms—the difference for example between being convicted criminals and prisoners of war—is dramatized in the 1996 film, *Some Mother's Son*, based on the hunger strike of the Irish Republican Army members in the British prison in 1981.

6. We acknowledge that the discursive effects of amnesty-seeking campaigns are not total. They may open up discursive shifts to demand funda-

mental changes in a political entity; they may wage a revolution and subvert a regime; and they may also be co-opted as exceptions and then be erased from history. For this latter possibility, see Kaminsky's (1994) discussion of erasure in terms of granting privileges to racial and gendered transgressions declared as exceptions (p. 10).

7. For a detailed discussion of treating privileged Chinese as whites, see Loewen (1988). C. W. Sidney, a Chinese in Mississippi, changed his name from Sit to Sidney. However, the Rotary Club still barred his membership in the late 1960s. This was changed in the early 1980s. "When the Civil Rights Movement made whites feel guilty about their racism, they accepted Chinese, as if to say 'I'm not a racist, it is just blacks who are the problem'" (p. 195).

8. This 1940s usage appears in McCarthy (1992, p. 14).

9. This project recalls the analysis of equality in Condit and Lucaites (1993).

10. Kaminsky (1994) labels her method as "a comparative, gender-conscious approach to examine configurations of race" (p. 7). However, given her emphasis on discontinuities obliterated by the official naming process in the United States, we regard it as a superb piece of scholarship challenging the discursive amnesia in North Americans' use of the term *Hispanics*.

11. The Supreme Court, under Chief Justice Marshall, tried to moderate this theft (Frickey, 1993).

12. According to Harris (1993), a classical definition of *property* denotes "everything that is valued and to which a person has a right." She uses Reich's work to advance a modern concept of property, defined as "jobs, entitlements, occupational licenses, contracts, subsidies, and indeed a whole host of intangibles that are the product of labor, time, and creativity, such as intellectual property, business goodwill, and enhanced earning potential from graduate degrees" (p. 1728). It also focuses on the relative relations as defined by a particular definition of property.

13. What prevailed was the "one-drop" rule or, in anthropological terms, the "hypo-descent" rule, which means a single drop of blood from an inferior or subordinate race would make a person belong to the inferior or subordinate race (Harris, 1993, p. 1740).

14. See the discussion of the famous case *Plessy v. Ferguson* in 1896 (Harris, 1993, pp. 1746–1750).

15. President Clinton, having removed much of the welfare safety net, has been wheedling corporations to hire people off the roles. This will not provide enough jobs either for them or for those losing their jobs to outsourcing and downsizing.

16. We recently ran into two family friends at a Christmas concert. They were wife and husband, both white, middle aged, and middle class. The wife was in the process of getting a therapist license. But the husband, a computer engineer, told us a terrible story. On the day he received a twenty-five-year service award from his company, he was told to pack his bags because of reorganizing.

17. For the connection between these constructed spaces and racism, see Ford (1994).

18. The crime-action drama in the big city is a genre, but there are others that explore love affairs (*Crossing Delancy* in 1988) and character and relation-

ships (*A Bronx Tale* in 1993, *Smoke* in 1995, and *Blue in the Face* in 1995). Compare the perspective of these last two films starring Harvey Keitel with his character in *Bad Lieutenant* in 1992.

19. Studying the people who commit crimes in the media, we note that in the 1920s and 1930s, Irish American criminals flourished. From the 1930s through to the 1970s, Italian Americans emerged. Most recently, African and Hispanic Americans predominate.

REFERENCES

Afary, J. (1989). Comment: Some reflections on third world feminist historiography. *Journal of women's history* 1: 147–152.

Burton, A. (1991). The feminist quest for identity: British imperial suffragism and "global sisterhood," 1900–1915. *Journal of women's history* 3: 46–81.

Butler, J. (1991). Imitation and gender insubordination. In *Inside/out: Lesbian theories, gay theories*, ed. D. Fuss. New York: Routledge.

Canning, K. (1994). Feminist history after the linguistic turn: Historicizing discourse and experience. *Signs: Journal of women in culture and society* 19: 368–404.

Chaudhuri, N., and M. Strobel. (Eds.). (1992). *Western women and imperialism: Complicity and resistance*. Bloomington: Indiana University Press.

Condit, C., and J. Lucaites. (1993). *Crafting equality: America's Anglo-African world*. Chicago: University of Chicago Press.

duCille, A. (1994). The occult of true black womanhood: Critical demeanor and black feminist studies. *Signs: Journal of women in culture and society* 19: 591–629.

Ford, R. T. (1994). The boundaries of race: Political geography in legal analysis. *Harvard law review* 107: 1841–1921.

Foucault, M. (1993). *The archaeology of knowledge and the discourse on language*. New York: Barnes and Noble.

Frickey, P. P. (1993). Marshaling past and present: Colonialism, constitutionalism, and interpretation in federal Indian law. *Harvard law review* 107: 381–440.

Harris, C. I. (1993). Whiteness as property. *Harvard law review* 106: 1707–1791.

Holmes, S. A. (1996). Census sees a profound ethnic shift in U.S., by 50, non-Hispanic whites will decline to a slim majority. *New York Times*, March 14, p. A8.

hooks, bell. (1981). *Ain't I a woman?* Boston: South End Press.

hooks, bell. (1984). *Feminist theory: From margin to center*. Boston: South End Press.

Kaminsky, A. (1994). Gender, race, Raza. *Feminist studies* 20: 7–32.

Lam, M. C. (1994). Feeling foreign in feminism. *Signs: Journal of women in culture and society* 19: 865–893.

Lee, W. S. (1997). Patriotic breeders or colonized converts: A postcolonial feminist approach to anti-footbinding discourse in China. *International and international communication annual*. In press.

Loewen, J. W. (1988). *The Mississippi Chinese: Between black and white*. 2nd ed. Prospect Heights, Ill.: Waveland Press.

McCarthy, M. (1992). *Intellectual memoirs: New York 1936–1938*. New York: Harcourt, Brace & Jovanovich.

McLaughlin, K. (1994). Prop 187, immigration battle will move to courts after splitting state along ethnic lines. *The Mercury News*, November 9, pp. 1EL, 18EL.

Mohanty, C. T., A. Russo, and L. Torres. (Eds.). (1991). *Third World women and the politics of feminism*. Bloomington: Indiana University Press.

Moraga, C., and G. Anzaldua. (Eds.). (1981). *This bridge called my back*. New York: Kitchen Table, Women of Color Press.

Pieterse, J. N. (1995). White negroes. In *Gender, race and class in media*, ed. G. Dines and J. M. Humez. Thousand Oaks, Calif.: Sage.

Roediger, D. R. (1991). *The wages of whiteness: Race and the making of the American working class*. New York: Verso.

Sawicki, J. (1991). *Disciplining Foucault: Feminism, power, and the body*. New York: Routledge.

Sievers, S. (1989). Dialogue: Six (or more) feminists in search of a historian. *Journal of women's history* 1: 134–146.

Terkel, S. (1992). *Race: How blacks and whites think and feel about the American obsession*. New York: The New Press.

Wander, P. C. (1968). The image of the Negro in three movements: Abolitionist, colonizationist, and pro-slavery. Ph.D. dissertation, University of Pittsburgh.

Wander, P. C. (1971). Salvation through separation: The image of the Negro in the American Colonization Society. *Quarterly journal of speech* 57: 57–67.

Wander, P. C. (1972). The savage child: The image of the Negro in the pro-slavery movement. *Southern journal of communication* 37: 335–360.

Chapter 11

The Search for Intimacy
in American Politics

Roderick P. Hart

In light of contemporary mediated politics, Harry Truman surely seems an albatross. Blessedly, his presidency was spared today's electronic scrutinies, which allowed Truman to conduct himself rather nakedly. This is important because Harry Truman was, as they say, colorful. His brusqueness and witticisms are legendary, as was his salty but functional use of the English language. The reporters of his day carefully edited this private Truman; thus, colloquialisms that might have seemed tatty in one circumstance seemed merely quaint after having been massaged by the press prior to deadline. Somehow, the republic managed to survive these suppressions.

Things are different today. In an era of sound bites and computer-generated campaign ads, of "60 Minutes" exposés and salacious Supreme Court hearings, and in an age in which citizens know as much about the president's liaisons as they do about those of a rock star, a fellow like Truman is surely a man in a plain brown suit. To our ears, Truman's following theory of mass persuasion sounds inane: "[When speaking] I just stood there and I didn't have to make any fancy speeches or put on any powder or paint. I just told people the facts, and the people believed me" (Miller, 1973, p. 145). During his own times, however, few could resist his clarities.

On American enterprise, Truman said, "Business was never so productive, vital, and energetic as it is today. All this talk about weakening private enterprise is sheer political bunk" (Truman, 1950a, p. 497).

On the Korean conflict, Truman said, "There is no intention of running out on the obligation we undertook to support the principles of the Charter. We made our decision, it was the right decision, and we are going to follow it out—and that is that" (Truman, 1950b, p. 35).

On Texans who voted for Nixon, Truman said, "They ought to go to hell" (Cochran, 1973, p. 226).

Nuance was not Truman's strength, largely because he so sharply distinguished between his private and public selves. With no apparent need for prime-time purgation, Truman declined to show the nation his surgical scars, as did Lyndon Johnson, or to describe his underwear to a teenage audience, as did Bill Clinton. Truman did not sit with his arm around his wife in front of a roaring fire, as did Jimmy Carter, and he did not weep in public about his parents, as did Richard Nixon. Truman did not grant interviews with the press while sitting on a chair lift in Vail, Colorado, as did Gerald Ford, and he did not chop wood in his undershirt, as did Ronald Reagan. But Harry Truman never forgot the following principle that his successors never managed to learn:

You see the thing you have to remember. When you get to be president, there are all those things, the honors, the twenty-one gun salutes, all those things, you have to remember it isn't for you. It's for the Presidency, and you've got to keep yourself separate from that in your mind. If you can't keep the two separate, yourself and the Presidency, you're in all kinds of trouble. (Miller, 1973, p. 288)

This chapter examines why Truman's model of the presidency, and of politics in general, no longer fits our experience. It argues that the American people are on a generalized quest for intimacy and that they have extended their search into the political realm. This quest is an odd thing and, I shall argue, a dangerous thing. When a nation attempts to refashion political life into something it is not, nor never can be, it deludes itself and, worse, it shortchanges its political vision. Democratic politics is a great and wonderful thing, and so, too, is television. But in the American experience, they have not been good for one another. I shall try to explain why.

THE RICHMOND DISCLOSURES

The 1992 presidential campaign brought forth changes in media formatting that have continued apace during the 1996 campaign. The 1992 campaign found the candidates on both morning and evening chat shows, often with coffee in hand and sprightly chatter at the ready. They performed these feats on both network and cable programs and one of them even played the saxophone on late-night television. Some commentators praised these proletarian activities—returning government to the people, and all of that—but what it really did was cordon off the working press. Puckish though he was, Arsenio Hall could not conduct a political interview in the style of Mike Wallace.

The 1996 campaign continued the trend. The magnificently dour Robert Dole of Kansas found himself on a bus trip with the inveterate MTV reporter, Tabitha Soren, who probed the candidate's soul for his knowledge of rock music. Dole flunked the interview, and his failure called to mind a telling exchange four years earlier when the three presidential candidates were asked (in a "citizens debate" in Richmond, Virginia, on October 15, 1992) what their personal experience had been with economic adversity. During that exchange, Ross Perot got a "B," Bill Clinton got an "A," and George Bush got an "F minus." The debate segment began as follows:

CITIZEN: How has the national debt personally affected each of your lives? And if it hasn't, how can you honestly find a cure for the economic problems of the common people if you have no experience in what's ailing them?

Ross Perot leaped at the chance to answer the question and immediately ventured into the interiorities of his age by offering the following:

PEROT: Believe me, if you knew my family and if you knew the private life I have, you would agree in a minute that that's a whole lot more fun than getting involved in politics. But I have lived the American dream. I came from very modest background. Nobody's been luckier than I've been, all the way across the spectrum, and the greatest riches of all are my wife and children. That's true of any family. But I want all children—I want these young people up here to be able to start with nothing but an idea like I did and build a business. But they've got to have a strong basic economy and if you're in debt, it's like having a ball and chain around you. I just figure, as lucky as I've been, I owe it to them and I owe it to the future generations and on a very personal basis, I owe it to my children and grandchildren.

Being far more skilled at such matters, Clinton fashioned his answer from equal parts heart and head, carefully dovetailing his personal experiences with his oft-stated campaign themes which were, by this time, well-honed. He replied as follows:

CLINTON: I see people in my state, middle-class people—their taxes have gone up in Washington and their services have gone down while the wealthy have gotten tax cuts. I have seen what's happened in this last four years when—in my state—people lose their jobs, there's a good chance I'll know them by their names. When a factory closes, I know the people who ran it. When the businesses go bankrupt, I know them. And I've been out here for thirteen months meeting in meetings just like this ever since October, with people like you all over America, people who have lost their jobs, lost their livelihood, lost their health insurance. I think what we have to do is invest in American jobs, American education, control American health care costs, and bring the American people together again.

For his part, George Bush seemed completely baffled by the question and not a small amount irked by the questioner as well. He responded as follows:

BUSH: Well, I think the national debt affects everybody.

CITIZEN: You personally.

BUSH: Obviously it has a lot to do with interest rates.

MODERATOR: She's saying, "You personally." You, on a personal basis. How has it affected you? Has it affected you personally?

The initial exchange had not gone well. But George Bush was a trooper and so he continued:

BUSH: I'm sure it has [affected me]. I love my grandchildren.

CITIZEN: How?

BUSH: I want to think that they're going to be able to afford an education. I think that that's an important part of being a parent. If the question— maybe I—get it wrong. Are you suggesting that if somebody has means that the national debt doesn't affect them?

CITIZEN: What I'm saying is . . .

BUSH: I'm not sure I get—help me with the question and I'll try to answer it.

At this point, we are nine turns of speech into the exchange and Bush has still not answered the question. His problem seems not so much cognitive as cultural. The young woman asking the question was one with her times, her times being sociocentric and televisual. Raised on a diet of Phil Donahue and Oprah Winfrey revelations and of Larry King and Howard Stern therapies, she assumed that everyone on television— presidents of the United States included—has a soul to sell. Generously, she threw out a lifeline to the floundering chief executive by offering the following:

CITIZEN: Well, I've had friends that have been laid off from jobs.

BUSH: Yeah.

CITIZEN: I know people who cannot afford to pay the mortgage on their homes, their car payment. I have personal problems with the national debt. But how has it affected you, and if you have no experience in it, how can you help us, if you don't know what we're feeling?

Despite his interlocutor's helpfulness, Bush is clearly on another planet here. His chief offense was in not answering the question quickly; speed of disclosure is the key test of emotional credibility in the age of television. Also, unlike Bill Clinton (and even Ross Perot), Bush did not seem to understand the question itself and also seemed oblivious to the watchwords of the 1990s, namely, *authenticity, empathy, angst,* and *solidarity.* Bush compounded his problems when drawing a heretical distinction between a president's personal and institutional roles, as seen in the following:

BUSH: Well, listen, you ought to be in the White House for a day and hear what I hear and see what I see and read the mail I read and touch the people I touch from time to time. I was in the Lomax AME Church. It's a black church just outside of Washington, D.C., and I read in the bulletin about teenage pregnancies, about the difficulties that families are having to make ends meet. I talk to parents. I mean, you've got to care. Everybody cares if people aren't doing well.

Bush's attempt here is a game one: He uses a first-hand encounter with a second-hand reality to qualify himself as an existential pol. But in the argot of his time he failed to "get it," distinguishing as sharply as he did between a public and private presidency. He continued:

BUSH: But I don't think it's fair to say, "You haven't had cancer. Therefore, you don't know what's it like." I don't think it's fair to say, you know, whatever it is, that if you haven't been hit by it personally. But everybody's affected by the debt because of the tremendous interest that goes into paying on that debt everything's more expensive. Everything comes out of your pocket and my pocket. So it's that. But I think in terms of the recession, of course you feel it when you're president of the United States. And that's why I'm trying to do something about it by stimulating the exports, vesting more, better education systems.

The word *systems* is an appropriate one to end on here for it encapsulates the president's main shortcoming. Like Bush himself, the word *systems* is gray and lifeless, a term stained with the blood of bureaucrats and reeking of antiseptic. Bush was a *systems* man from the beginning of his career, and he treasured this persona. Yale University had taught him that systems are inevitable in a complex political state and that they are redolent of rules (to keep things fair) and orderliness (to make things possible). Systems have emerged because the United States is a technocratic nation and because it houses a bewilderingly diverse citizenry that delights in making persistent, often exotic, demands upon itself. Bush learned to trust systems because he was a capitalist to the core, as well as a fairly congenial pluralist. On television, however, systems-talk is dreadful.

TELEVISION'S AGENDA

The Richmond Debate (1992) is a synecdoche for all televised politics. Unlike traditional presidential debates, it was informal (because it
used ordinary citizens rather than members of the press) and largely
unscripted. Guests and audience members were physically proximate,
as they are on "Sally Jesse Raphael," and the candidates were given
only stools to perch on during the questioning. For their part, members of the press denounced the debate's vapid exchanges, claiming
that *the people incarnate* delivered only softball questions to the candidates. But television executives found superior production values in
the Richmond conversations and, as a result, few doubted that the 1996
campaign would reuse the format.

George Bush's poor performance is out of step with the last forty years
of American politics, an era in which politicians have increasingly tried to
dominate the people's emotional lives with their emotional lives. The
nation's media have helped them do so. Hart, Jerome, and McCombs
(1984) have shown, for example, that the president is almost always
the lead-off hitter on the nightly news, even if it has been a slow news
day—especially if it has been a slow news day. Jimmy Carter pounding
some nails, Ronald Reagan brushing his horse, and Bill Clinton jog-
ging in place outside McDonald's are now familiar images. They allow
us, ostensibly, to see the person behind the person, and they dovetail
with the point-and-shoot mentality of much electronic reporting. Admittedly, these scenes of domesticity are often overridden by a sono-
rous voice announcing the governmental things the president has done
that day via fax and phone, but the pictures—always the pictures—
linger in our heads, drawing the president closer and closer to us.

As I argue here, such intimacy comes at a price: When we become
familiar with a person in these day-in and day-out ways, we develop
the sorts of expectations that any intimate association promises. But
intimacy with a politician is a special sort of intimacy. Because it is
political, it is fractious, and because it is electronic, it is fragile. It is
intellectual intimacy, not affection-based intimacy. We come to know
politicians, not necessarily to like them. It is the sort of intimacy that
people who were once married still retain for one another, a deep knowledge that produces a knowing glance and a snarl simultaneously. Political intimacy is almost always a case of bait and switch. The politician
opens up his heart. We are drawn in. He or she then does something
craven or stupid, an inevitability in politics. We jump back, scorned
again. We declare the lot of them toxic waste. Then television brings us
a new, more vulnerable soul to probe. The soap opera continues.

Presidents, as a result, have become expert at speaking the language
of relationships. Miller and Stiles (1986), for example, tracked what
they called *verbal familiarity* in nomination speeches and inaugural ad-

dresses between 1921 and 1981. For Miller and Stiles, verbal familiarity emphasizes *you* talk as well as *I* talk, addresses experiential rather
than abstract matters, and avoids impersonal commands. Previous research had shown that married couples' verbal familiarity was much
higher than unmarried couples and that physicians sharply increased
their verbal familiarity when conducting intimate physical examina-
tions (vs. taking medical histories). As might be expected, given the
increased coverage the networks have devoted to political speechmaking over the years, verbal familiarity is now at an all-time high.

Intimacy, unfortunately, is a double-edged sword. The closer we get
to someone, the more pain we suffer when they hurt us. When Newt
Gingrich behaves like a prima donna, when Christy Todd Whitman
raises taxes for public education, or when Jesse Jackson sandbags Bill
Clinton, love can turn to loathing instantly. How dare such close friends
act like politicians? we reason. How can persons who have bared their
souls to us now behave like martinets? How can they woo us only to
rape us? Phrased this baldly, such reactions seem preposterous. But
television's intimacies, I argue, encourage just such overreactions. With
television, politics becomes melodrama and the following cycles set
in: charm begets adoration begets disappointment begets cynicism. The
extraordinary thing about all this is how resilient some voters are in
spite of it all—the senator from Alabama is caught with his hand in the
till but the new senator from California seems the genuine article. This
is television's morality play.

Jamieson (1988) has suggested that Ronald Reagan's personalized
style punctuated this growing trend toward intimacy, producing a femi-
nized presidency in which the language of relationships supplanted
the language of public policy. Hinckley (1990) has shown this to be
true even when presidents talk about the economy. She reports, for
example, that when delivering such addresses, presidents use substan-
tially more thinking and feeling verbs than action verbs. In other words,
presidents may not be able to fatten our wallets but they can be distressed by our condition.

This is not a cynical statement. It simply dramatizes the powerful
option television makes available. The world politicians inhabit—the
real world, that is—provides few things that they can manage with
confidence. Wars break out suddenly, the stock market careens out of
sight, and urban unrest explodes without warning. A president is therefore constantly overpedaling to keep from backpedaling. The language
of intimacy gives him an edge. With it, a president can show that he
knows what he feels even if he does not know what to do. The language of intimacy gives him control of something.

Politicians alone are not responsible for this new style of politics.
Media personnel abet them. Consider, for example, the near-psychiat-
ric interview that Walter Cronkite conducted with Gerald Ford during

the 1980 republican national convention. At the time, speculation was adrift that Ronald Reagan might ask Ford to join him on the ticket. Cline (1985) has shown the eerie parallel between Cronkite's interviewing style and the question–answer frame of the standard therapeutic encounter. Cline suggests that Cronkite's deft probing of Ford's psyche caused Ford to think seriously about a Reagan–Ford ticket for the first time. There, on national television, with Ronald Reagan watching with his mouth agape, Cronkite asked his most tantalizing question, as seen in the following:

Mister President, the—there are a lot of governors and senators here who are talking about a "draft Ford" movement, and there's even been some suggestion that Governor Reagan would support such a movement from the floor just to convince you, if you need any convincing—I don't think you do after the demonstration for you the other night here, but if you need any convincing—that the party wants you, needs you, feels that it is your duty to answer a call. What would happen if they got out there on that floor tonight or tomorrow and said, "It's got to be Gerald Ford"? (1985, p. 102)

What followed was much waxing and waning on Ford's part, much double thinking and question begging, but also some soul searching. The best evidence suggests that the interview threw a substantial wrench into Reagan's convention machinery, as Ford explored Ford's feelings live and in color. Reagan, of course, ultimately took a different tack, but Jack Kemp was surely correct when complaining that "television literally affected Reagan's decision. I got the feeling that Walter Cronkite was in the middle of history" (Cline, 1985, p. 93).

In an era of intimate politics, feeling good about oneself is everything. It is as if the Rogerian 1960s were collectively thumbing their noses at the Trumpian 1990s and declaring interiority the king. At times, one has to pinch oneself to be reminded that all of this going to-and-fro is going on in public. Even alone, on a couch in his office, Jim Wright would have been pitiable when resigning his Congressional post. But standing in the well of the House with the C-SPAN cameras rolling, he was infinitely sadder when he said the following:

Have I contributed unwittingly to this manic idea of frenzy, of feeding on other people's reputations? Have I caused a lot of this? So maybe I have. God, I hope I haven't. But maybe I have. Have I been too partisan? Too insistent? Abrasive? Too determined to have my way? Perhaps. If I've offended anybody in the other party, I'm sorry. I never meant to. I would not have done so intentionally. (Wright, 1989, p. A18)

Viewers at home, needless to say, take in such stuff in great gulps. They are, by now, addicts of intimacy. Some might be tempted to dismiss such disclosiveness as mere rhetorical fashion—we speak emotions today, computer chips tomorrow. But the language of intimacy is wider and deeper than politicians. They speak it but it also speaks them. It speaks the media, too, and it speaks much of the U.S. citizenry. It also speaks a new model of politics and that is its most troubling feature. But one cannot dismiss its effects on politicians themselves. When the Self is transformed into political barter, after all, what is left inside the politician to be traded or savored?

INTIMACY AND DRAMA

Politicians have become more intimate because television has goaded them into it, although as Schudson (1982) reports, the tendency to make politics personal had been growing in the print press prior to the 1940s. When it took to the airwaves, television made this tendency an act of faith. As a result, says Meyrowitz, the "electronic media of communication have been eroding barriers between the politician's traditional back and front regions [thereby upsetting] the traditional balance between rehearsal and performance" (1985, pp. 270–271). This new tradition has found its way into schoolchildren's textbooks, which now emphasize politicians' lives much more than they did before. Smith-Howell (1993) found, for example, that eighth grade and high school government textbooks (the sorts of textbooks that used to explain the Constitution), refer to individual chief executives today three times more often than they did forty years ago. Newspapers behave similarly, giving almost 90 percent more coverage to "robust, outgoing presidents" than to "quiet, reserved presidents" (Streitmatter, 1985, pp. 68–69).

Textbook authors and journalists who write in these ways are no doubt practicing their crafts admirably, making otherwise dull materials passably interesting. Television does them one better. Because television is a quintessentially visual medium, it does for the eye what the print media can only do for the imagination. For example, consider the size of the average television screen. What can it show well? When it gives viewers a wide-angle shot, for instance, the objects in its foreground are only slightly larger than those in its background. When it uses multicamera techniques, it can move our eye around from place to place to simulate movement but it never really feels like a car chase in a twelve-screen movie theater. Television gives us the best it can—faces. Faces fit its technology and faces fit its psychology. Faces fit its politics, too.

That is how television's pictures of politics became its model of politics. Graber (1990) has documented, for example, that in a study of over 2,000 visual scenes in 189 news stories, close-ups of politicians were the single most dominant visual image; over 70 percent of the news stories had them and most stories had more close-ups than anything else. Kem (1989) shows this to be especially true for U.S. political coverage (as opposed to news broadcast in the United Kingdom). Keeter (1987) has detailed the unsurprising results of facial politics: Candidates' personal qualities were found to be of far greater importance to television viewers than newspaper readers, a trend that has held constant for every U.S. election since 1964.

This, then, is television's model: know the person, know the vote. With this model, television has given us a whole new world, a world that changes how we think as well as how we see. In a strange, deconstructive turn, one of television's greatest inadequacies—its small space—becomes a primary gateway to perception. It makes us a nation of adventurers, persons willing to explore the visualized minds of politics wherever they can be found.

And so it is little wonder that "the character issue" now dominates political reportage. Each evening, we embark on television's journey to the soul. Consider the following data: (1) television reporters consistently probed the personalities of antiwar activists in the 1960s, thereby turning a political movement into a psychological excursion (Gitlin, 1980); (2) television reporters addressed personality issues far more frequently during the 1980 presidential campaign than did print reporters (Robinson and Sheehan, 1983); (3) television reporters spent almost 50 percent of their time profiling the families and friends of those who were hijacked on TWA flight 847 in 1985, whereas the *New York Times* gave such matters only 13 percent of its coverage (Elliott, 1988); and (4) television reporters primarily use voter profiles to talk about a political candidate's personal strengths and weaknesses rather than the candidate's stands on the issues (Smoller, 1988).

Rhetorically, of course, the character model is ideal for television. With vaults of video footage at their disposal, television producers can find evidence for any claim they might want to make. The incumbent is alleged to be worried about the polls—show him shaking hands nervously. The challenger feels intimidated by his wife's growing popularity—assemble a montage of his public speaking gaffes. Through it all, the character model says the following to voters: Watch television. Issues confuse, character endures. And the character model says the following to reporters: Determine your argument. Supporting evidence is everywhere.

Evidence is everywhere because character is nowhere, literally. No matter how hardy it might be from a moral point of view, character is a pure reification for the media. In the hands of a television journalist, character comes into being the moment it is discussed. It then hovers around a candidate and ceases to exist only when it no longer creates interest. Because character attaches to a politician's inside and not his outside, it can never be falsified completely. But it can be altered, which is to say, its plot usefulness can change. As a result, Bill Clinton can be made to seem an incompetent in the area of health reform in 1993 and a savior of Medicare three years later. Because television's pictures are so mesmerizing and because character is such an elastic concept, politicians have learned how to produce their own character profiles (e.g., Clinton's gorgeous 1992 convention film, *A Place Called Hope*) and the result is precisely what Jamieson suggests in the following: "Television's close-ups give us a more detailed look at our leaders than we have of most of our friends" (1988, p. 62).

Or so it seems. In fact, television gives us nothing of the kind. The look it gives us is precisely that—a look. Television gives us a seeing, an ogling more often, but it provides not even a soupçon of friendship. We all know that real intimacy cannot be found in politics. But the mass media tell a different story. The technology of television socializes its workers: Because television can only deliver close-up pictures, its employees learn to write close-up stories. The result is that voters have close-up feelings, at first, and far away feelings, ultimately.

While personality politics keeps the media's narrative fluid, and while it keeps politics itself tidily compartmentalized, it comes at a price. For one thing, it perverts the notion of character. To make character *specular*, something that is read onto another, is to make people one-dimensional. Real character is an aggregated phenomenon fashioned each day out of life's experiences. Character, the genuine article, is best seen in the clinches. It presents itself when least expected.

Televised character is none of these things. Its roots lie in air, not in earth. It is a manufactured product, not something that grows out of lived reality. For voters, overindulgence in personality politics becomes innervating, as they nourish themselves on less and less civics and on more and more nuance and imagery. For the media, learning the sentiment beat in Washington can result in media pontificating, in the aggrandizement of power, and in reportorial laziness. For government leaders, psychological politics can divert them from their appointed rounds as they watch themselves being watched by the media's always engaging watchers. Despite its attractions, personality politics can make a society sick.

WHY INTIMACY?

Thus far, we trace the rise in personality politics to largely technological factors. Television features people because it is only a box with wires. As such, it does better with emotions than with ideas, the former being more visual than the latter. Also, personality politics is attractive to the electronic media for rhetorical reasons. Television specializes in narrative and is therefore always hungry for a story. Since narrative requires skillfully drawn characters and since political affairs have a colorful supply of same, a match is made.

But personality politics springs from other sources as well. Philosophically, for example, there is something typically Western about this model. Its roots lie in the "Romantic assumption that style could be read to uncover the character, or soul, of individuals and nations" (Cmiel, 1990, p. 156), and they lie, too, in the classic American belief that people, especially great people, make a difference. As Cook has said, the current focus of news on "individual actors within continuing stories . . . dates back to the Progressive Era's emphasis on cleaning up the system by placing well-qualified individuals in positions of power to administer in a nonpartisan manner" (1990, p. 9). Carey (1987) extends this theme when contrasting U.S. news coverage to Soviet coverage. In the Soviet press, says Carey, "individuals merely personify these larger forces [capitalism, history, imperialism] which are in the saddle driving the actions of individuals. But for us [Americans], individuals act. Individuals make history. Individuals have purposes and intentions" (p. 182).

The happy side of personality politics, therefore, is a bedrock belief in the resiliency of the individual, in a New Progressivism. But there is also something quite old about personality politics—an almost premodern faith in the ability of the solitary individual to conquer great odds, even great technological odds. Television does particularly well with such stories, as seen in the following: Christopher Reeve, now a quadriplegic, conducts an upbeat interview from his wheelchair; and O. J. Simpson stands defiantly alone, thumbing his nose at the nation's legal machinery.

But there is something even older about personality politics, an almost Calvinist determinism whereby in-born character sets one's eternal clock in motion. Television appreciates this theme, too, since essentialism makes storytelling simple. That is why television's situation comedies feature stereotyped characters—the mouthy bartender, the doe-eyed librarian—and it is also why the mass media work so hard to get an early reading of the candidates' personalities during a political campaign. Who will be the establishment figure, the nasty spoiler, the unknown marauder?

Merelman (1984) provides another way of explaining the politics of intimacy. He notes that a large, complex society such as the United States is a loosely bounded culture in which the day-to-day tendernesses once afforded by rural life are no longer possible. In a mass society, says Merelman, intimate disclosures become a token of group commitment ("one holds nothing back") and sharing emotions becomes a way of reestablishing tribal connections (p. 106). According to Sennett (1977), the middle class is especially attracted to the myth of the private man inside the public man that results in such a society, ostensibly because the middle class can literally afford to be speculative.

If Offe (1987) is correct that the traditional political structures of class, ethnicity, and region are breaking down in mass society, it may also be true that modern Americans are willing to pay any price for intimacy; that is, their loving Bob Dole or hating Bob Dole may have nothing to do with governance at all. Instead, politics may simply be a convenient site for making contact with others. Life at city hall, of course, has always given people something to talk about at work. But television brings voters closer to their political leaders, thereby making each of them a political authority and, hence, an important communal participant.

Perhaps the most direct explanation for personality politics is temporal. The great bloc of active voters in the 1990s, after all, are either children of the 1960s or have been "culturally contaminated" by the 1960s. They are the children of Abraham Maslow and Carl Rogers, of Consciousness IIII, and of group therapy and psychobabble. They are the children of mind-expanding drugs and nude encounters and of acid rock and bralessness. They are the children of Freud, not Marx. Even today, the language of the 1960s remains. More important, it has crept into politics. As a "society obsessed with 'personality,' self-cultivation, and the search for uninterrupted exuberance," says Barber (1989, p. 52), how could it not? But it did more than creep into politics. It now threatens to dominate it.

Although examining the private lives of politicians has long been fair game for the press, it now seems to be the only game. During their lives, for example, numerous presidents were denounced from the pulpits of the day, as seen in the following: George Washington for not taking communion; Thomas Jefferson for sleeping with his slaves; Andrew Jackson for being an adulterer; Grover Cleveland for having a bastard child; and Woodrow Wilson for remarrying too soon (Goldman, 1963). But the following two points need to be made about these cases: (1) media outlets at the time were less intertwined and less imitative and so such attacks could not constitute a theme as easily as today; and (2) the presidents' putative behaviors, not their motives, dominated the agenda.

Things are different today. Today, all is motive. At first such a notion seems absurd, but that discounts its rhetorical power. Consider the following, for example, which shows how Richard Nixon once explained Watergate:

I'm convinced that if it hadn't been for Martha [Mitchell], and God rest her soul, because she, in her heart, was a good person. She just had a mental and emotional problem that nobody knew about. If it hadn't been for Martha, there'd have been no Watergate, because John wasn't minding that store. He was letting Magruder and all these kids, these nuts, run this thing. Now, am I saying here, at this juncture, that Watergate should be blamed on Martha Mitchell? Of course not. I'm trying to explain my feeling of compassion for my friend, John Mitchell. (Rosenblatt, 1982, p. 95)

We have here the following primer for intimate politics: Offer an opinion, not a fact; make it psychological, not moral; make it personal, not institutional. Who can resist such psychodrama? John Mitchell's head was in the wrong place and so he goofed. The perpetrator of the villainy, Martha Mitchell, did not mean to sin. The criminal children of Watergate—the Hunts and the Colsons—were mentally unstable and hence forgivable. Nixon felt compassion and that gives him two points—one for feeling an emotion (a universal good in personality politics) and another for feeling an unselfish emotion (the best kind). By the 1990s, language of this sort has become so common that it is hard to imagine how politics could be different. But politics can be different, and indeed, it must be different if the nation's citizens are to exercise their franchises in an enlightened, consensual manner.

SUMMARY

Because the electronic media are so good at what they do, it is often hard to remember that television is an arbitrary art form. Nothing requires that television make politics personal. Instead of asking a Buffalo congressman couch questions, for example, a television reporter could film pollution in Lake Erie. Instead of letting him discuss his boyhood experiences in Catholic grade schools, for example, Pat Buchanan could have been made to explain his odd attraction to racist groups when he ran for the presidency in 1996. Television patrols the intimacy beat because that is the simplest and most dramatic thing to do. Often, this turns politics into pure representation: Each evening on the nightly news, greed, lust, envy, and, occasionally, honor, stride the boards. The drama of politics becomes the human drama and governance is reduced to a mere theatrical convenience.

But notice what is happening here: (1) politics is becoming unmoored from statecraft, with the nation's politicians worrying more and more about the appearance of their psyches and less and less about leadership; (2) voters use hyperpersonalized criteria when choosing their leaders, thereby producing leaders who can please them emotionally but who cannot lead them; (3) policy information becomes increasingly devalued as journalism becomes theater and as journalists become character actors; and (4) with politics becoming entertainment, citizens turn into spectators rather than involved, democratic workers. This is what results from intimate politics, namely, preening leaders, decentered elections, bankrupt journalists, and lazy citizens.

What is a nation to do? For one thing, it can satisfy its needs for intimacy at home, or in a parked car, or in church, or at the movies—anywhere but politics. Television will make this hard to do because it is so good at producing feelings of political intimacy and for increasing our appetite for same. But political intimacies are false intimacies largely because politics deals with the least intimate things imaginable, namely, roads paved, wars fought, taxes collected, treaties signed, and wildernesses protected. These are the crucial matters of public life and television's intimacies distract us from them.

During the Richmond Debate (1992), George Bush became distracted in just these ways. When he haltingly tried to utter sweet nothings to his viewers, he stopped being a president and became a national paramour. Every fiber of his being argued against his doing so and yet he did it, or tried to. This was a sad thing to witness but the following is a sadder thing: Because he was so worried about his performing Self, Bush failed to discuss economic matters, the ostensible focus of the question asked of him. As a result, the American people missed the chance of hearing their president think through the economic conditions plaguing them, namely, job creation, tax reform, and international competition. Nothing of consequence was learned on October 14, 1992 because television's agenda, not the people's agenda, had a vice-like grip on the leader of the free world.

Things can be different but only if our leaders decide to lead. Television's agenda can become their agenda only if they allow it. Harry Truman would never have permitted such a thing. On those few occasions when the press tried to pry into his personal life (e.g., with regard to his daughter's musical talents), he tore into them like the offended father and offended leader that he was. Today's politicians use members of their families for political fodder and their own souls for national titillation. All the while, the people's business is held in abeyance and governance is held in the grip of a medium that knows no master but itself. Harry Truman would have called this an outrage. And so it is.

REFERENCES

Barber, J. D. (1989). The candidates' analysts. In *The 'Barberian' presidency*, ed. W. D. Pederson. New York: Peter Lang.

Carey, J. (1987). The dark continent of American journalism. In *Reading the news*, ed. R. Manoff and M. Schudson. New York: Pantheon.

Cline, R. (1985). The Cronkite–Ford interview at the 1980 republican national convention: A therapeutic analogue. *Central states speech journal* 36: 92–104.

Cmiel, K. (1990). *Democratic eloquence: The fight over popular speech in nineteenth-century America*. New York: Morrow.

Cochran, B. (1973). *Harry Truman and the crisis presidency*. New York: Funk and Wagnalls.

Cook, T. (1990). Thinking of the news media as political institutions. Paper presented to the American Political Science Association, San Francisco, California, August 1990.

Elliott, D. (1988). Family ties: A case study of coverage of families and friends during the hijacking of TWA flight 847. *Political communication and persuasion* 5: 67–75.

Gitlin, T. (1980). *The whole world is watching: Mass media in the making and unmaking of the new left*. Berkeley and Los Angeles: University of California Press.

Goldman, E. (1963). Can public men have private lives? *New York Times Magazine*, June 16, pp. 13, 60–61.

Graber, D. (1990). Seeing is remembering: How visuals contribute to learning from television news. *Journal of communication* 40 (3): 134–155.

Hart, R., P. Jerome, and K. McCombs. (1984). Rhetorical features of newscasts about the president. *Critical studies in mass communication* 1: 260–286.

Hinckley, B. (1990). *The symbolic presidency: How presidents portray themselves*. New York: Routledge.

Jamieson, K. (1988). *Eloquence in an electronic age: The transformation of political speechmaking*. New York: Oxford University Press.

Keeter, S. (1987). The illusion of intimacy: Television and the role of candidate personal qualities in voter choice. *Public opinion quarterly* 51: 344–358.

Kem, M. (1989). *Thirty-second politics: Political advertising in the eighties*. New York: Praeger.

Merelman, R. (1984). *Making something of ourselves: On culture and politics in the United States*. Berkeley and Los Angeles: University of California Press.

Meyrowitz, J. (1985). *No sense of place: The impact of electronic media on social behavior*. New York: Oxford University Press

Miller, M. (1973). *Plain speaking: An oral biography of Harry S. Truman*. New York: Berkeley Medallion.

Miller, N., and W. Stiles. (1986). Verbal familiarity in American presidential nomination acceptance speeches and inaugural addresses, 1920–1981. *Social psychology quarterly* 49: 72–81.

Offe, C. (1987). Challenging the boundaries of institutional politics: Social movements since the 1960s. In *Changing boundaries of the political: Essays on the evolving balance between the state and society, public and private*, ed. C. S. Maier. Cambridge: Cambridge University Press.

Robinson, M., and M. Sheehan. (1983). *Over the wire and on TV: CBS and UPI in campaign '80*. New York: Russell Sage.

Rosenblatt, R. (1982). The staff ate my homework. *Time*, March 8, p. 95.

Schudson, M. (1982). The politics of narrative form: The emergence of news conventions in print and television. *Daedalus* 3: 97–112.

Sennett, S. (1977). *The fall of public man*. New York: Knopf.

Smith-Howell, D. (1993). Using the past in the present: The rhetorical construction of the presidency. Unpublished Ph.D. dissertation, University of Texas at Austin.

Smoller, F. (1988). Presidents and their critics: The structure of television news coverage. *Congress and the presidency* 1: 75–89.

Streitmatter, R. (1985). The impact of presidential personality on news coverage in major newspapers. *Journalism quarterly* 62: 66–73.

Truman, H. (1950a). Democratic aims and achievements. *Vital speeches of the day* 16(16): 496–502.

Truman, H. (1950b). Peace comes high. *Vital speeches of the day* 18 (2): 34–36.

Wright, J. (1989). Partial text of Wright's resignation speech. *The Washington Post*, June 1, p. A18.

Chapter 12

Continuing the Conversation in a Democracy Always at Risk

Patricia M. Sias

The goal of this chapter is defined by what it is not, rather than by what it is. The goal is not to review and rehash the public voice chapters. It is not to provide a synthesis of the preceding chapters, nor is it to critique the chapters. Simply put, this chapter's goal is not to draw conclusions from this book's chapters regarding the topic of the public voice in a democracy at risk. Rather, the purpose of this chapter is to provide an impetus for continued study and discussion of issues relevant to the book's theme. Accordingly, this chapter identifies a number of loose ends suggested by the public voice chapters that, rather than being tied up, are proposed as topics for continued dialogue among citizens concerned with the relationship between democracy and the media. Finally, ideas for encouraging further interdisciplinary dialogue regarding these issues are provided.

PUBLIC VOICE OR PUBLIC VOICES?

We begin by problematizing the term *public voice*, which implicitly assumes a single, unified public voice—an assumption questioned by the authors of the chapters in this book. In Chapter 7, Campbell explicitly acknowledges this assumption in her title, "Collaborating to Hear Public Voices." She argues that democracy requires the voices of all citizens be heard; in particular, she notes how the voices of women and citizens of various ethnic backgrounds are often muted by a dominant voice typically reflecting a white male perspective. Breaking down the notion of a unitary public voice further, Cohen observes in Chapter 4 that the individual citizen carries several identities presumably accompanied by several voices. My voices regarding various public issues, for instance, spring from multiple identities as a woman, scholar, daughter of a Mexican mother, daughter of an Anglo father, mother, wife, and so on.

While democracy may be ideally shaped by multiple voices, however, the public voice expressed through the American mass media too often fails to capture the complexity and variety of perspectives and interpretations of public issues. In a process akin to what Lee and Wander (Chapter 10) call *collective remembering*, the media tend to construct a public voice as "pure, homogeneous, and devoid of shifts and discontinuities."

Along these lines, several of the public voice chapters identify media as a reason American democracy is at risk. In Chapter 11, Hart chastises the media for enabling politics to become more concerned with the intimate and personal (and presumably, the entertaining), rather than with clear, reasoned debate regarding public issues. Several contributors, including Hobbs (Chapter 5) and Campbell (Chapter 7), note that the media's preoccupation with the horse race features of political campaigns prevents citizens from obtaining basic facts regarding relevant and important political issues. This lack of information limits our ability to vote for the candidate most likely to effectively represent our voices in designing and implementing legislation that affects our lives. In a similar vein, Burns (Chapter 6) accuses the media of classifying people into markets and producing consumers instead of citizens. Willard (Chapter 3) explains that the mass media (in Latitude One of his latitudes of comprehension) are the least able to encourage thoughtful deliberation and citizen participation in public issues. To reach the largest audience possible, the mass media aim for the lowest common denominator. Consequently, "mass politics is and can be little else than the marketing of mass commodities, and mass journalism can be little more than a contradiction in terms." In fact, according to Willard, reporting political horse races is the best the mass media can do.

Several of the public voice chapters maintain that the mass media, more suitable for entertaining than enlightening, do not enhance an informed citizenry able to effectively deliberate public issues. Rather, they present an homogeneous, abstract public voice that neglects the diverse perspectives of American citizens.

If democracy requires public deliberation reflecting a diversity of opinions, how can the media encourage a more heterogeneous public voice? Examination of this question requires consideration of the extent to which media organizations are themselves heterogeneous and diverse institutions.

DEMOCRACY *THROUGH* THE MEDIA
AND DEMOCRACY *IN* THE MEDIA

Burns, Cohen, and Hobbs (in Chapters 6, 4, and 5, respectively) each note that for schools to teach the skills necessary for democracy (e.g., leadership, critical viewing, and media literacy), schools themselves must employ democratic practices, including practices that encourage "political conversations across divisions of race, class, religion, and ideology" (Meier, 1995). Unfortunately, such practices do not characterize most educational institutions. Changes in school climates, then, are important steps toward an invigorated public voice and several of the public voice chapters note programs dedicated to effecting such changes.

But what of the other institutions involved? Must media organizations, like schools, practice democracy to enhance democracy? More to the point, must media organizations reflect diversity to enhance a diverse public voice? According to Federal Communications Commission (FCC) chairman Reed Hundt, the answer is a resounding yes. In recent years, Hundt has lobbied for a new social compact between broadcast media and the American public. Inspired by Boris Yeltsin's claim that television saved democracy in Russia, Hundt argues, "The time has come to reexamine, redefine, restate, and renew the social compact between the public and the broadcasting industry" (McAvoy, 1994). A key component of that social compact, according to Hundt, is the belief that to foster democracy, the media must present a diverse public voice. Toward this end, Hundt explains, "We want to have the ownership and management ranks in this sector look more like the people they serve" (McAvoy, 1994, p. 6). In other words, if the media are to reflect a diverse public voice, then the producers of media messages must themselves reflect diversity.

So how diverse are media institutions? Not diverse enough, according to recent statistics. While women made up 45.6 percent of the nationwide workforce in 1993, they comprised only 39.6 percent of the broadcast workforce. Similarly, although minorities comprised 22.6 percent of the workforce nationwide in 1993, they made up only 18.2 percent of the broadcast workforce (excluding cable networks where they made up a more impressive 25.3% of the workforce) (Stern, 1994). Based on the 1993 statistics, the FCC concluded that the "1993 percentages of women in the broadcast and cable industries and minorities in the broadcast industry overall remain below comparable figures for the 1993 overall national work force" (Stern, 1994, p. 58). Worthy (1996) notes that the situation remained largely unchanged in 1996 with minorities still underrepresented in the broadcast workforce.

The situation appears to be no better in the print journalism industry. As Bramlett-Solomon (1993) points out in the following:

The figures speak for themselves. In 1978, minorities constituted 6.3% or 3,402 of the 54,000 newspaper journalists in the United States. Since 1978, the average annual percentage increase for minorities at daily newspapers has been about a third of a percentage point [Anderson, 1988; Garneau, 1988; Rosenfeld, 1987]. At the end of 1992, minorities made up 9.4% or 5,120 of the 54,530 newspaper work force [ASNE 1992 Newsroom, 1992]. However *51% of the nation's newspapers still have no minorities at all* [emphasis added; ASNE 1992 Newsroom, 1992; ASNE Finds, 1990; Anderson, 1988] and among newsroom executives, minorities comprise less than 5%. [Newsroom Integration, 1989; Minority Task Force, 1991; ASNE 1992 Newsroom, 1992]

Bramlett-Solomon concludes that, although the number of minority journalists has increased since 1978, "U.S. newsrooms appear to be making only modest progress in hiring and promoting journalists of color" (1993, p. 203).

Let us consider some of the implications of these statistics. Although hardly a melting pot, the broadcast media tend to be more representative of ethnic diversity than are newspapers. Two statistics are particularly disturbing. The first is that, as recently as 1992, over one-half of the newspapers in the United States employed no minority journalists. The second is that less than 5 percent of newsroom executives (presumably the people with the most control over the content of the news reports) are minorities. Postman (1987) makes a strong case for the argument that the print media are better suited for intelligent, rational, and informed deliberation. Television, in contrast, is more amenable to entertainment. In fact, Postman claims, the advent of telegraphic technology (which led, of course, to the development of radio and television broadcasting) marked the end of the age of exposition and the beginning of the age of show business. As Postman explains in the following:

Telegraphy made relevance irrelevant. The abundant flow of information had very little to do with those to whom it was addressed; that is, with any social or intellectual context in which their lives were embedded. . . . Telegraphy also made public discourse incoherent. The principal strength of the telegraph was its capacity to move information, not collect it, explain it or analyze it. (1987, pp. 67, 69)

If Postman is correct, we are led to the following conclusion: The more diverse of our media (television and radio broadcast organizations) are the media best suited for entertaining; the media best able to enhance intelligent deliberation are woefully unrepresentative of diversity. Taken together, these sobering statistics indicate that media organizations have much work to do if their employees are to look more like the people they serve and, as a consequence, enrich the mass-mediated public voice.

MEDIA-PUBLIC *INTERACTION* AS SOLUTION

Although the public voice chapters direct blame at the media for the precarious condition of the public voice, they also suggest possibilities for media technology to enhance, rather than hinder, democracy and consider media technology as a potential partner in public deliberation. The underlying thread among the chapters is that for media to enhance a heterogeneous voice and, consequently, a participative democracy, they must enable interaction among citizens rather than the one-way communication typical of mass media. This is consistent with Dahlgren's recent claim that sociocultural interaction is "a key dimension of the public sphere" (1995, p. 132). Taking a social constructionist stance, Dahlgren argues that because social reality is constructed through talk, "The public sphere is—and must be—larger than that of media representations. It must also include sociocultural interaction. This dimension takes us into the realm of people's encounters and discussions with each other, with their collective sensemaking and their cultural practices" (p. 18). It is in interaction, rather than abstract, one-way mass-mediated messages, that public sphering is accomplished.

This perspective is apparent in the encouraging examples of media enhancement of democracy provided in this volume. In Chapter 7, for instance, Campbell uses the Anita Hill/Clarence Thomas case to show that mass media and citizens can collaborate in effective democratic deliberation. That case illustrates how an issue perfectly suited for the mass media (i.e., filled with conflict, novelty, and drama) sparked dialogue among experts and citizens regarding an important social problem. In Chapter 8, Lambeth, while noting a variety of criticisms, provides several examples illustrating the ways public journalism can contribute to effective public debate reflecting multiple perspectives on important public issues. A critical component of public journalism, Lambeth notes, is citizen participation in deliberation of public issues. In other words, public journalism works when newspapers enable and encourage citizen interaction, rather than the traditional information dissemination activity of newspapers. Finally, in Chapter 9, Pride provocatively details his role as an on-line media critic, demonstrating the ability of interactive computer-mediated communication to stimulate reader interest and debate regarding local issues. In particular, Pride discusses how on-line critics can encourage readers to see issues from a variety of perspectives not typically acknowledged by newspaper accounts of events and to engage in on-line interaction regarding those events. These authors suggest that it is by enabling interaction that media foster an effective and diverse public voice and function as partners in democracy.

Despite the successes cited in these chapters, however, recent research indicates that the potential of media-public interactive technologies for enhancing democracy faces important obstacles. Perhaps the greatest of these obstacles is the deeply ingrained perception of citizens as consumers. McMillan and Campbell (1996), for example, examined the extent to which cities throughout the United States used interactive media technology to develop a virtual public sphere. They note that computer-mediated communication (CMC) appears to fulfill the following key elements of a public sphere: open access, voluntary participation not based on institutional roles, generation of public opinion through physical copresence and rational discussion, and freedom to express opinions and criticize (McMillan and Campbell, 1996). To determine whether cities are using CMC to its full potential in creating a public sphere, McMillan and Campbell examined the Web sites of 140 randomly selected cities throughout the United States to determine the type of information available on those sites and the extent to which citizen involvement was included. They also sent a brief survey, via e-mail, to the designers of those sites to determine perceptions regarding the mission and communication benefits of the Web site.

The results were, to say the least, disappointing and suggest a view of citizens as consumers, rather than producers, of information. Specifically, McMillan and Campbell note, "Only three of the 140 sites analyzed (2.1 percent) provided an electronic community forum for citizen participation" (1996, p. 13). Instead, the most frequent types of content on these pages were "the digital equivalent of a phone book and a city brochure" (p. 13). This is not surprising given the results of the e-mail survey: The majority of respondents perceived that the communication benefits of such Web sites are primarily one way, rather than interactive, and saw the site primarily as a tool to boost tourism (i.e., sell their city to potential tourist consumers). As McMillan and Campbell note in the following:

An overwhelming majority (64.6 percent) agreed with the statement that the primary benefit of online media for cities is that the new communication tool "provides an ideal way for the city to deliver information." Only 20 percent agreed with the statement that the medium "makes it easier for citizens and city officials to develop a dialogue." And a mere 4.6 percent agreed with the statement that online media "enables citizens to take an active role in shaping city government." (pp. 15-16)

The authors concluded that city officials' general perceptions about the potential for two-way or truly interactive communications could be limiting Web developments; rather, they "seem to foster development of 'consumption communities'" (McMillan and Campbell, 1996, p. 21).

The citizen-as-consumer mentality is a formidable obstacle to progress toward an effective, interactive public voice. Campbell notes in Chapter 7 the paradox of the 1996 National Issues Forum—politicians did not attend because the event would not be covered by national newspapers and television networks; national journalists did not attend because important politicians would not participate. Clearly, both the politicians and the journalists in this case viewed the forum as a media event for public consumption, not public participation. Similar to the city Web sites examined by McMillan and Campbell (1996), the 1996 forum shows how the consumer mentality hinders the ability of the media to enhance democracy. An important step toward effective use of media involves altering our view of citizens as consumers of, rather than participants in, mediated communication.

CONTINUING THE CONVERSATION: ADVOCACY DOMAINS

There is the need to carry on a dialogue regarding a variety of issues relevant to media, the public voice, and democracy. Among other things, scholars and practitioners must continue discussing the following:

- Ways to encourage a public voice representative of a diverse citizenry.
- Ways to improve the diversity of the producers of mass-mediated messages.
- Ways to fully realize the potential of interactive mediated communication to enliven citizen participation in civic matters.

This list is, of course, incomplete, and represents only the few loose ends considered in this chapter. Effective dialogue regarding these issues and others should possess two important characteristics: It must be both interdisciplinary and interactive. As evidenced by the chapters in this book, democracy transcends disciplines. Democracy concerns all of us, regardless of our specialty. It was for this reason we designed this collection as an interdisciplinary reader. Just as democracy is enhanced by a diverse public voice, our continued dialogue regarding the issues listed will be most effective if people (both scholars and practitioners) from a variety of disciplines and backgrounds participate in that dialogue. Sociologists, computer scientists, businesspeople, elected officials, and other citizens from all walks of life have unique contributions to make to our conversation and should be sought out for participation.

The important work of citizens in shaping and maintaining the public sphere occurs through interaction. Accordingly, continued dialogue must be just that, a dialogue. It should encourage interaction, not reaction; it should involve multi-way, not one-way, communication.

Toward this end, Dahlgren provides a useful distinction between the common domain and the advocacy domain. The *common domain*, represented by the dominant media, "strives for universalism" and serves as the provider of broad, abstract information for the masses. The *advo-*

cacy domain, in contrast, is "the setting for all citizens who wish to pursue special interests, and generate group-based cultural and political interpretations of society" (1995, p. 156). Communication in this domain occurs through a variety of media, including newsletters and electronic bulletin boards. An advocacy domain provides a setting for dialogic and contesting voices which, Dahlgren argues, "counter the prevailing understanding that there is only one version of what constitutes truth or reality and only one way to talk about it" (p. 156). We should consider the concerns expressed in this volume as comprising an advocacy domain and do our best to continue our interdisciplinary dialogue through a variety of communication media.

SUMMARY: STRIVING FOR DEMOCRACY CONTINUALLY AT RISK

The latter part of this book's title reflects an important assumption— the assumption that American democracy is, in fact, at risk. In my view, this is an accurate and necessary assumption. American democracy is at risk, has always been at risk, and should always be considered at risk. The more we value something, the more concerned we are with protecting it. This simple logic keeps insurance companies in business. If we truly value democracy, we must continually be concerned with protecting it. If we get to the point where we think we have solved the issues treated in this volume, if we get to the point where we believe democracy is safe and certain, then our democracy will be more at risk than ever.

REFERENCES

American Society of Newspaper Editors (ASNE). (1992). Newsroom employment survey. *ASNE bulletin* (May/June): 33.

American Society of Newspaper Editors (ASNE). (1990). ASNE finds scant progress for minorities. *Presstime* (May): 76.

Anderson, M. A. (1988). The goal: Full minority representation. *Presstime* (April): 24.

Bramlett-Solomon, S. (1993). Job appeal and job satisfaction among Hispanic and black journalists. *Mass communication review* 20: 202–211.

Dahlgren, P. (1995). *Television and the public sphere: Citizenship, democracy, and the media.* London: Sage.

Garneau, G. (1988). Not enough progress. *Editor & publisher* (May): 14–15.

McAvoy, K. (1994). Hundt's new deal. *Broadcasting & cable* 124: 6, 8.

McMillan, S. J., and K. B. Campbell. (1996). Online cities: Are they building a public sphere or expanding consumption communities? Paper presented at the annual meeting of the Association for Education in Journalism and Mass Communication, August 9–13, Anaheim, California.

Meier, D. (1995). The power of their ideas: Lessons for America from a small school in Harlem. Boston: Beacon Press.

Minority task force regroups. (1991). *Presstime* (March): 43.

Newsroom integration still crawling at a snail's pace. (1989). *NABJ Newsletter* (April): 1.

Postman, N. (1987). *Amusing ourselves to death: Public discourse in the age of show business.* New York: Penguin Books.

Rosenfeld, A. (1987). Minorities in the newsroom. *ASNE bulletin* (May/June): 16.

Stern, C. (1994). FCC says EEO efforts above average. *Broadcasting & cable* 124: 58.

Worthy, P. M. (1996). Diversity and minority stereotyping in the television media: The unsettled First Amendment issue. *Hastings communications and entertainment law journal* 18: 509.

Index

Politics. *See* Media
Populism, 26
Postman, N., 52, 194
Pride, R. A., 139–140, 141–143, 146–147
Public sphere, 44, 110, 195. *See also* Knowledge, public
Public voice(s), 4, 12, 35, 43, 62, 107, 110–111, 134, 169, 191–192

Reagan, R., 178–179
Rhetoric: 41–43; 49–50; 182. *See also* Public voice(s)
Richards, I. A., 43
Roediger, D. R., 159, 160, 162, 163
Rogers, C., 185
Rosen, R., 105, 108, 115–116
Ruby Ridge, 132–133

Schudson, M., 110
Solow, R., 26–27

Television. *See* Media
Thomas, C., 100–103
Tinker v. Des Moines School District, 69
Truman, H., 173–174, 187

Waco controversy, 132–133, 141–142
Washington, G., 185
Watergate, 132–133, 185–186
Weaver, R., 43
White, T., 15
Whitewater controversy, 133
Williams, P., 45
Wilson, W., 185

Yeltsin, B., 193

About the Editors and Contributors

JOHN S. BURNS is Assistant Professor in the Department of Educational Leadership and Counseling Psychology at Washington State University, and he is the Coordinator for the Interdisciplinary Undergraduate Minor in Leadership Studies, as well as Coordinator for the Higher Education Administration Program. He was the Director of the U.S. Department of Education Eisenhower Leadership Program Grant to develop Leadership Studies courses in business administration, communications, comparative American cultures, political science, and women's studies. He also worked in partnership with Eisenhower Projects at the University of Maryland and Harvard University which produced the 1996 report, "Democracy at Risk: How Schools Can Lead."

KARLYN KOHRS CAMPBELL is Professor of Speech-Communication at the University of Minnesota. She is the author of *Man Cannot Speak for Her* (1989), coauthor of *Deeds Done in Words: Presidential Rhetoric and the Genres of Governance* (1990), and editor of *Women Public Speakers in the United States, 1800–1925* and *1925–present* (1993; 1994). She received the Woolbert Award for scholarship of exceptional originality and influence (1987), the Winans-Wichelns Book Award (1990), and the Ehninger Award for outstanding scholarship in rhetoric (1991); in 1992 she was selected as one of the first five distinguished scholars honored by the Speech Communication Association (SCA). She was awarded a fellowship at the Barone Center of the John F. Kennedy School of Government at Harvard University in the fall of 1992. In 1996, she received the Francine Merritt Award for significant contributions to the lives of women in SCA and the communication discipline.

JODI R. COHEN is Associate Professor of Speech Communication at Ithaca College where she teaches courses in public communication, rhetorical theory, and critical research methods. She has published articles on communication and culture, communication and democracy, as well as critical studies of specific texts. Her book, *Critical Powers*, was to be published in 1997.

RODERICK P. HART is the F. A. Liddell Professor of Communication and Professor of Government at the University of Texas at Austin. He is the author of *Public Communication* (1975; 1983), *The Political Pulpit* (1977), *Verbal Style and the Presidency* (1984), *The Sound of Leadership* (1987), *Modern Rhetorical Criticism* (1990), and *Seducing America: How Television Charms the Modern Voter* (1994). He has published in such journals as the *Quarterly Journal of Speech, Presidential Studies Quarterly, Philosophy and Rhetoric, Critical Studies in Mass Communication*, and *The Journal of Communication*. He has received grant support from the Ford Foundation, Carnegie Foundation, Exxon Foundation, David Ross Foundation, University Research Institute, the Television and Politics Center, and the Kaltenborn Foundation. A former Woodrow Wilson Fellow, Hart is currently listed in *Who's Who in America*. He has been named a Research Fellow of the International Communication Association and a Distinguished Scholar by the Speech Communication Association.

RENEE HOBBS is an Associate Professor of Communication at Babson College and Director of the Media Literacy Project at Clark University. She created KNOW-TV, a curriculum for analyzing nonfiction television that won the 1996 Golden Cable Ace Award for Public Service programming, and she developed the Harvard Institute on Media Education, the nation's first national level educational program on media learning from audiovisual media; the uses and misuses of visual media in the kindergarten through twelfth grade classroom; and the impact of media culture on youth socialization and intellectual development.

EDMUND B. LAMBETH is Professor of Journalism at the University of Missouri and funding director since 1984 of the National Workshop on the Teaching of Ethics in Journalism. A former Washington correspondent, Nieman, and Congressional fellow, he is the author of *Committed Journalism: An Ethic for the Profession* and holder of the Thomas Jefferson Award of the four-campus University of Missouri system.

WEN SHU LEE is Associate Professor of Communication Studies at San Jose State University. Her research interests include deep code (humor and idiom) in intercultural communication, anti-footbinding rhetoric in China, and postcolonial feminisms.

RICHARD A. PRIDE is Associate Professor of Political Science at Vanderbilt University. He recently published *The Confession of Dorothy Danner: Telling a Life* and "How Media and Activists Frame Social Problems" (*Political Communication*, 1995). His current research focuses on the redefinition of the problem of racial inequality in America.

MICHAEL SALVADOR is Associate Professor of Speech Communication in the Edward R. Murrow School of Communication at Washington State University. His research centers on rhetoric, organizational advocacy, and public decision making. His dissertation on the American consumer movement won the Speech Communication Association Dissertation Award, and he has published numerous articles on social movement organizations involved in consumer and environmental advocacy. His current research focuses on how competing cultural discourses, particularly Native American organizations, frame environmental awareness and action.

ROBERT SCHMUHL is Professor of American Studies at the University of Notre Dame. He is also Chairman of the Department of American Studies and Director of Graduate Studies. His teaching and research areas include American political life, communications, and contemporary affairs. Among the eight books he has written or edited are *The Responsibilities of Journalism* (1984), *Statecraft and Stagecraft: American Political Life in the Age of Personality* (1990; 1992), *Demanding Democracy* (1994), and *Wounded Titans: American Presidents and the Perils of Power* (1996).

PATRICIA M. SIAS is Assistant Professor of Speech Communication in the Edward R. Murrow School of Communication at Washington State University. Her research focuses on organizational communication and leadership, in particular examining the ways leader behavior influences coworker communication and coworker relationships. Her research has been published in a variety of academic journals including *Communication Monographs, Human Communication Research, Communication Reports,* and *Communication Research Reports.*

PHILIP C. WANDER is Professor of Communication Studies at San Jose State University. His research interests include rhetorical criticism, media criticism, and African-American and Native American rhetoric. His recent work is on postcolonialism and rhetorical contextualization.

CHARLES ARTHUR WILLARD is Professor and Chair of the Department of Communication, University of Louisville. His books include *Liberalism and the Problem of Knowledge* and *A Theory of Argumentation.* He has published in such journals as *Communication Monographs, The Journal of the American Forensic Association* (now *Argumentation and Advocacy*), and *Argumentation and Social Epistemology.* He is one of the founding Co-Directors of the International Society for the Study of Argumentation, based at the University of Amsterdam.

ISBN 0-275-96013-7

90000>

EAN

9 780275 960131

HARDCOVER BAR CODE